Inquest

Concentrating on the much-publicised inquest on the
death of Helen Smith in Jeddah, this book is a serious
contribution to the debate which continues to rage
about the case. It gives the background story to the
British nurse's death, examines the conflicting
evidence produced in court and looks into the whole
accident theory and the politics of cover-up, pathology
and inquests.

Gordon Wilson and Dave Harrison are both journalists
who sat through every minute of the three-week
inquest on behalf of their newspapers. Gordon Wilson
reports for the weekly *Leeds Other Paper*, a radical,
non-party newspaper which he co-founded in 1974. He
is also a part-time tutor for the Open University on
social and political control of technological change,
dealing partly with the use of experts in decision-
making.

Dave Harrison provided reports both the top-
selling Danish newspaper *Ekstrabladet*, which had a
special interest in the case, and for various Bradford
groups.

Since his return to Britain in 1979, he has spent two
years on the Yorkshire Ripper inquiry and a year
collecting evidence for the Bradford 12 Defence. He
has worked as a freelance writer for the Danish media
for twenty years. He also works for the Campaign
Against Racist Attacks, Bradford.

INQUEST
Helen Smith
The Whole Truth?

GORDON WILSON and
DAVE HARRISON

METHUEN LONDON

A Methuen Paperback

First published in 1983
© 1983 Gordon Wilson and Dave Harrison
Printed in Great Britain for
Methuen London Ltd
11 New Fetter Lane, London EC4P 4EE
by Richard Clay (The Chaucer Press) Ltd
Bungay, Suffolk

ISBN 0–413–53170–8

Contents

Illustrations

PLATES

DIAGRAMS

Acknowledgements and thanks for permission to re-produce photographs are due to the Press Association for plates 1a, 1b, 2a, 2b, 3a, 3b, 4a, 4b, 5a, 5b, 5c, 6a, 6b, 6c, 7b and 8b; to Times Newspapers Ltd for plate 7a; and to the *Leeds Other Paper* for plate 8a.

The diagrams were re-drawn by Neil Hyslop.

1. *Helen Smith*

'They're talking about my daughter in there,' said Ron Smith. It was around 5.00 p.m. on Thursday 9 December 1982, in the dank, draughty, emulsioned corridor that does a 'dog-leg' around the old Leeds Crown Court No. 1. Nearby stood his son, Graham, his solicitor, Ruth Bundey, and the two barristers representing the Smith family, Geoffrey Robertson and Stephen Sedley. Not far away was Richard Arnot with his solicitor, Sir David Napley. Media people were everywhere, although they were by now almost outnumbered by the empty soup cartons and plastic coffee mugs littering the floor. The corridor looked a slum as, whatever our background, we settled down to the same conditions of existence.

The jury had been out since 11.15 a.m., discussing how Helen Smith had met her death at Richard Arnot's flat in Jeddah, Saudi Arabia, some three and a half years previously. It was not to return finally and deliver its verdict for another one and three-quarter hours. *They're talking about my daughter in there.* Perhaps it had something to do with the circumstances, but more it was the way he said it that caused Ron Smith to inject fresh life into a well-worn cliché.

That simple sentence also brought back to life Helen Smith, and not for the first time during the fifteen days the inquest sat. Suddenly that lump of meat that had been passed from pillar to post, talked about, at times almost character-assassinated, was there in the background smiling, a pleasant, cheerful smile with dimples prominent, looking slightly confused but also flattered that such a fuss was being made about her. The fuss and the expense is because she was once alive and we do not know how she died. Human life is too important not to ask why once it ceases.

Helen Smith was a young woman whom we would have liked to have known. She was variously described at the inquest by those who knew her as: 'a great character' . . . 'someone with a large circle of friends' . . . 'basic' . . . 'not very ladylike' . . . 'could be stroppy and abusive' . . . Much of the popular press reported and interpreted this in a predictable way. But to us she was obviously little different from most single people in their early twenties – of either sex.

Except, when you come to examine people as individuals more closely, rather than *en masse*, they are, of course, different from one another. And Helen was at times examined in fine detail at the inquest.

She was born in Leeds and spent her childhood and adolescence in the city or not far away. Her father was a successful businessman who had at one time been a policeman. After leaving school, Helen thought of joining the police herself, but instead trained as a nurse at St James's hospital in Leeds.

In 1978, British staff were being recruited for a private hospital which was about to open in Jeddah. This hospital was named after its owner, Dr Bakhsh. Helen, at that time living in Leeds but away from home, applied and got a job there. She went out to Jeddah in December 1978.

No doubt at the time she was fired by a sense of independence (she was, after all, living apart from both her father and her mother in Leeds – Ron's marriage to Jeryl Smith had broken up in 1977) and a desire 'to see the world'. Perhaps it is this that makes her stand out from the mass a little. Many young, single people talk about going out 'to see the world'. Helen actually did it.

A young woman from a northern-English industrial city, with a pretty ordinary upbringing from a father who had formed part of the backbone of Britain – the country's thriving small businessmen – Helen Smith for at least one period of her life asserted a will to break the mould, to be independent, to make choices. If she had not made those choices she would probably be alive and living in Leeds today with 2.1 children. But then, if she had not made them, she would not be Helen Smith.

We do not wish to elevate Helen Smith to the level of saint, but nor should she be lowered to the level of immoral whore, as some sections of the press have done. So what if she wanted a good time, enjoyed company, knew how to abuse people and enjoyed sex? Plenty of people of both sexes are exactly the same, newspaper reporters as much as the next man or woman.

In late November 1978, former Scarborough surgeon Richard Shackleton Arnot also went to work at the Bakhsh hospital. Joining him were his wife, Penelope, and two young children. 'I think I met Helen some two or three weeks later,' he told the inquest. 'We were invited to a party at the Embassy. I went to the hospital to look for a babysitter and found some nurses sitting around. I asked whether one of them would be prepared to babysit and Helen, who was among them, was the first to volunteer. She became the favourite babysitter of the children.'

Richard Arnot also explained to the inquest how he and Penelope became friendly with a group of workers at a German salvage company in Jeddah harbour, called Harms Salvage. A member of the hospital staff was going out with one of them and they eventually married. Dr Arnot said that he and Penelope 'had an open house to Harms Salvage because they enjoyed associating with family life'. They were family men themselves, but far away from their wives and children.

Richard Arnot added that there was nothing unusual about this 'open house' arrangement. It was commonplace among the expatriate community in Saudi Arabia, where people would be thrown very much back to entertainment at home. 'Casual acquaintances became close friends,' he said.

Working for Harms Salvage was a New Zealand diving instructor called Timothy Hayter. He apparently became friendly with Helen Smith, and Richard Arnot claimed at the inquest that it was she who introduced the two men to each other: 'My wife and I expressed an interest in learning to scuba dive. Helen brought Tim into my office towards the end of January; then I took him up to my flat and introduced him to my wife.'

On 20 May 1979, Tim Hayter was due to go away for some weeks on leave. The Arnots therefore offered him the use of their sixth-floor flat next to the Bakhsh hospital for a farewell party. Richard Arnot ordered a crate of whisky from another British expatriate acquaintance, Dr Alan Kirwen. Alcohol is strictly forbidden in Saudi Arabia but Dr Kirwen worked for Lockheed and was therefore in close contact with the American community in Jeddah, which was apparently a good source of black-market supplies.

The party was thrown on Saturday night, 19 May. The arguments continue to rage as to exactly who attended, but by 2.00 a.m. on Sunday 20 May there were at least the following in or around the Arnots' flat: Tim Hayter, five Germans from Harms, a French friend of Tim Hayter called Jacques Texier, Richard and Penelope Arnot, Helen Smith and a Dutchman called Johannes Otten. Otten was a tugboat captain in Jeddah harbour, who was not actually employed by Harms but was well-associated with the company and took his meals on its accommodation barge. He had come to the party with some of the Germans in their company jeep and, according to all witnesses at the inquest, he and Helen had become more attached to each other as the party wore on.

At approximately 5.45 a.m., Richard Arnot was telephoning the police to say that Johannes Otten and Helen Smith were dead. Johannes was impaled on the ornamental railings on top of the wall surrounding the small courtyard to the flats. Helen was lying on the marble floor of the courtyard nearby.

The Arnots and their guests were rounded up for questioning and taken to the Sharifia police station, and their blood was tested for the presence of alcohol. With the exception of Penelope Arnot and one of the Germans, all proved positive. Although they were told initially that nobody was being arrested, they were kept at the police station for nineteen days. They were then transferred to prison, where they were kept for between three and five months before being allowed out on bail. Richard Arnot was eventually sentenced to a further jail sentence and a flogging, Penelope to a flogging, but diplomatic efforts saved both.

Ron Smith had been a police officer for a few years in the early 1950s, but left and started up his own highly successful television repairs business in Leeds. He heard about the death of his daughter while at home on Sunday 20 May 1979.

He immediately arranged to fly to Jeddah – 'to identify my daughter and pay my last respects,' he told the inquest. He also tried to tell the inquest, but was stopped by Coroner Philip Gill, that there had been a 'bureaucratic foul-up' at the Foreign Office in relaying the message.

Six days later, Ron Smith was talking to Richard Arnot in the courtyard of the Sharifia police station. The British Embassy Consul, Francis Geere, had driven him there past the Arnots' flat. Ron Smith was not happy with some things that Richard Arnot told him and at one point there was a heated exchange. They spoke for about ten minutes and then, after speaking to the hospital owner, Dr Bakhsh, he was taken to the mortuary to see Helen.

He had been told that Helen had fallen by accident from the Arnots' balcony on the sixth floor – obviously some considerable distance from the ground. She had supposedly fallen onto a solid marble floor. He was well prepared for the shock of seeing a badly injured body.

And it was a shock when he saw her. Far from being

mutilated, Helen's body appeared to him to be in near-perfect condition. She did not look as if she had fallen from anywhere. He did notice a small indentation in her forehead – 'like a mosquito bite in reverse'. From that moment onwards he suspected murder and, during his stay in Jeddah, he found that this was a view shared by many of Helen's former colleagues at the hospital.

Ron Smith discovered that Penelope Arnot had talked to a British Embassy official, Vice-Consul Gordon Kirby, about the deaths. This had been at the Bakhsh hospital on Sunday 20 May, while the police were still at the scene, and before they took her away. Both she and Richard had been able to move quite freely after the police arrived and she had taken their two children into the hospital. Kirby had written up his conversation with her and was apparently not happy with some aspects of what Penelope Arnot told him, especially her description of who was at the party and her account of her own movements that night.

Ron Smith wanted to see the document, but the Embassy would not allow it. He fought his way up the hierarchy of the Embassy and got to see the Counsellor, Michael Weston – number two to the British Ambassador. 'When I walked into his office he was stroking a white pussy cat which he continued to stroke throughout our conversation.'

Michael Weston telexed the Foreign Office in London, but there was still no joy for Ron Smith and he left Saudi Arabia empty handed as far as the document was concerned. Being refused it, however, only added fuel to his fire. Back in Britain, after further unsuccessful dealings with the Foreign Office, he tried to tell the press that his daughter had been murdered and that this was being covered up by the British Embassy in Jeddah and the Foreign Office in London.

Alas, the press, cautious because of the laws of libel, printed very little in the period immediately after Helen's death. The Bradford-based *Pennine Radio* did a programme in the spring of 1980, but in the main it was the satirical magazine, *Private Eye*, which took up the cudgels on Smith's behalf.

Elsewhere in the world, the *New Straits Times* of Malaysia printed some major articles in 1981. Later still, in England, the radical weekly, *Leeds Other Paper*, printed Ron Smith's case in full.

Ron Smith had left Helen's body in Jeddah while the Saudi police were investigating, but when nothing came of this, he decided to try to force an inquest in Britain. In June 1980, therefore, just over a year after the deaths, he returned to Jeddah and put Helen's body on a plane to bring her back to England – to Leeds, her home city. At that time he received encouraging noises about an inquest from the then Leeds coroner, John Walker.

But Walker fell ill and Ron Smith returned to Leeds to find that his deputy, James Miles Coverdale, had taken over. He remembers well his first meeting with Coverdale on 24 June 1980:

> Several other persons were there including, to my surprise, the then Assistant Chief Constable for the West Yorkshire Police, Jim Hobson. He was then in charge of the Yorkshire Ripper murder inquiries.
>
> I told Coverdale that I desired an inquest in order that I would be able to exercise my legal privilege in a court of law (i.e. an inquest) in the witness box and thus circumnavigate the pernicious laws of slander and libel ... because the British media present in court would be able to report freely and accurately without fear of recrimination re the said libel laws.
>
> Coroner Coverdale said that under no circumstances would he allow me to use his court as a mouth-piece and further stated that he would sign an immediate order releasing Helen's body for disposal.
>
> I told Coroner Coverdale that Helen's body was vital evidence as to the manner in which she and Captain Johannes Otten met their deaths and that under no circumstances would I accept Helen's body for disposal.

By law, Ron Smith had put Coverdale in a cleft stick with his stance. The coroner could only 'dispose' (i.e. bury or cremate) of the body if: a) he decided there was no need for an inquest *and* obtained the consent of the next of kin (i.e. Ron Smith); or b) he ordered an autopsy (a pathological examination) and the results satisfied him completely that there should be no inquest.

Coroner Coverdale ordered an autopsy which was performed three days later by Dr Michael Alan Green, Home Office pathologist and senior lecturer in forensic medicine at Leeds University.

For weeks afterwards, Ron Smith haunted the Leeds coroners' office and when he eventually collared Coverdale there was a row. Coverdale did not want to let Ron Smith have a copy of the autopsy report, but in the end conceded the request provided Ron Smith gave his word that he would not reveal its contents. There were also dire warnings about the Official Secrets Act if he did so. Ron Smith takes up the story again:

The following night at 8.00 p.m. I was in my home. Two police officers in uniform arrived in a patrol car. They handed me a sealed envelope and quickly departed. The envelope contained Green's autopsy report and a 'press release' statement. I read the autopsy report and was aghast at what I read.

I do not like breaking my word, I do not think I had ever done so before, but after reading the document and realising the implications of what I had read, I immediately photostated scores of copies and despatched them to the media, my friends and colleagues and to many leading pathologists. I still await arrest for contravention of the Official Secrets Act.

The report bore little relation to what Ron Smith knew of Helen's injuries after talking to pathologists in Saudi Arabia. The press release was a short summary of the report and ended by saying that the present evidence available did not warrant holding an inquest, but if more came to light then Coroner Coverdale would reconsider the matter.

Ron Smith therefore decided to commission, at his own considerable expense, an independent autopsy on Helen's body. His faith in the British establishment being at a low ebb, he asked Danish pathologist, Professor Jorgen Dalgaard, to do it. Professor Dalgaard is regarded as one of the world's top pathologists and, among other things, has done much work for the United Nations.

The coroners' office asked Professor Alan Usher, who holds the chair in forensic medicine at Sheffield University, to attend and observe the autopsy. Professor Usher, in fact, ended up doing a joint autopsy with Professor Dalgaard. Dr Green was in attendance.

The autopsy took place on 16 December 1980 and Professor Dalgaard's interpretation of their joint findings was emphatic. Helen had been beaten around the head. If she had fallen, it had only been from a moderate height – not the seventy feet that Ron Smith had estimated as the height of the Arnot balcony. Professor Usher felt that she had fallen no more than thirty feet, and emphasised genital injuries which suggested rape.

Meanwhile, back at the Foreign Office, Ron Smith was having fresh problems regarding the report of the first autopsy carried out on Helen, which was done in Jeddah eleven days after she died. This was an important document as it was the only autopsy that included an examination of the internal organs. After the autopsy, they had been removed and the body embalmed.

The Foreign Office sent Smith a photostat copy of the Arab original, together with their own translation, which he received on 20 December 1980. It consisted of two pages, but the copy was impossible to follow as the left-hand edge of the text had not been photostated properly.

Ron Smith therefore asked for, and received, the original. He noticed that at the top left-hand corner of the two sheets there was a punch-hole that appeared to have been made in the original after the bad photocopies were made, as there was no sign of it on them.

The text read OK. It would not have done so, however, had that punch-hole not been there. Page one had ended with a full stop and the punch-hole at the start of page two had obliterated a hyphen which would indicate that the first words at the top of page two were mid-sentence, not the start of one.

In fact, page two was not page two at all, but page three. The real page two, which detailed the internal injuries, was missing, only to turn up eighteen months later, in May 1982, and then only after a persistent campaign by Ron Smith, who knew what it should contain after conversations in Jeddah. The Foreign Office claimed, once the inquest was over, that it had not originally been sent the missing page and did not notice the mistake at first because the text seemed to make sense.

Scattered over the Foreign Office translation of the Saudi autopsy report were the words 'accident', 'accidentally' and 'accidental' in relation to Helen's death. These were translations of the Arab symbol, ESABYA, in the original. In fact, ESABYA means nothing of the sort. 'Traumatic' would be a more accurate translation.

Then there was the matter of the Jeddah police report into the deaths of Helen and Johannes. Ron Smith received a translation of this from the Foreign Office and was told that a copy had also gone to the Leeds coroners' office.

One night, Ron Smith was sitting at home with Chief Inspector Peter Smalley, the investigating officer for the West Yorshire police, whom he had known from his own days with the force. They started discussing the Jeddah police report and produced their respective copies. Suddenly it became apparent to both men that, although appearing identical, these were not copies at all. In particular, a phrase was missing from Peter Smalley's translation.

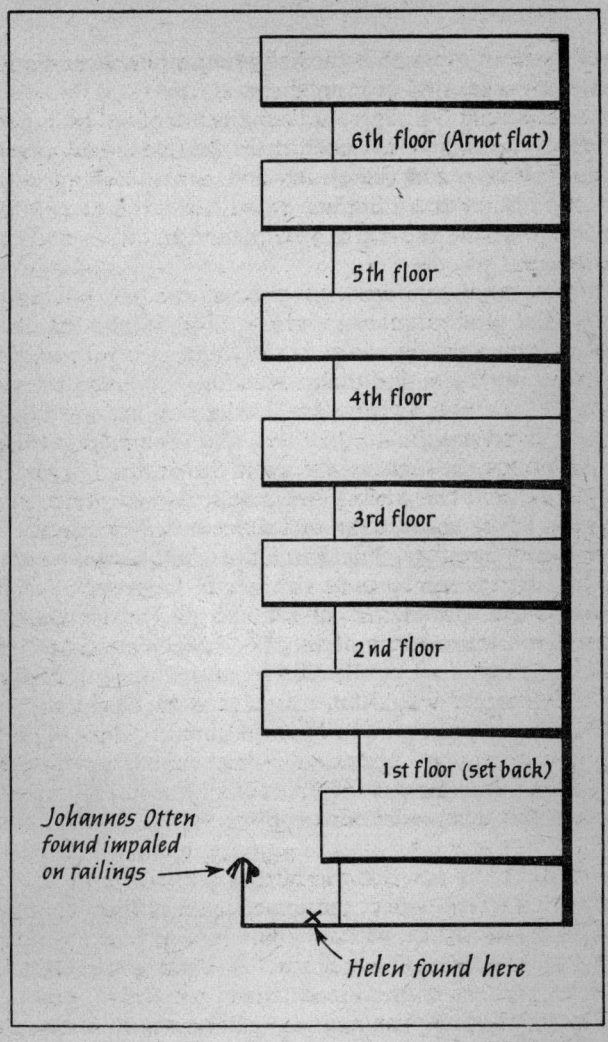

6th floor (Arnot flat)

5th floor

4th floor

3rd floor

2nd floor

1st floor (set back)

Johannes Otten
found impaled
on railings →

Helen found here

The block of flats in Jeddah, showing where the bodies were
found and indicating the unlikelihood of Helen's having
fallen from the sixth floor in view of the position of her body.

Referring to the positions of the bodies, Ron Smith's version ran: 'Mr Johannes Otten the Dutchman was found impaled on the railings on the top of the wall (about two metres high) surrounding the building. His legs and thighs were impaled with his upper torso downwards in the direction of the building and the girl had fallen on her face inside the courtyard, behind the wall, and both were dead.'

The equivalent part of Peter Smalley's 'copy' was: 'Mr Johannes Otten the Dutchman was found impaled on the railings on the top of the wall (about two metres high) surrounding the building. His legs and thighs were impaled with his upper torso downwards in the direction of the courtyard behind the wall and both were dead.'

In other words, the reference to the position of Helen's body was missing from Peter Smalley's version.

Ron Smith called in an old police colleague to examine the two documents. John Conway, who had some twenty years' experience as an 'Examiner of Questioned Documents' and who had given evidence in court on this on many occasions, concluded that both documents probably emanated from one translation because of their close similarities (even punctuation mistakes were repeated) apart from the missing phrase. He also noted that some punctuation marks had been added or changed later in Peter Smalley's copy as they were out of alignment. These were all present in Ron Smith's copy, so Peter Smalley's was probably re-typed from this, leaving out the phrase that referred to the position of Helen's body.

Taken in isolation, these anomalies regarding the Saudi autopsy and police reports might not amount to much, but coming at the same time as Professor Dalgaard's autopsy report, they were dynamite to Ron Smith. Calls for an inquest were intensified, and questions were asked in the House of Commons by Bob Cryer, the Labour member for Keighley.

The coroners' service in West Yorkshire was reorganised in July 1981. Leeds and Wakefield combined to form a single district and, as Coroner Walker had retired ill, the Wakefield coroner, Philip Gill, became the man in charge. Deputy Leeds coroner Coverdale was moved to North Yorkshire, which meant that Philip Gill took over the Helen Smith case.

At the time time he was replaced, Coverdale was still prevaricating over an inquest on the basis of his press release a year previously. Within a month of officially taking over, Gill stated there could be no inquest anyway. The death had occurred abroad and the body was therefore outside of his jurisdiction.

More outrage followed on the part of Ron Smith. The West Yorkshire County Council tried to intervene. But although it pays coroners out of the rates, it cannot tell them what to do, or replace them. Only the Lord Chancellor can do that. Instead, the County Council asked the Attorney General, Sir Michael Havers, to conduct a full inquiry into the case. But he too refused.

End of story; or was it? Ron Smith took Gill to the High Court in London, but it upheld the coroner's view in a judgement delivered on 2 April 1982. Smith appealed, and this time, almost four months later, the judges ruled in his favour. There had to be an inquest.

Philip Gill formally opened the inquest on 16 August 1982. It was a short hearing mainly for identification purposes. But it was not without incident. Ron Smith boycotted it and his solicitor, Ruth Bundey, told Gill that he should hand it over to another coroner.

Her main argument was that justice must not only be done, it had to be seen to be done, and by persistently refusing to hold an inquest until ordered to do so, he could appear to be biased against Ron Smith. She referred to various allegations made during the previous twelve months by Smith against Gill, all of which he had strenuously denied, but which, even if totally untrue, would lead any reasonable man to be prejudiced against Smith.

Philip Gill rejected the arguments, stating that he had merely expressed a legal view that he did not have juris-

diction and he could not feel that there was any substance
in allegations of prejudice or bias.

Ron Smith had stood alone in the street outside while
all this was going on because he did not wish to appear to
be recognising Gill as the rightful coroner. When the
hearing finished, he immediately sought to remove him
via the High Court again. As West Yorkshire Council
was refusing to pay his legal expenses in connection with
litigation over the Helen Smith case, Gill was not represented at the first hearing on 25 October 1982, even
though he was present as a spectator. This made the
hearing completely abortive as the judge, Justice Webster,
ordered that his case should be represented – by an *amicus
curiae*.

This literally translates as 'friend of the court'. It is
someone appointed by the Treasury to 'put the other side'
when a matter of public interest is at stake. At the second
hearing, on 4 November, the duly appointed *amicus*
argued that Gill would not even be subconsciously biased
and should therefore be the man to conduct the inquest.
He won.

The inquest proper opened a fortnight later on Thursday 18 November 1982, amid much ballyhoo, a special
press briefing the day before, and a row going on because
Gill would not tell the interested parties in advance who
the witnesses were likely to be. 'It is not my intention to
publicise in advance a list of the witnesses who may give
evidence. Arrangements in this respect are extremely
delicate and still in progress. You may rest assured that I
am doing everything possible to secure the attendance of
every person of whom I am aware, who is able to give
material evidence to assist the jury at the hearing,' he
wrote to Ron Smith's solicitors in a letter dated 10
November. A list of essential witnesses sent to him by
Ron Smith a month earlier had apparently been lost in
the post. Also, Gill made it clear in the same letter that if
Ron Smith was to appear in the witness box it would
only be if he could give 'admissible' evidence:

You are doubtless aware that at an inquest, it is the duty of all persons who are able to assist the Enquiry with relevant and admissible evidence to do so. I do not know whether Mr Smith is in a position to give such evidence concerning the circumstances of his daughter's death to his own knowledge. I understand that he was not present at the time, nor even in Saudi Arabia. Nevertheless, if you feel that he is able to assist the court with evidence which would be admissible, I should be glad to have particulars.

The inquest was held at the old Crown Court No. 1 in Leeds Town Hall. The Crown Courts themselves had recently moved to a new, purpose-built building next door, and as the Leeds Coroners' Court is very tiny, this was a much better venue.

West Yorkshire Council had budgeted £50,000 for the inquest, which included paying all the expenses of witnesses who came from abroad. Some of these expenses were likely to be considerable. Richard Arnot, for example, was brought over from Australia, where he had taken up his medical career again. Apart from his return air fare and living expenses while in Leeds, the County Council had to pay for a substitute surgeon in Australia while he was away. Richard Arnot had also appointed Sir David Napley, one of Britain's top and most famous solicitors, to represent him. Napley had defended Jeremy Thorpe in his trial in the summer of 1979 and once defended Princess Anne on a speeding charge.

In a press statement shortly before the inquest ended, the County Council leader, John Gunnell, expressed surprise at Richard Arnot having chosen Sir David Napley to represent him, but added: 'Sir David is well aware that his fee will be paid out of public funds. He has been asked to ensure that his fee will be reasonable. After all, this has become in terms of public interest, the inquest of the century. All lawyers taking part in it are receiving considerable publicity.'

John Gunnell promised a breakdown of the figures once they became known. This had not been given by March 1983, but it was widely expected that the £50,000 budget would be exceeded. Coroner Gill at this time would not supply Sir David Napley's bill to the County Council leader, but at a news conference on 8 March, Gunnell estimated it to be £20,000 – over £1,000 per day that the inquest sat. At the same time, old wounds were reopened over the coroner's accountability to his pay-masters.

The opening day dawned. The press assembled, the public queued. The inquest was generating an enormous amount of interest – so enormous that the obvious question was in danger of being forgotten. How *did* Helen Smith die? There were basically two theories from which to choose:

1. She died accidentally in a fall from the Arnot balcony while making love to Johannes Otten. This was the original story.
2. She was not on the Arnot balcony at all at the time of her death, but in a first-floor flat in the same block, belonging to an absent lover – Dr Sachel – to which she had a key. She was murdered there and dropped outside. This theory found favour in the Smith camp, especially after the joint autopsy of Professors Dalgaard and Usher in December 1980, which suggested a fall only from a moderate height, if at all.

It neared 10.00 a.m. Ron Smith walked the short distance from the office of his solicitor, Ruth Bundey, through the barrage of cameras and microphones. Then a gold Rolls Royce drew up outside the Town Hall. In it were Richard Arnot, Sir David Napley and his assistant. As he stepped outside, Sir David posed momentarily – an old hand at dealing with the press.

The Inquest

2. The Pathologists

Day One

10.00 a.m., Thursday 18 November 1982. 'All stand please,' the usher called out to the packed court. Coroner Philip Gill made his entrance.

He was clearly nervous as first he had to deal with a welter of applications on behalf of the interested parties.

Stephen Sedley stood up. Whereas Geoffrey Robertson was representing Ron Smith, he wished to represent Helen's two brothers, Graham and David, and her mother, now living in the USA. There was no disagreement within the family, he said, but all had a legitimate interest. Would Mr Gill accept the Smith family, outside of Ron Smith, as being a properly interested party in its own right and allow him to represent it? Gill granted the request.

Next on his feet was barrister Andrew Collins, representing the Foreign Office together with barrister Timothy Hartley. He told Gill that he recognised that, strictly speaking, the Foreign Office was not an interested party at the inquest, which could only address itself to the questions of how, when and where Helen Smith died. 'One cannot ignore, however, the fact that serious allegations have been made against the Foreign Office and its staff who were in Saudi Arabia at the time,' he added, and pointed out that five of these staff were being called as witnesses.

'Some of these allegations may be of relevance to how, when and where Helen Smith died,' McDermott continued. 'I want the opportunity, if the need arises, to make an intervention. I will be happy to be present keeping a note and keeping a watching brief.'

'Wait and see how things go,' Gill replied, and gave him the liberty to intervene as the need arose.

Coroner Gill then addressed the jury of seven men and four women (inquest juries have between six and eleven members – at the discretion of the coroner – and, unlike courts, they are not chosen at random but by the coroner's office). He told them that this was a complex case that had attracted a great deal of publicity. They should try to do the impossible and put all they had heard, read and seen to one side. They had to make up their minds on the evidence presented to this inquest – and that evidence alone. Gill's summary of the events as known was then brief and uncontroversial.

When he had finished, Sir David Napley, representing Richard Arnot, stood up and asked for the order of witnesses. Gill said he still did not know exactly who would be attending and efforts were continuing at that moment to contact people. The first witnesses, however, would be the four pathologists who had, at various times, examined Helen's body.

Geoffrey Robertson was next to get his word in. He made an application for the documents relating to the case that had been supplied to Coroner Gill. He was thinking particularly of Foreign Office documents and a supplementary autopsy report written by Dr Michael Green. Robertson also pointed out that Ron Smith had spent three and a half years investigating the case and it 'would be a tragedy' if one of those documents contained a vital clue as to how Helen met her death, and he missed it.

Gill held his ground: 'The documents are of a confidential nature, supplied to the coroner,' he said, at which Stephen Sedley jumped to his feet to state that a coroner normally takes the view that they can be shown, although he would (and not for the only time) have to accept Coroner Gill's ruling.

Gill compromised. He would make available the pathology reports now, and those relating to other witnesses as they attended.

The preliminaries were now over, and Dr Michael Alan Green stepped into the witness box. He told the court that he was instructed by Deputy Coroner Coverdale to carry out a post-mortem examination on Helen Linda Smith, aged twenty-three years, on Friday 27 June 1980. He read from his report of that examination:

At 10.00 a.m. on Friday 27 June I attended at Leeds City Mortuary where I met Mr Coverdale, Sergeant Craig (the coroner's officer), Detective Chief Inspector Smalley and other police officers. I was introduced to the father of the deceased, Helen Linda Smith.

The body was in a wooden coffin, the lid of which had been sealed and screwed down. Mr Smith confirmed that the seals were intact as when he last saw the coffin in Saudi Arabia. The lid of the wooden coffin was then removed. The body was further enclosed in a light metal shell. This was opened and Mr Smith again confirmed that there was nothing to suggest that the body had been tampered with. Mr Smith then left the mortuary and the examination was commenced.

The body was that of a young, Caucasian, dark-haired girl which was wrapped in a white linen shroud. This was removed and the body was prepared for radiographic examination.

The X-rays were carried out by Mr H. Bentley, the Principal of the School of Radiography at Leeds General Infirmary. The plates showed multiple fractures of the pelvis, a fracture of the right eighth rib, and . . .

Dr Green faltered momentarily. Ron Smith, sitting only a few feet away, was staring hard at him. Dr Green departed from his script: '. . . and what I interpreted at the time as a fracture through the right shoulder joint.' Then he returned to the script to say: 'There were no other fractures obvious on X-ray.'

But the departure was highly significant. One of the

reasons for Ron Smith being aghast when he first read Dr Green's report two and a half years previously was that he *knew* that Helen had no right shoulder fracture.

Dr Green went on to describe his external examination of the body (no internal examination was possible as the organs had been removed in Saudi Arabia). He pointed to the difficulties presented by a body that had become shrunken and dried and said that some marks were obviously due to post-mortem spillage of embalming fluid. However, he could identify several areas of bruising. There was a brown mark over the point of the right shoulder and a dark-red one over the right iliac crest which extended down to the groin. On the lower half of the body there was extensive red discoloration on the outside of the right thigh, a bruise lower down and on the front of the right thigh, and an abrasion mark over the right kneecap. The left thigh had two bruises on the inside only and there was a faint bruise on the inside of the left shin. Both feet and ankles had lacerations.

Throughout this description, Dr Green twisted and turned in the witness box to show visually the positions of the various marks. Then he described the head and face.

Helen had bruises on the right forehead and on the right cheek. She also had bruises over the left eyebrow, in the left eyelid, on the left ear and on the left cheek. She was bruised on top of the nose, under the angle of the jaw, over the right mastoid process, and on the right side of the neck near her Adam's apple.

Dr Green next looked more closely at the skeletal system. Besides the fractures he had already mentioned, he noted that the spine was intact. Bruising on the insides of both thighs, he said, 'were consistent with secondary impact following a fall'. (Dr Green meant here that if Helen fell on her side, then her thighs would slap together.) 'There was bleeding around the heads and necks of all the ribs on both sides; this was more prominent on the right than on the left,' he added.

Dr Green could not confirm any hair-line skull fractures as noted by a Saudi pathologist, but he did note a fracture of the large breast bone, the sternum. Because there was little evidence of bleeding around it, he thought it must be a post-mortem change caused during autopsy in Saudi Arabia and therefore it had nothing to do with the circumstances in which she died. Fractures caused during life would have extensive bleeding around them, but after death the blood would have drained away to the lowest part of the body.

Dr Green turned to his 'Summary of the Principal Findings and Opinion as to the Cause of Death'. He could not say how Helen had died due to the removal of the internal organs, but the objectives of his examination were to determine: 'a) Whether this girl's injuries were due to a fall from a height, and b) whether she was in fact alive when she fell from a height.'

As for a), he concluded: 'The principal injuries are consistent with a fall from a height.' He added that the pelvic fractures, which were principally right-sided, the eighth-rib fracture and the principal areas of bruising were entirely consistent with the body having fallen thirty feet or more and landing on the right side. Such a fall 'would also account for the minor areas of bruising on the inside of both thighs and shins, and the minor lacerations on both forefeet which are approximately in the line of the upper of a shoe or sandal'.

A fall onto the right side would also account for a right shoulder fracture which in turn, Dr Green wrote in his report, 'would account for the bizarre position of the right arm described by the father and other witnesses of the scene of the incident'. (When Ron Smith first viewed Helen in the mortuary, her arm was bent over her head in a *rigor mortis* position, as if she was shielding it.)

But, of course, Dr Green had just admitted there was no right-shoulder fracture and, anyway, it was the left arm that had been noticed in the 'bizarre' position. Dr Green did say there was a tiny 'flake fracture' on the right shoulder but that this was of 'no relevance'.

'I was mistaken very much. I was quite frankly wrong,' he added.

But the non-shoulder fracture held another significance. Dr Green had found no skull fracture, and it was reasonable to presume, if Helen fell on her right side, that the right arm was protecting the head in some way as she hit the ground. This would explain the presence of one fracture and the absence of the other. Now the explanation no longer held.

Addressing himself to his second objective, he concluded that Helen must have been alive when she fell because of the extensive bleeding around the injuries to the trunk which would not be there if they had been caused after death.

Dr Green now looked at some of the other injuries he had found – especially those on the face, head and neck. These were distributed all over, favouring neither the right nor the left side. They could not have been caused by one impact.

'The minor bruises around the face are not entirely consistent with a fall of the type which I have described. They are more consistent with slaps with the open hand or punches with the fist,' he told the inquest. 'However, none of them are particularly severe, and in the absence of the brain and its coverings it is not possible to say whether this girl sustained any head injury which could have caused unconsciousness or impaired consciousness before her fatal fall.'

Questioned further on the subject by Coroner Gill, he painted three possible scenarios: 1) she had become hysterical and was slapped to quieten her; 2) she was drunk and she had been slapped to revive her; 3) she had been indulging in sexual horseplay, had withdrawn consent, and her partner had become violent.

Dr Green had already sent journalists scurrying off once that morning with their copy over his 'right-shoulder fracture', but soon he dropped another bombshell when he told the inquest that he had also found injuries around

Helen's genital region and her anus, but had not in-corporated these into his autopsy report. 'Coroner Coverdale asked that they were not included,' Green ex-plained, although he later made a supplementary report for the police and the pathologists who examined Helen six months later. He paused and then added: 'Mr Cover-dale did not wish to cause Mr Smith any further distress.' He said that these injuries were consistent with 'forceful sexual intercourse' and agreed that the bruises to the insides of the thighs could also be explained in this way.

Dr Green summarised his evidence by referring to the joint autopsy carried out by Professors Dalgaard and Usher in December 1980, which he attended. All three pathologists were agreed, he said, that the injuries to the face and head had been sustained during life, and that Helen had had forceful sexual intercourse. Where they differed was on the height of the fall.

'Professor Dalgaard thought it was no more than a few feet, Professor Usher thought it was less than thirty feet. I would say she fell a considerable distance and I cannot exclude the possibility that she fell seventy feet,' he said.

To back up his point, Dr Green then dramatically waved yards of computer paper at the inquest. It was a print-out of a statistical survey he had done of falls from a height. The study was of eighteen females and thirty-one males. Its purpose was to show how unpredictable such falls are.

Hearts tended to rupture in falls over seventy feet, the aorta (the main blood artery) in falls over ten feet. Be-tween ten and forty feet, the liver would rupture.

The vast majority who fell more than forty feet had fractured skulls but a considerable number did not. Simi-larly, a surprising minority (20 per cent) showed no obvi-ous external injuries after a long fall.

At this point Coroner Gill advanced for the first time what was to become his own pet theory – that Helen's fall had been broken in some way, which accounted for the lack of some of the injuries one would expect. Supposing Helen and Johannes had come down together, he had hit the railings and she had bounced off him? Green was not happy with this theory, as he felt they would have separated during their flight.

What, then, if they had separated but Helen had hit Johannes on the railings and then bounced off him, Gill persisted? It was a possibility that Dr Green had not thought of before, but definitely a possibility.

The inquest adjourned for lunch. More than one journalist would have liked to contact ex-Coroner Coverdale to ask why he requested that the genital injuries be omitted. Unfortunately, Coroner Coverdale had died of a heart attack some six months previously, a few days after the Appeal Court had ordered that an inquest should take place.

Geoffrey Robertson started his examination of Dr Green immediately after lunch. It should be pointed out here that at an inquest you *examine* witnesses, not *cross-examine* them. You are not allowed to attempt to discredit the witness, who has come to assist the coroner. You may only ask questions relevant to how, when and where the deceased died and those that directly ascertain information. This difference was to lead to many an altercation between Coroner Gill and counsel for the interested parties (especially the two barristers for the Smiths) during the course of the inquest.

Robertson reminded Green that at the start of his autopsy, back in June 1980, Ron Smith had been ushered away by the coroner's officer, Sergeant Craig. This was unfortunate as he had not been able to discuss with Ron Smith some of the background facts and, as a result, Green had been wrong on a number of points.

For example, it was the left arm that had been positioned in front of the head, not the right. No Saudi pathologist had told him of hair-line skull fractures as he stated in his report (Dr Green could not now remember where this information came from). And as for the lacerations in the shoe line – Helen was barefooted when found.

Green had been asked to consider whether the injuries were consistent with a fall and whether she was alive when she fell, and had answered yes to both questions, Robertson continued. But the injuries to her face and head could have contributed to her death. 'There was a real prospect that they could have impaired consciousness,' agreed Green.

'Well, you can't get up and fall over a balcony if you're unconscious,' retorted Robertson, and followed up by asking about evidence of an extensive wound to the left side of Helen's forehead. This had not been mentioned by Green in his report, but Professors Dalgaard and Usher drew particular attention to it in their later joint autopsy.

'When I saw it at the time of my autopsy, I was not convinced it was a bruise. By the time of the second autopsy I agreed it was one,' replied Green. 'I omitted it from my report. I thought it might be a henna dye,' he added.

Robertson was quick to point out that this head wound added weight to the theory that Helen had been subjected to violence before her death.

Green was then asked about the genital injuries which he had failed to mention in his original report, and those to the insides of the thighs. 'I thought they had no direct bearing on the cause of death,' he said, but Robertson wanted to know how he could draw such a conclusion. 'I accepted the express request of Coroner Coverdale,' said Green.

Robertson returned to the head injuries. One of Green's own hypotheses was that Helen had been beaten because she withdrew sexual consent. Did these not indicate sexual assault, taken together with the thigh and genital injuries?

'Mr Coverdale took the decision that no references be made to the genital injuries,' repeated Green.

Robertson now produced the press release that Cover-dale put out shortly after the autopsy. Green agreed that he had been shown it and had approved its contents. Yet these too said nothing of the genital and thigh injuries, and described the injuries to the face and head as super-ficial bruises that did not contribute to death.

'With hindsight it would have been fairer to say that it was extremely unlikely they contributed,' replied Green.

Robertson next referred to Green's computer print-out. 'The Leeds computer print-out takes no account of the nature of the surface,' he commented. (If you fall from the same height onto a road, a flower bed or a cow pat, the extent of the injuries is bound to be different.) Green took the point but added that the vast majority of his forty-nine cases had been in an urban area.

Robertson therefore invited him to consider a fall of seventy feet onto a hard marble pavement. The speed of the body on impact would be about 48 m.p.h. This is what is claimed to have happened to Helen Smith, yet she had 'no skull fracture, her leg joints were perfect, and she had no serious fracture to her right arm . . .'. Robert-son broke off here. 'That was quite a bad mistake, wasn't it?' he asked.

'It was one which I should not have made,' agreed Green.

Robertson referred to the rib fractures – the later autopsy of Dalgaard and Usher had found more than the one Green had found, but two of them were left, not right, ribs. And the pelvic fractures – there were only two, yet Green had referred to them as multiple fractures. Nor was it strictly accurate to say that these pelvic frac-tures were on the right side of the body.

'Yet she fell on the right side or nothing?' Robertson asked. Green agreed: if she fell on her head, the skull would have smashed, if she fell on her feet, the major injuries would be to her legs. There was nothing in the pattern of injuries to suggest she fell on her left side, her front or her back.

Yet surely, Robertson pressed, if she had fallen seventy feet onto a marble floor, there would be more extensive injuries to her right side. There would be some evidence of skull, right arm and leg fractures. 'I would have expected more extensive injuries,' said Green, but, returning to his computer print-out, added that a surprising number who fall this distance would not have them.

Robertson finished his examination by stating that if the deaths had occurred in Britain, Green's findings would have resulted in a criminal inquiry. Green agreed and said: 'Mr Coverdale was aware of those findings, and I expressed my concern. He said he would ask for a supplementary report as and when it became necessary.'

Sir David Napley rose. He had now had time to study the Saudi pathology report handed over by Coroner Gill only that morning, and this formed the basis of his examination. It detailed extensive damage to the organs, such as tears of the liver. 'The internal injuries do add to the probability that she fell from a height?' Sir David queried.

Green brightened. 'We're moving up the scale rather than down it,' he said enthusiastically.

Sir David followed up Coroner Gill's theory that Helen's fall might have been cushioned by Otten. 'The more I hear of the internal injuries, the more I'm inclined to favour a straight fall to the ground of seventy feet,' said Green, with the tone of a man who suddenly felt vindicated.

Sir David's examination was fairly short and he was followed by Stephen Sedley, who began by suggesting to Green that he had looked only for evidence that suggested a fall from a height.

'I did look for other things,' Green replied.

'Did you consider that Helen might have been rendered unconscious and then dropped?' Sedley asked.

'Yes, I did consider that possibility,' replied Green. But he had not suggested it anywhere in his report, so had he rejected it? 'It is possible she was badly injured and then dropped,' he added, but he did not sound sure. Sedley pressed the point and Green said: 'Yes, it is a

possibility, but a seventy-foot fall is the more likely.'
Sedley would not accept the answer.

'It's a perfectly good possibility. Why are you being so
grudging about it?'

'I cannot exclude the possibility,' was the only reply.

Stephen Sedley left the point and discussed the head
and face injuries. The left forehead injury found by Professors Dalgaard and Usher had caused bleeding on the
top of the brain. It must have been caused by an impact
capable of rendering Helen unconscious, Sedley suggested. Green agreed that if it was sustained before she
fell, it must have been a heavy blow.

Of the thigh and genital injuries, Sedley drew the distinction between *forceful* and *forcible* sexual intercourse
(the latter being rape, the former rough, but consenting,
sex). 'What you meant was *forcible* intercourse,' he suggested.

'The two are very difficult to sort out. The injuries
(especially to the thighs) are more indicative of forcible
intercourse,' Green replied.

'So, the more realistic hypothesis is that she was beaten
up, raped and thrown out unconscious,' ventured Sedley.

'The injuries are consistent with her having been
beaten up and raped. They are consistent with her having
been thrown out,' Green conceded.

Sedley now referred to the condition of Helen's clothing when found. She had been wearing a dress, her beige
silk bra was intact and in position, but her pants had
been removed from one limb. 'Is that not the classic picture of a victim of rape?' he asked.

'Yes,' agreed Green, and Sedley continued:

'Because, if she was willing . . .'

'She would take them off both legs,' interrupted
Green.

It was mid-afternoon by the time Saudi pathologist Dr
Ali Muhammad Kheir stepped into the witness box.
Speaking through an interpreter, he told the inquest that

at 8.00 a.m. on Sunday 20 May 1979, the police informed him of two dead bodies in the vicinity of the Bakhsh hospital – fallen from the fourth or sixth floor.

Dr Kheir arrived at the scene around 9.00 a.m., but the bodies had already been transferred to the hospital. He was shown where Helen and Johannes were found and was then taken up to the Arnot flat. There he went onto the balcony, but noted nothing in particular about it. There was a sunlounger in the corner, he said.

Dr Kheir estimated the height of the balcony balustrade as 75 cm (2 feet 6 inches), and when shown a model prepared for the inquest, agreed that it was accurate. The top balustrade railing would be about level with the top of the thighs of a normal-sized person.

Inside the flat, Dr Kheir found nothing of significance. There was no evidence of blood to suggest a struggle may have taken place. There were some flasks containing wine or gin, however.

He examined Helen externally that afternoon, internally some eleven days later, after Ron Smith had given permission. He thought she was a woman in the fourth decade of her life and she had 'bruises and contusions of various sizes on the limbs'. Some of these appeared to be due to scraping with a rough surface, and Dr Kheir explained that when he arrived, certain repairs were going on and the marble courtyard floor was not smooth because of sand and cement. There was also bruising to Helen's head.

He estimated the height of the balcony above the courtyard to be forty-five feet and he felt satisfied there had been a fall from this balcony. (No official measurement of the height had been released to the inquest but seventy feet – Ron Smith's estimate – had been the one so far assumed.) There were 'no signs of injury to the cerebellum matter [the brain] suggesting the use of criminal violence'.

Dr Kheir finished the first day's evidence by describing some of Johannes Otten's injuries. The railings had impaled him to a considerable depth in the groin and abdomen, he said.

Day Two

Friday 19 November. Coroner Gill continued to ask Dr Kheir about Johannes Otten. Did the fact that he was lying on the railings some distance away from Miss Helen in the courtyard cause any concern? Did he feel the body had been projected forward and away from the building in some way? Dr Kheir thought that Johannes had definitely come off the balcony with some momentum, rather than simply overbalancing and falling. Otherwise he would have been nearer to Miss Helen.

Dr Kheir said that Johannes was wearing 'shorts' (underpants) and a tee-shirt only. The shorts were torn. Gill asked if the damage was a result of the railing spikes going through the shorts when they impaled Johannes's body or whether it occurred when the body was pulled off. 'Both,' was the reply.

Coroner Gill said there was evidence that Johannes's watch had stopped at 3.10 a.m. and this was the time of his death. Dr Kheir said that, according to his medical experience, he would favour around that time too. He was told at the time that early morning prayer-goers had first reported the deaths to the police at 4.00 a.m.

Dr Kheir then turned to his internal examination of Helen. He had established the presence of semen in her, but no grouping test had been carried out so it was impossible to say who it had come from. He explained that the word 'accidental' in the translation of his report into English should really mean 'injurious' and had nothing to do with his opinion as to the cause of death. What he had been doing in the report was stating the obvious – Helen had died from her injuries.

He was also shown the two English versions of the Saudi police report and confirmed that Ron Smith's was the correct one. He contradicted one part of it, however, where it said that he accompanied the police when they were first called to the scene. He had only come later, after the bodies were removed.

Geoffrey Robertson started his examination by pressing home the point that Johannes had probably left the balcony under some momentum. Then he asked Dr Kheir who had shown him around the Arnots' flat. 'Just one senior officer,' he replied and added that Mr and Mrs Arnot gave him a sandwich.

Robertson asked about the sunlounger in the corner of the balcony. 'Was it unfolded?'

'No,' was the reply, and Kheir added that all balconies in Jeddah possessed a sunlounger.

Geoffrey Robertson was also concerned with injuries noted in Kheir's pathology report that related to the left side of Helen's body. These were numerous and were not consistent with a fall on the right side. Kheir had noted bleeding too just under the skull, on the covering to the brain. He confirmed to the inquest that these injuries were present.

Robertson concluded by asking Kheir if he remembered telling Ron Smith there were no fractures to the skull or spine. 'Yes, I remember telling him.' He had felt that this lack of injuries was 'a problem'.

Sir David Napley rose to complain that his examination of witnesses was sandwiched between that of Geoffrey Robertson and Stephen Sedley for the Smiths. Gill acknowledged the complaint and shuffled the order. But Stephen Sedley had nothing to ask, so Sir David went ahead.

'Is it right you found no abrasions inconsistent with a fall?' he asked. They were all consistent, Kheir replied, and he agreed there was no sign of blood on Helen's ears, nose or mouth when he examined her. Nor did he see any abrasions on her neck.

Sir David then turned to Helen's clothing. The translation of Kheir's pathology report said she was wearing a light, silk dress and a 'pantie-girdle' which was only around one leg.

'Was it an elasticated girdle?' he asked.

'Yes,' came the reply.

'They're difficult to remove, aren't they? They don't come off easily. If one is pulled down to the knees, do you agree it would be impossible to have intercourse?'

'Difficult, but not impossible,' said Dr Kheir.

'And the same would apply if it was around the ankles?'

Dr Kheir nodded.

'So the pantie-girdle could be only on one leg and it could still be consent,' Sir David rammed his point home. Helen may simply have taken one leg out herself to ease sex.

'It is a possibility,' said Dr Kheir.

Sir David then turned to the state of the pantie-girdle. There was no sign of grabbing or pulling of that article. And Dr Kheir had already said he found no genital injuries. Rape can only be concluded when there are such injuries, both men agreed.

Sir David now referred to Dr Kheir's earlier comment that Johannes must have fallen with some momentum: 'If Otten fell backwards, might he have somersaulted on the way down?'

'It is possible. God knows,' replied Dr Kheir.

'One of two witnesses we're not calling to this inquest,' ventured Sir David sharply, drawing the first relieving laugh of this tense session.

Sir David finished his examination by investigating the position of Johannes Otten's shorts. Dr Kheir had inferred that these were up in position, because the spikes that had penetrated his groin and abdomen had also torn his shorts.

'My client, Mr Arnot, says that when he saw the body, the shorts were around the knees and ankles and not in the normal place,' Sir David commented. 'Might the tears have been caused instead by pulling him off the railings?'

'I can dispute it, because the tearing of the shorts

corresponded with the injuries on the body,' replied Dr Kheir, holding his ground.

World-respected Danish professor in forensic medicine, Jorgen Dalgaard, followed Dr Kheir into the witness box. Specially commissioned by Ron Smith, he performed an independent autopsy on Helen on 16 December 1980. Professor Usher from Sheffield University was there, as was Dr Green. Dalgaard asked, when doing the autopsy, for Dr Kheir's report, but for some inexplicable reason had never been given it. He did have some photographs of Helen in the coffin in Jeddah, taken by Ron Smith a year after her death.

Although Dalgaard 'had the knife', Professor Usher joined in the examination. They each took away sections of the same tissue for independent microscopic examination and then met to compare results. Some lesions, they noted on external examination, looked as if they might be post-mortem changes in Helen's body, but once they confirmed blood to be present in their sections, they could also confirm a genuine lesion sustained in life.

Of the head injuries, Professor Dalgaard confirmed for the most part Dr Green's findings, stating that their distribution on both sides meant that they could not have originated in a fall. He did find one extra important lesion, however, over the left side of the head, which he numbered as lesion 13. 'It was a very distinct lesion,' he said. 'It was not a hair dye as Dr Green had thought.' Questioned further by Coroner Gill, who suggested that it may have developed and become more obvious since Green's examination, Professor Dalgaard said: 'I'm sure it was there and Dr Green observed it in his examination. The colour might have changed a little, but I think I can also see it from the photograph of Helen in the coffin in Jeddah.'

Professor Dalgaard confirmed that on the right shoulder there was a very small 'emulsion' or flake fracture. The outside of the right thigh had a very conspicuous bruise, as Dr Green had found, but there were no breaks.

He also found bruising on the left shoulder and arm, and on the left index finger, which Dr Green had missed. And there were 'very convincing' bruises on the insides of the thighs, possibly due to Helen's legs being forced apart, and some 'very small haemorrhages around the pubic region', indicating 'rough but not dangerous sex'.

Turning to the skeleton, Professor Dalgaard found that there were fractures in most of the right ribs, although none were actually dislocated. There were also two left-rib fractures. He found some pelvic fractures, but there was only a small amount of blood around those fractures that suggested she fell on her right side. What was most significant about the skeleton, however, he told the inquest, was what he did not see: no fractures of the main bones of the arms, legs, hip, feet, hands, face or skull.

When Professor Dalgaard examined the skull base, he found blood there and saw that this extended some way down the spinal column. This blood appeared to be associated with the lesion 13 that Dr Green had thought might be henna dye. It was natural now to equate it with Dr Kheir's discovery of blood on the brain covering. Because the blood had seeped down the spinal column some way, Professor Dalgaard considered it to be a most severe lesion, which had probably been caused by a blow with the open hand to the head. 'This blow would have caused unconsciousness and may by itself have caused death. It was very definitely *not* due to a fall from a height.'

In conclusion, Professor Dalgaard said that the right-side lesions of Helen's body were the only ones that could be due to a fall.

'But they do not indicate a fall of a considerable height. More serious lesions would be expected. There was no fracture of the rim of the pelvis, or of the leg, or of the arm. When the head hit the ground, you would expect a great fracture of the skull, maybe the neck and spine too.'

Professor Dalgaard mimed the side of the head hitting

the floor. If the skull was not fractured, it could only be because the arm was protecting it, in which case the arm should be broken. And he pointed out that Helen was only wearing a thin dress at the time, which would offer virtually no protection to the rest of her body. 'Who can show me a body falling on a marble floor on the right side from such a distance (the sixth floor) and not sustaining these lesions?' he asked rhetorically. He had examined 250 cases over the years of people falling from heights, of which 42 were in the fifteen- to seventy-feet range. 'Thirty-three displayed much more lesions and three fell onto soft ground.'

'I have never seen a body falling from this height sustain such small lesions. The ribs should be all over the place, like matchsticks. I would not be surprised if she fell only from the first floor.' Professor Dalgaard stressed here that it was very difficult to say exactly from what height Helen fell, if any. But in any case, he thought the head lesion 13 that caused the brain bleeding was the most serious in causing Helen's death: 'I am not certain whether she was dead because of this when she fell. I am certain she was unconscious.'

Coroner Gill at last got a word in to advance his cushioned-fall theory, to explain the relative lack of injuries. Could Helen have bounced off Johannes?

'I accept it as theoretical. If you fire a bullet in the air it might happen you find a sparrow hit, but it is not very likely,' Professor Dalgaard replied.

Geoffrey Robertson began by questioning him further about the severe blow to the head. Professor Dalgaard thought it was with the open hand because the lesion was curved from the forehead over the top of the scalp. Its nature also indicated that something had hit Helen, rather than the other way round.

Robertson asked him about Dr Kheir's evidence, where he stated there was nothing about the injuries being inconsistent with a fall.

'There are many injuries consistent with blows and not with a fall. I disagree with Dr Kheir,' was the reply.

'Your conclusion was that the death was not accidental,' continued Robertson.

'Yes,' said Professor Dalgaard. He added that her injuries were like those of a motor accident victim. If she had been taken to hospital, she could have survived: 'There was a hospital just there nearby.'

Professor Dalgaard then agreed with Stephen Sedley that the inside thigh bruising and the genital bruising was consistent with rape, and the bruising on the face and head were consistent with the 'domestic form of violence'.

Sir David Napley's exchanges with Professor Dalgaard were short and sharp. 'Pathology is not an exact science,' he began.

'No,' Professor Dalgaard agreed.

'You often have to indulge in speculation and guesswork.'

'I try not to, but sometimes it is necessary.'

Sir David pointed out that Dalgaard had dealt with a body that was nineteen months old, and had had to cope with shrinkage and embalming of that body. Professor Dalgaard replied that much of his work was in the USA, where they embalm all bodies.

Sir David then suggested that Helen might have fallen from the Arnot balcony, hitting her head against something which had caused the major head wound, lesion 13. 'If you are in the air, you cannot climb back in,' retorted Professor Dalgaard. If she had hit her head against a wall on the way down, she would have scraped it and sustained a completely different type of lesion, he expanded.

Sir David asked about the degree of injury one would expect to be inflicted during rape. 'Rape is not life-threatening. It can occur without any lesions,' Professor Dalgaard said.

'Have you seen a fair amount of rape?' continued Sir David.

'What is a fair amount?' Professor Dalgaard replied.

Sir David next tried to press him on the height of the

fall, especially as Dr Kheir had now given evidence that the Arnot balcony might only be forty-five feet from the ground, not seventy feet. Did he think she could not possibly have fallen from there? 'I should say she fell twenty to twenty-five to thirty feet. I could accept ten feet as a possibility. I believe it not to be seventy feet, but to exclude the possibility . . .'

'The difficulty is that it is so variable, the statistics are not reliable,' interrupted Sir David. Professor Dalgaard said that, in looking at his own statistics, he had counted the falls that seemed most relevant in this case, but no, he could not exclude the possibility that she fell from a greater height. It was not probable, however.

Sir David ended his examination by referring to a talk Professor Dalgaard had given about the Helen Smith case to other pathologists in Denmark. 'Some had very grave doubts about what you said,' he ventured.

'Two out of 150,' replied Professor Dalgaard. Sir David suggested it was more. 'If there were, they did not tell me,' Professor Dalgaard flashed.

Day Three

Monday 22 November. The media had concentrated its reporting of the first two days on the blows to the head and the possibility of rape. Interest was still high after the weekend, about forty reporters being present for Monday's opening session.

Professor in forensic medicine at Sheffield University, Alan Usher, went into the witness box. He was the last of the pathologist witnesses who examined Helen and he said that he had performed 10,000 autopsies, including 600 murders, in a career spanning twenty-two years. He had originally been called in to watch Professor Dalgaard, but the two pathologists had decided to work together as a team instead.

'We are absolutely agreed on the injuries that did occur,' he said, adding, 'it was one of the most difficult autopsies I have ever been involved in. There was a complete lack of information of what went on in the flat. We were asked to consider a fall of seventy feet; now we are being asked to consider one of forty-five. We were told the surface was absolutely flat, now we are told there was rubble there.'

A second problem, Professor Usher told the inquest, arose because of the length of time that had elapsed between the death and his examination of the body. It had been removed from the scene, examined, brought to Britain and examined again. Changes had occurred due to the sheer length of time that had elapsed. It was very difficult to come to conclusions.

Summarising the lesions that were definitely present, Professor Usher confirmed all of Professor Dalgaard's findings, including the head injury, lesion 13, which Dalgaard thought may have itself caused death. Professor Dalgaard had discounted that this could have been caused by a fall, but Professor Usher was not so sure. Hitting your head in a broken fall can give rise to that sort of haemorrhage, he said, to give the first real credence to Coroner Gill's theory.

Professor Usher referred to bruising in the groin region, which was mysterious as it did not relate to any of Helen's pelvic fractures. The pubic bruising could be due to heavy intercourse, rape, or Helen could have been kicked between the legs. Some of the lesions on the right upper arm suggested she had been restrained by the arms. The bruise on the outside right thigh, together with the extensive right-rib fractures, was the best evidence that she fell on that side. There was only a little haemorrhaging around these rib fractures, however, and Professor Usher commented: 'I am unable to say whether they occurred in life or death.' Some of the inner thigh injuries could be due to the legs being forced apart, or they could be 'cross-over' injuries – the thighs slapping together on impact with the ground. The problem with the 'cross-over' theory, however, was that the relevant bruises on the right and left thighs should have matched each other exactly, but they did not.

He and Professor Dalgaard found four pelvic fractures, all accountable for by impact with the ground. But three of them could also be explained by kicks to the abdomen.

Interpreting the injuries, Professor Usher said he would have thought Helen fell twenty to thirty feet, but it was very difficult to quantify. The injuries not related to a fall raised the possibility that violence had been used towards this girl.

Geoffrey Robertson suggested to him that, although it had been one of the most difficult post mortems he had ever carried out, it had also been one of the most thorough. He and Professor Dalgaard had erred on the side of caution and, indeed, Dr Kheir had noted lesions (for example on the left foot) that they had later discounted because, although they saw them, they could not be sure they were sustained while Helen was alive. 'Yes, I think that is true,' said Professor Usher.

Professor Usher agreed that it was possible Helen Smith had not fallen at all, and the injuries he and Professor Dalgaard discovered would, if the deaths had occurred in Britain, have resulted in a thorough police investigation. He also agreed that the severe head injury was much more likely to result from one or more blunt impacts to the top of the head than a glancing blow against the wall as Helen Smith fell. The bruising to the pubic area and the insides of the thighs were 'the sort of injuries in size and sight, typical of rape victims'.

Geoffrey Robertson then asked Professor Usher to consider the mysterious sternum (breast bone) fracture. This had been briefly alluded to in the examination of the other pathologists. It had so far not been explained because of the absence of bruising around it, which sug-gested it occurred after death. Dr Green had thought that Dr Kheir may have broken it during his autopsy, but Kheir said it was already broken when he examined the body.

Professor Usher had told Coroner Gill a few moments earlier that it would have needed a massive, localised impact to break this very strong bone. Gill suggested that Helen's chest might have hit the lamp on the railings wall, just to the right of where Johannes Otten was impaled, since Dr Kheir had said this light was broken.

Geoffrey Robertson now took up this theory.

'If the chest hit the lamp first . . .' he began.

'You would have wounds in the chest,' replied Professor Usher.

'And a large area of bruising?'

'Yes.'

'But there was virtually none?'

'Yes.'

'There was no sign of a vital [i.e. in life] chest injury.'

'Yes.'

'If she hit the rubble in the courtyard, to hit the chest would require a fall on the front. But the evidence is for a fall on the right side. If she fell on her front, you would expect a smashed-in nose, for example; you would expect a completely different pattern of injury.'

'Yes, there is no evidence for a fall on the front.'

'The sternum can fracture with a very heavy punch, sometimes seen in violent heart resuscitation [i.e. heart massage].'

'Very heavy.'

'We have seen there are fractures of the seventh and ninth left ribs. The ninth left rib is also out of alignment.'

'The ninth rib was fractured twice. Rib seven is also fractionally further round than it should be.'

'The left-side fractures are not associated with a right-side fall. But they could be associated with a vigorous attempt to resuscitate Helen Smith, which could have caused the sternum to fracture.'

Professor Usher looked at Robertson as if he was a very bright student in a tutorial group before delivering his reply: 'Yes, this is a much more convincing explanation for the sternum fracture.'

'And a much more convincing explanation for the lack of blood and bruising, if Helen Smith was dead at the time.'

'Yes.'

The sternum fracture very neatly explained! It was probably Geoffrey Robertson's best moment of the inquest and should have been of great significance. If someone had attempted to revive Helen Smith from the dead, who was it, and when and where was it done?

Stephen Sedley established with Professor Usher that the probability was against Helen's head striking the wall as she fell. And Professor Usher thought it would have been 'remarkable' if she had struck Johannes Otten on the railings. Moreover, to account for her head injuries being sustained in the fall, she would have had to strike him with her head, and such an impact would have dislocated her neck. Sedley asked Usher if he thought Dr Kheir was wrong when he claimed all the injuries could be attributed to a fall. 'I have to say, yes,' replied Professor Usher.

Sir David Napley began as he did with Professor Dalgaard. 'Even at best, it is very rare that you don't have to engage in speculation?' he asked.

'Yes,' said Professor Usher.

He challenged Professor Usher on his estimated height of the fall. Professor Usher was not prepared to state that it was unthinkable she fell seventy feet, and Sir David Napley mooted the 'new' height of forty-five feet as being a 'real, solid possibility' from the point of view of the injuries. 'Yes,' was the reply.

Sir David turned to a bruising of Helen's nostrils, which Professor Usher said could have been caused by an assailant's hand. 'You have to strain the imagination,' he commented.

'I would not have thought so. I can go on my experience over the years; I accumulate experience,' replied the very mild-mannered Professor Usher.

Despite Professor Dalgaard having told him earlier that there need be none at all, Sir David Napley still wondered to what extent the genital injuries indicated rape. He suggested that Helen's genital bruises may simply have been the result of 'stroking the woman's pubis'.

'She would have to be handled very forcibly to produce such bruises,' Professor Usher retorted. Sir David also thought the bruises on the insides of the thighs that were typical of rape were actually 'very slight'.

'I can't accept that,' was the reply.

Sir David still did not want to leave the sexual line of questioning. He said that two of Helen's lovers had had problems with the Saudi authorities. He suggested to Professor Usher that these injuries could have occurred at any time during the previous week. She was supposed to have had a close relationship with both a Saudi and an Iranian doctor, so it was possible the sexual injuries could have occurred in some other way. Professor Usher could not exclude the possibility.

Professor Usher was followed by a Dr Albert Goonetilleke, senior lecturer in forensic medicine at Charing Cross hospital, London. He had never seen Helen's body, but was doing research into the statistics of falling bodies. It had not been fully written up yet, however, and the Smith barristers were clearly unhappy about him being there – no warning had been given that he would be. He found that 7 out of 25 people who fell on their sides from between 11 and 130 feet had no serious skull fracture, but the ground that the bodies fell onto varied from grass to tarmac. Questioning from Stephen Sedley also revealed that the clothing worn by the fallers was quite variable – from December outdoor clothes to tee-shirt and jeans. In several cases the clothing was not even known.

Dr Goonetilleke's evidence was never referred to again in the inquest.

3. From Harms Salvage to the Bakhsh Hospital

Day Four

Tuesday 23 November. Sitting on the witness bench waiting to be called are Martin Fleischer, Klaus Ritter and Manfred Schlaeffer, three of the party guests from Harms Salvage. The air is expectant – these are the first party guests to give evidence. On the previous afternoon, Sir David Napley had already effected the transition from the evidence of the pathologists to the evidence of the party witnesses, and laid down the foundations of one of his main lines of argument. Helen echoed in the court as 'immoral'; echoed in the comments of passing women, complaining bitterly of character assassination.

Sitting on the bench, stripped of their distance from us and the weight of our images, the three employees of Harms look like any other men on the street. We are surprised. Fleischer looks so young, his blonde hair tousled, round-cheeked, wearing the student's Oxfam jacket. Alongside him sits Klaus Ritter, the company cook, a massive man with genial eyes, black hair brushed back, his black beard trimmed around his chin, a belly for his children to bounce on. Then Manfred Schlaeffer, the crane operator, his facial bones and gestures sharp-lined, needing the technology of progress and examination of machines to draw him out.

Coroner Gill enters and Fleischer takes the witness stand first. An interpreter stands with him but Fleischer's English is good and he does most of the talking. Once he corrects the interpreter.

GILL: Mr Fleischer, you are not under any obligation
to answer any questions which might be incriminat-
ing. I say that, having regard to not only the law of
this country but to the law of Saudi Arabia, because
there are matters which might not be of a criminal
nature in this country, but which might have punitive
consequences there.

Fleischer nods, thoughtful. It is established that he
arrived in Jeddah three weeks before the party. Harms
employed him as a buyer. He lived on the company accommodation barge in Jeddah harbour. Another of the
Harms employees, diving instructor Tim Hayter, was due
to leave for Singapore and a party was arranged for him
on Saturday 19 May.

Gill asks if it was arranged by Mr Arnot and his wife.
'I would say that Tim arranged the party, but in Arnot's
flat,' Fleischer replies.

It is established that Fleischer and Hayter had visited
the flat two days previously at a birthday party for one of
the Arnot children. There, he met Helen Smith for the
first time and they discussed Tim Hayter's party. Fleischer understood he was welcome.

Saturday 19 May: Fleischer arrived at the Arnot flat
between 8.45 and 9.00 p.m., he tells the inquest. He
walked up the stairs, passing Mrs Arnot and Tim
Hayter on the way down, 'going to the shop to buy
drinks.'

'Were they to be alcoholic or soft drinks?' Gill asks.

Fleischer smiles. 'You don't get alcoholic drinks in the
shops. They were soft drinks,' he says.

Inside the flat, Fleischer met other Harms employees
already there – Klaus Ritter, the company cook, Manfred
Schlaeffer, the company crane operator, Dieter Chapuis,
the company engineer. They had come together in the
company jeep and brought with them a Dutch tugboat
captain, Johannes Otten.

GILL: When you arrived at the flat, what were people doing?

FLEISCHER: Sitting in the chairs and talking.

GILL: Was any form of refreshment available?

FLEISCHER: Yes.

GILL: Did that include alcoholic drinks?

FLEISCHER: Yes.

GILL: What was the nature of the alcoholic drinks?

FLEISCHER: Some bottles of whisky.

GILL: Anything else?

FLEISCHER: I don't know.

GILL: Soft drinks?

FLEISCHER: Yes.

Fleischer then tells the inquest of the arrival of the other guests. Helen Smith and the Harms Salvage boss Harry Gutzeit arrived more or less at the same time. Later a Frenchman called Jacques Texier came with a Chinese friend of Tim Hayter – 'Jimmy' – who only stayed a few minutes. Richard Arnot arrived an hour later when he came off duty, and a German called Peter turned up later still. He only stayed about two hours.

GILL (leaning towards the witness): So far as the events which followed are concerned, these were the only people in the flat?

FLEISCHER: Yes, that's correct . . . the children were there also.

Fleischer gives the flat details. There was a living room and a dining room, nominally separated by a big sliding door which was open for the party to create one large room. In the living room, the larger of the two, were chairs and a sofa, and the smaller room was clear for dancing.

GILL: Helen was coming to the party. Can you tell us the circumstances in which she came?

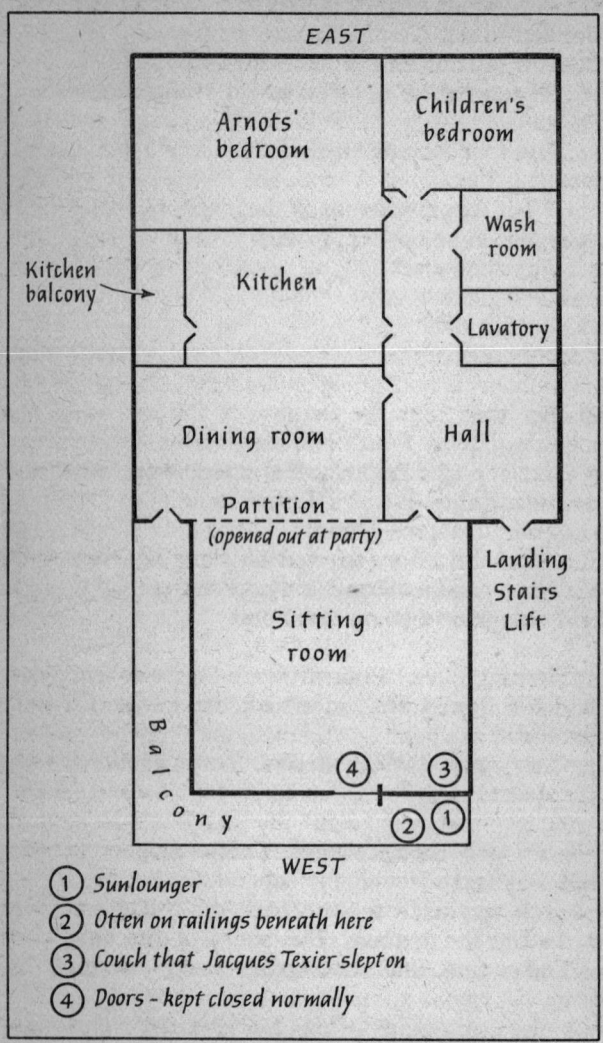

Ground plan of the Arnots' flat in Jeddah.

FLEISCHER: When Mrs Arnot came back from the shop I talked to her about who else was invited. She said she was not sure if her husband had already invited Helen at work or not yet, so she suggested to me, 'Why don't you go to the hospital because now she's finished work and ask her to come . . .?' The hospital has a reception hall. I asked for Helen there and she came within some seconds and told me, 'Yes, I'm already invited, I'll finish now. I'll go upstairs and get dressed and I'll be there in about twenty minutes.'

Fleischer returned and Harry Gutzeit arrived, then Helen. Fleischer talked to Helen 'socially', as Gill puts it. He danced with her only once.

GILL: Am I right in assuming there were only two females, Helen and Mrs Arnot?

FLEISCHER: Yes, that's right.

GILL: Therefore, if some men are dancing, they must take it in turns to dance with the ladies?

FLEISCHER (grinning broadly): Yes.

The narrative now unfolds. In the party's first half, Helen spoke to the others, in the second only with Otten. She was holding a glass all the time but Fleischer did not notice how she mixed her drinks. Yes, she did drink a considerable amount. Yes, you could see how she became more drunk during the night. She laughed and danced, yes, there was a noticeable effect. She did not become unsteady, though.

Gill suggests that the word 'merry' might be more appropriate than 'drunk'. Fleischer repeats the word 'merry' and grins. English language has its charm. Yes, Helen was happy.

What about Johannes Otten? Fleischer sat next to him at first and they spoke for half an hour to an hour. They talked about drinking. Otten said he liked whisky, liked it

very much and had no problems consuming it. He drank
continuously, but was always under control. Helen and
Johannes began, as the evening wore on, to dance together, 'in a close way'. They sat next to each other on
the sofa in a 'rather affectionate way . . . embracing each
other'. Fleischer never saw them leave the room together
– always they were in one or the other of the two rooms.
Fleischer was aware that there was a balcony. At the children's party, fetching a drink, he had looked through the
window and seen it. There were two doors to the balcony
but he never saw any open and never saw anyone go out
on the balcony. He did not know if it was locked with a
key. The rooms had two doors leading to the hall and
front door. There was no trouble, no violence: 'No, no
arguments, it was a friendly party.'

2.30 a.m., 20 May: Fleischer left and drove back to the
accommodation barge – consisting of two large containers
slotted together. The barge clock showed 2.50. He had
departed alone. Jimmy had gone, Peter had gone, the
others remained. Helen and Johannes were dancing in
the small room when he departed. Everyone else sat in
the larger room.

Next? 'At 6.30 in the morning Tim Hayter woke me
up. He told me to get up quickly. He said, "John . . .
Johannes . . . is dead." I asked what happened. He said,
"He was trying to screw Helen and they both fell down
the balcony." I apologise to the court for the words but
that was what he said.'

GILL: If mentioned, so be it. He asked you to do
something?
FLEISCHER: I, of course, wanted to know more, but he
told me, 'Stop asking questions, go and inform Harry
Gutzeit . . .' He told me to hurry up, be quick . . .
'Hurry up, no time for questions, go!' I could not go
to the toilet, he chased me away . . . When I left the
party I saw Harry in an armchair sleeping so when
Tim Hayter said go and inform Harry I asked,

'Harry, is he still there?', and then Tim said, 'Yes, stop asking questions, hurry up' ... so I thought Harry was still in apartment of the party, but later I found it was misunderstanding because Harry did not live in barge, but in an apartment in the city, and of course, Hayter wanted me to drive to the apartment and inform Harry but I misunderstood this ... I know this was not logical. I came out of bed, no breakfast, no drink, no toilet, and drove to the Arnots' apartment, I know this was wrong ...

GILL: At the apartment?

FLEISCHER: I found Dr Arnot, Dr Bakhsh and some policemen in front of the main door and I saw two bodies covered with sheets.

Hayter had only said they both fell over the balcony. Fleischer saw Otten's body hanging over the railings, Helen in the yard. His memory was that Otten's head faced the building, but he had no proper view of Helen in the courtyard.

A sheet was blown up by the wind and he saw Otten's naked chest – bloodspots. He needed to use the lavatory but Arnot barred him from the flat and directed him to the hospital instead. On returning he noticed the lamp, on the railings in the middle section, was bent over. He cannot recall if the glass was shattered. Someone came over and asked him to bring the party guests together for short interviews.

GILL (staring): Who asked you?

FLEISCHER: May I think ...? I think there was a plain-clothes policeman, he spoke good English ... There was also an employer at Bakhsh hospital to help and interpret [this refers to the hospital owner, Dr Bakhsh].

GILL: A plainclothes officer asked you?

FLEISCHER: Yes or maybe Arnot because they had asked him. I do not remember who had put this question

... I, together with Arnot, made a list on paper of guests at the party and then I gave it to one policeman who put it in his pocket, and then I went with two other policemen.

They drove to Harry Gutzeit's but he was not at home. They drove to the port where Fleischer, at police bidding, assembled Hayter, Ritter, Schlaeffer and Chapuis. No arrests, the police ensured them. In two cars, company and police, they drove first to the hospital to give blood samples, then to the police station. They were kept in the police yard for a day and night. Then they were put in cells, one and a half by two metres, four people, sometimes five to a cell. After two or three days they were questioned and after ten days they were moved to the jail.

They spent five months in prison, with one examination from a judge during that time. The German Embassy had told them that no one would be arrested. Even after they were released, they could not leave the country for five months. During that time they were called to the court and Fleischer was charged with joining a party 'where women and men could celebrate together and where there was dancing and also drink'. 'A moral offence,' are Gill's words. The time in jail was considered sufficient punishment for Fleischer.

The prison was in sections. Each section was the size of a flat, twenty to forty metres square. In each section were between eighteen and thirty prisoners, sometimes more. Inside the police-station cell, Fleischer had been with Ritter, Arnot and Chapuis. They talked of the night continuously. All Fleischer could learn, and repeat to the court, was that after the other Harms workers had left, a short time after he himself had left, some overnight guests went on to the balcony for fresh air and saw bodies below. Richard Arnot called the police.

GILL: Your colleagues could not tell you more?
FLEISCHER: No.

Arnot, as Fleischer remembers it, retired to bed just before he left. Otten's papers? He did not see them. Many times he has been asked about Otten's papers. He now details for the inquest those documents required for working in Saudi Arabia: passport, residence permit, igana (Saudi work permit) and a portpass (required by all those working inside the harbour). Guards were at the harbour gate. 'Similar to Europe,' Fleischer explains. You need a pass, but you are not always checked, especially at 2.30 in the morning. The pass may be held against the car window; the guard peers in, and waves you on.

Gill has no more questions. Geoffrey Robertson rises. He needs to establish a footing. That party was his third visit to the flat, Fleischer had told Gill at one point.

ROBERTSON: There was a birthday party, when was the other occasion?
FLEISCHER: Some days before. I don't know the date. Because I didn't know people privately I asked Tim to introduce me to some friends, so one night he took me to the Arnots.

Fleischer explains that he studies electronics. One year's practical experience was required, so he joined Harms Salvage. Otten was not a company man. He had a tugboat. The Harms accommodation barge was near to him, and he used it for food and showers. They then discuss Hayter.

ROBERTSON: Tim was leaving next day?
FLEISCHER: He wanted to leave.
ROBERTSON: He planned to leave?
FLEISCHER: He wanted to go on holiday.
ROBERTSON: What time next day was he leaving?
FLEISCHER: I don't know.
ROBERTSON: Did he have luggage with him?
FLEISCHER: I didn't notice.

Otten wore blue jeans and a white shirt for the party. He wore glasses, but Fleischer could not recall shoes or socks. Otten arrived at the party in the company car.

Robertson asks about the party: 'Were any photos taken?'

FLEISCHER: I made some photos but the film was completely spoilt ... a little difficult ... this film was used two times ... I rewind film not enough so little piece still on reel, so second time I thought film was new.

A pause – this is the first grit of the morning.

ROBERTSON: Double exposure?
FLEISCHER: Yes.
ROBERTSON: Nothing of the party came out?
FLEISCHER: No.
ROBERTSON: Others took photos?
FLEISCHER: I can't remember.

In an inquest there is no cross-examination so barristers must meander sometimes to get the answers they need. Nobody knows the Frenchman, Jacques Texier, who was at the party, and rumour has it that he will not be attending the inquest. Robertson discusses him with Fleischer. Yes, he spoke with Texier at the party. It was about Vietnam – not the war, but its historical past.

Robertson turns to Richard Arnot and Fleischer's impression that he went to bed shortly before he left the party.

ROBERTSON: You can't remember him wishing goodnight?
FLEISCHER: No.
ROBERTSON: You can't recall where he went?
FLEISCHER: No.
ROBERTSON: Why did you leave at 2.30?
FLEISCHER: I was tired.

ROBERTSON: When you saw Helen, what was your interest in asking her if she'd come?
FLEISCHER: I think parties are boring with no girls.

Fleischer smiles. For him it is a natural answer. There
are echoing smiles around the court.

ROBERTSON: Had Hayter indicated to you that there
would be girls?
FLEISCHER: No.
ROBERTSON: Had he indicated to you there would be
nurses?
FLEISCHER: No.
ROBERTSON: Who did you expect to see?
FLEISCHER: I didn't know. That's why I asked Mrs
Arnot.

They now discuss Hayter's 6.30 a.m. arrival back at
the barge and Fleischer driving to the Arnots' flat by
mistake. He confirms it was he from Harms who first saw
the police at the scene.

ROBERTSON: You first saw the police, isn't that the case?
Tim was somewhat angry that you went back to the
flat?
FLEISCHER: I think so. He did not shout at me.
ROBERTSON: He was clearly very angry. You disobeyed
orders. You hadn't done what he'd told you?
FLEISCHER: Yes.
ROBERTSON: You simply got it wrong?
FLEISCHER: Yes, and because I'd seen Harry asleep.

Fleischer explains that when he left the party he asked
if anyone would like to go with him but they said they
had their own car. No, he could not remember if anyone
was the driver and therefore was not drinking. Robertson
presses: 'Was anyone not drinking?'

FLEISCHER: I don't like question ... nobody seemed drunk ... everyone behaving ...

ROBERTSON: No one rolling drunk?

FLEISCHER: No, I said already, people sitting on chairs.

ROBERTSON: Everyone had been drinking?

FLEISCHER: Of course ... everyone had glasses. I don't know what they had and how they mixed their drinks.

Robertson sits down shortly afterwards. The pathologists, on the whole, had been good for the Smith camp. Martin Fleischer gives us the hint, however, that the witness evidence is going to be rather different. Stephen Sedley, a wiry and more impatient man than the mellifluous, rolling Robertson, stands.

Fleischer tells him about Harms – how it is involved in underwater exploration at Jeddah harbour. It brings up wrecks. Sedley asks if he met someone by the name of Dr Kirwen at the party. 'No,' is the answer. They turn to the subject of girls.

SEDLEY: One of the problems, is it not, is that most people you meet are men? There are very few women to associate with.

FLEISCHER: Yes, that is right.

SEDLEY: There is a shortage of girls?

FLEISCHER: If you want to call it that way.

SEDLEY: It is difficult to find a girlfriend?

FLEISCHER: That is one thing, and then it is criminal.

SEDLEY: Sexual relations are criminal?

FLEISCHER: Yes.

SEDLEY: Relationships as friends are difficult. How do you manage?

FLEISCHER (smiles): I take it as it comes.

They establish that there were always two or three bottles of whisky on the table, and the inquest adjourns for lunch. Fleischer looks slightly bewildered as he leaves

the Town Hall with two plainclothes policemen around
him to meet a solid phalanx of photographers. He is
whisked away by a waiting car.

The afternoon session starts with Fleischer confirming that the Bakhsh hospital and Harms Salvage
connect through the Arnot–Tim Hayter friendship.
He also confirms that when Hayter rushed in at
6.30 a.m. that morning he did not actually mention
that Helen was dead.

Sedley is interested in why Hayter did not go himself
to see Harry Gutzeit or even phone him. Fleischer says
that Gutzeit had a telephone but he did not know whether
the Arnots had one. There are public telephones in
Jeddah, however, and it would anyway have been much
quicker for Hayter to have driven directly to Gutzeit
rather than go to the port. This is packaged as one of the
inquest's mysteries.

Like Robertson, Sedley is also interested in Jacques
Texier. Fleischer says that at the police station he was in
another cell. At the prison all except Texier were in one
section. Fleischer does not know why. Why these questions about Texier? the press gallery murmurs. Little do
they know what will be said the next day.

Sedley asks Fleischer if he ever discussed with the
others in prison what to say to the police. 'No,' he replies,
and eyebrows raise all round the court.

Sedley finishes, and next to him Harold Fowler, representing all the Germans, rises, paper in one hand,
white-haired, his delivery slow and enunciated – choosing
his words, compelling attention to what he has to ask.
He establishes Martin Fleischer as an intelligent human
being – a university student. He establishes Martin
Fleischer as a sensitive human being – he went later
than the others to the party because he was making a
plant box and wanted to finish painting it before leaving
it to dry overnight. It is a nice touch for the inquest too
as something tugs at our hearts over what he has been
through since.

To complete his opening, Fowler establishes Fleischer as an ordinary young man. 'It was a friendly party,' Fleischer says, but he left early because, 'at that time the party had become boring, nothing going on . . . the only activity was on the dance-floor'.

This is as good a lead-in as any to the nitty gritty.

'Describe how Helen and Otten were dancing,' Fowler instructs.

'They were dancing very closely and in an affectionate way and only had interest for each other,' Fleischer replies.

'Not modern style . . . with their arms around each other?'

'I would say, more than old style,' says Fleischer.

Fleischer smiles again and the two men describe the graphic details of a smooch. Yes, Fleischer saw them embrace and sometimes kiss.

The other main argument for the accident advocates is the physical danger of the balcony. Fleischer saw it at the birthday party and realised it was very low. It looked dangerous and Mrs Arnot had told him she always kept the door closed so the children could not go out. At the adult party, curtains were across the window leading to the balcony.

Fowler ends by asking Fleischer what he felt when he was asked in Germany to assist at the inquest. 'I needed time to think about this . . . I wanted to help find the truth and I had to think because . . . as you know we have suffered very much because of this case . . . we have suffered very much and now I think . . . some people have made it more difficult than it was and it was difficult to decide and say, OK, you go through it again.'

FOWLER: . . . Was it part of your thinking to put an end to speculation?

FLEISCHER: I hope so. This is why I came. I can tell my story as it was. Nothing to hide. I did nothing criminal.

Fleischer steps down. His last words had a cadence, echoing, holding the court, his face impressively open. In that silence Dr Joe Deguara steps to the witness box, takes the oath, sits – black-haired, stocky, a Maltese. Gill establishes, Deguara's voice as stocky and emphatic as his build, that Deguara is now a pathologist in the Isle of Man. He worked from January 1979 until December 1980 as the pathologist at the Bakhsh hospital, living four floors below the Arnots in the same apartment block. He knew both Richard Arnot and Helen Smith professionally.

The first he heard of the events of 20 May 1979 was when the hospital anaesthetist arrived to take the children to school. He informed Deguara that there was a dead nurse outside.

Dr Deguara estimates the height of the Arnot balcony for the inquest at sixty to seventy feet. The balconies were dangerous, he agrees. From a door behind the witness box the wooden model of the balcony that was shown to Dr Kheir appears.

'Yes, just about . . . fair,' Deguara comments on its replication. Another rail was added after the tragedy, he mentions.

He saw Helen's body for about fifteen minutes a few days later. The hospital matron, Agnes Johnstone, was with Mr Smith at the time. 'She became very distressed and grabbed me to accompany her to the mortuary.' A British Embassy official was also present – Francis Geere.

Dr Deguara tells the inquest that when he saw the body he was 'struck by the lack of massive injury which I would have assumed with a fall from that height'. He had expected fractures of the legs and arms, and a crushing injury to the head. Gill asks if, as a pathologist, he examines bodies fallen from a height. 'Yes,' he replies.

He agrees that he did not examine Helen 'in a professional capacity', but he did proffer some advice to Dr Bakhsh. 'I was asked, what did I think about it, and I suggested the telephone number of a Home Office path-

ologist. It needed a much more close examination than
the Saudi facilities allowed. I suggested a proper pathologist ought to be sent out to do the job.'

'Was this acted upon?' Gill inquires.

'As far as I know, no,' replies Deguara.

Robertson stands and Dr Deguara tells him that when
he later came to London he met the pathologist in question. He had never been contacted.

When Dr Deguara left the Bakhsh hospital and came
to Britain in December 1980, he was soon contacted by
the West Yorkshire police investigating the Helen Smith
case. The date was 2 February 1981.

ROBERTSON: Were you invited to attend the meeting
    between Professor Usher, Professor Dalgaard and Dr
    Green some ten days later? [This was a meeting to
    discuss Usher's and Dalgaard's joint autopsy on
    Helen carried out in December.]

DEGUARA: No.

ROBERTSON: The police did not tell you about it or invite
    you to attend?

DEGUARA: No.

ROBERTSON: Your evidence today of a *prima-facie* case
    of murder has been available since 2 February 1981?

DEGUARA: Yes.

Gill looks up momentarily. Robertson and Deguara
now discuss the block of flats in Jeddah: the noisy,
inefficient air conditioner; the heat at all times of
the day; the cockroaches on the balconies at all
times of the day.

Back to Helen: yes, he noticed a depressed lesion on
her forehead when he saw her, between $\frac{1}{2}$ and $\frac{3}{4}$ of an
inch.

Robertson sits and Sedley shows Deguara a piece of
paper. It is a hospital memorandum dated 22 May 1979
advising all hospital staff that nobody is allowed to give
information to anyone regarding recent events at the hos-

pital, and that any information should only be given by the hospital administration. Deguara nods in recognition.

Slowly Napley stands. He is a broad, heavy man, black hair, balding, swept back.

As a pathologist who saw Helen within days of her death and who told the hospital owner he suspected murder, Deguara has cut a great swathe in Napley's client's interests.

Napley stares at Deguara a moment, hands in pockets, then attacks, his voice loud, a cutting edge at its peak.

NAPLEY: What sort of pathology are you engaged in?
DEGUARA: All kinds. We do forensic work as well.
NAPLEY: You've given us an estimation of the height. Have you measured it?
DEGUARA: No.

Napley would much prefer Dr Kheir's estimation of the height – forty-five feet. Firstly, it is less distance for Helen to fall, and secondly, it discredits Ron Smith, who has told anybody and everybody that the distance is seventy feet.

Deguara stands firm. He again states he would have expected more injuries from a fall from that height. Napley, his habit, moves slowly in a circle, hands deep in his pockets, glances at the jury, turns back, fires out the question at the point halfway between Gill and Deguara.

NAPLEY: Are you suggesting Helen was murdered?
DEGUARA: Yes.
NAPLEY: Rumour and dissatisfaction in the hospital was rife, was it not?
DEGUARA: Yes.
NAPLEY: You're not adding to it, are you?
DEGUARA: No.
NAPLEY: Either then or now?
DEGUARA: No.

Napley allows a long pause and then refers to Dr Sachel
– the Iranian doctor reputed to be Helen's lover. There is
a slight problem here. As her lover he fits neatly into the
'Helen was "immoral"' argument, but he is also reputed
to have supplied Helen with a key to his first-floor flat in
the same block as the Arnots. Napley needs to know
whether he was away that night. If he was, then why
would Helen go onto the balcony to make love to
Johannes Otten if she could find a bed several floors
below? But Dr Deguara cannot 'recall one way or the
other'.

A Foreign Office barrister now stands – his first entry
into the case. That Dr Deguara told the West Yorkshire
police in February 1981 that here was a case of suspected
murder has also cut swathes in the notion there has been
no cover-up. Deguara's comments do not necessarily
implicate the Foreign Office, but it is as well to set the
matter straight. He inquires if Deguara went to the Saudi
police with his views. 'No.'

It is around 3.40 p.m. as Deguara finishes his evidence.
Ritter and Schlaeffer still sit, waiting their turns. Availability of witnesses means they will have to wait until tomorrow. Call Dr Kirwen.

'Who's Kirwen?' a voice in the press gallery whispers.

'An interesting fellow, you'll like him. He supplied the
bottles,' a voice in the know replies.

'A bootlegger,' snipes another voice. 'Santa Claus for
dry mouths.'

'Well, if you can't get it, what can you do?' a Geordie
sage remarks.

Dr Patrick Alan Kirwen is a plump, blonde-haired
man, late-thirties, shiny skin, pale-brown glasses, wearing
a dark-blue jacket and striped tie. He crosses his legs in
the witness-box chair. His voice is slightly bored, dis-
dainful.

GILL: You supplied the whisky?
KIRWEN: Yes.

GILL: What steps did you take to protect your position?

Kirwen explains that, after being in touch with the Embassy, he brought forward by a few days some leave and returned to Britain.

GILL: In the event, what change of plans did you make?

KIRWEN: After I came back [to Britain] I spoke to the Foreign Office and they thought it was inadvisable for me to return at that time.

GILL: You have not returned to Saudi Arabia?

KIRWEN: No.

Robertson stands. The two men look at each other.

ROBERTSON: Dr Kirwen, you were named by Penny Arnot on the morning of the deaths [to the Embassy].

KIRWEN: So I believe.

ROBERTSON: You were not named by Hayter and Mr Arnot [to the police]?

KIRWEN: So it would seem.

ROBERTSON: Were you contacted by the Embassy?

KIRWEN: Four days later. They contacted me.

ROBERTSON: Mr Geere?

KIRWEN: Yes. He told me what had ensued.

ROBERTSON: What did he say?

KIRWEN: As far as I was concerned, Helen Smith, Johannes Otten were dead, everyone was in prison, he'd keep me informed.

ROBERTSON: Did he suggest you should leave?

KIRWEN: No.

ROBERTSON: Did you tell him you were leaving?

KIRWEN: Yes, he felt it would be wise for me to leave.

ROBERTSON: You supplied the drinks. Can you remember how much?

KIRWEN: It would have been a case. Twelve bottles of Johnny Walker Black Label obtained through American sources.

Kirwen has already told the inquest that he worked for Lockheed International in Jeddah as a medical adviser. He was able to obtain whisky relatively easily via the American community.

Robertson continues: 'And how much was the selling price?'

Kirwen smiles: '£20, £25 a bottle.'

'Were you ever paid for them?'

'I don't think I was.'

Kirwen smiles again, as he does throughout further questions about his contact with a Mr and Mrs O'Brien. They do not attend the inquest but they have claimed that Mr O'Brien – 'a larger bootlegger' – sold Kirwen the whisky.

ROBERTSON: Do you recall publicity from Mr and Mrs O'Brien?

KIRWEN: So it appears.

ROBERTSON: Mr O'Brien is a well-known bootlegger?

KIRWEN: So it would seem.

ROBERTSON: You bought the case there?

KIRWEN: Yes.

ROBERTSON: On this occasion?

KIRWEN: The alcohol I bought would have been bought two to three weeks earlier. Very difficult for British people to obtain. I would buy some in. If anyone wanted two or three bottles I could give it to them.

Kirwen said he knew the Arnots. They shared an interest in scuba diving. He knew the Embassy, played squash there and attended parties. He knew Hayter, from where he did not state. Arnot had rung him earlier that day, the 19th, and mentioned 'he had some people coming around and asked me if I could supply a case'. He took the case around at lunch-time. He attended the party himself for a short period of an hour or so. It was a 'quiet drinks party like one would have in this country'.

ROBERTSON: O'Brien said you came round early that
   morning very upset, saying all hell had broken loose
   at the Arnots'. No truth in that?
KIRWEN: No.
ROBERTSON: You went straight to bed?
KIRWEN: Yes.

Sedley takes over and mentions that Fleischer did not
remember him as having been at the party. Kirwen had
spoken to three or four who were not English at the
party.

SEDLEY: If Fleischer didn't know you, Arnot could have
   put you on the guest list?
KIRWEN: Yes.
SEDLEY: Arnot will tell us you were not seen by the
   police, you were not investigated?
KIRWEN: Yes.
SEDLEY: If so, it is clear you were deliberately omitted
   as the supplier of the drinks?

Kirwen makes a rare movement. He leans forward and
slightly tugs at the top of his sock.

KIRWEN: I think I would have been equally at risk as a
   party-goer.
SEDLEY: It was an offence to drink, and so as a supplier
   of alcohol, you had more to risk.
KIRWEN: Possibly.
SEDLEY: Near certainty?
KIRWEN (smiling): Speculation.
SEDLEY: Common sense.
KIRWEN: If you say so. [Kirwen grins, leans back,
   hands in his lap.]
SEDLEY: You were omitted to protect you?
KIRWEN: It makes sense, yes.
SEDLEY: Do you know anyone else to be protected?
KIRWEN: No.

Kirwen first heard of the deaths forty-eight hours afterwards from a friend who read the Arabic press. He did not know John Close, the man now married to Penelope Arnot, who was widely rumoured to be both at the party and a CIA man, his father the CIA collator at the American Embassy.

The inquest adjourns for the day. The press gallery was delighted with Kirwen. Copy was rung in. It produced a surprisingly small print. The day had produced a peaceful party, a murder, a bootlegger. It had also legalised alcohol consumption in Jeddah, at least within the inquest. The mood changed. Some tainted stone had been lifted and, as men of the world, recognising our needs, we could partake. Which of us would not have done the same?

Day Five

Wednesday 24 November: Martin Fleischer had established the foundations; Manfred Schlaeffer, Klaus Ritter, Harry Gutzeit would build the house. A happy party, no fights, violence, aggression, boring even. A harmonious evening. Always one or two bottles on the table. Remaining in the flat Texier, Mrs Arnot, Hayter. There would be a number of contradictions here and there, and unless the observer glanced sharply and remembered work experience, work roles, power shifts in a company of men, these contradictions would pass unnoticed.

Manfred Schlaeffer went to the party in the company jeep together with Dieter Chapuis, who was driving, Klaus Ritter and Otten. He describes the build-up of the party, the guests arriving. Gill, together with all of us, filling in the bricks. 'There were just two females. Who danced with whom?' he asks.

SCHLAEFFER: I had one or two with Mrs Arnot. Also Helen was dancing with some persons.

GILL: As the evening wore on, the situation changed?

SCHLAEFFER: Mrs Arnot was a good hostess, dancing with everybody. Helen at first danced with different persons but later on concentrated on Johannes Otten.

Schlaeffer confirms Fleischer on the drink. Otten was drinking; Helen 'was drinking whisky/orange fifty/fifty. It was really hard. It surprised me there was so much whisky,' Schlaeffer informs the court. Of their dancing, he says, 'First they danced normal, later on with slow movements. She put both arms around his neck. He did the same around her body.'

The sequence of events unfolds. The party divided into two halves, Otten and Helen dancing from midnight or thereabouts. Richard Arnot retired to bed, Schlaeffer sorry to see him go, since he found the party 'less interesting' without him. He was the host. Fleischer left at 2.30 a.m. The others left three-quarters of an hour later. Gutzeit went separately to his flat in town; the others drove to the port. They saw no body, heard nothing, smelt nothing on the street. They had a spot of bother with the lights on the jeep, the lights flashing.

Robertson takes over. He establishes that the harbour was top security, of great strategic importance, and was well-guarded. The previous day, the Friday before the party, Tim Hayter had showed up at the floating crane with Mrs Arnot and her children. It was the company's day off, and Tim was showing the Arnot family around. Mrs Arnot invited Schlaeffer to the party. Schlaeffer was hesitant in going that evening. Firstly, too many of the company were going; secondly, there may be too many others there.

ROBERTSON: Security?

SCHLAEFFER: Yes . . . party like that . . . two, three, four more safe than ten.

ROBERTSON: You came with Johannes Otten?
SCHLAEFFER: No . . . well . . .

Schlaeffer explains. Otten had arrived back after leave
in Holland ten days before the party. His tug was moored
alongside the accommodation barge. Every two or three
days, Schlaeffer would see him in the barge, as he used it
for meals, newspapers and showers.

ROBERTSON: Why give him a lift?
SCHLAEFFER: We had company cars . . . He was staying
    there alone. He took a shower in the barge . . . We
    try to behave [he pauses] . . . with us, if you want a
    lift and you want to come, we do it.
ROBERTSON: How did it happen?
SCHLAEFFER: Time we left, he was ready to go inside car.
ROBERTSON: No idea who invited him?
SCHLAEFFER: No.

They discuss the problem with the lights. Schlaeffer
was apprehensive in case the police came. He did not see
any bodies on the street thirty metres behind on the
corner railings. Nor did he look, since he was looking at
Ritter's driving. The time on the clock inside the jeep
showed 3.15 a.m.

ROBERTSON: Your attitude, in the car, was it not al-
    coholic?
SCHLAEFFER: Yes, but with alcohol, we have to drive
    back, just in front of port, few gates, gates are closed,
    you have to spread passport and harbour pass, they
    have to look . . . really dangerous if smelling of al-
    cohol, if drunk . . . really dangerous . . . not every-
    one drinking so much.
ROBERTSON: Were you drinking?
SCHLAEFFER: I can say on that, Saudi police asked me. I
    refused to have any drink, found me not guilty of
    alcohol.

Schlaeffer had told Gill the last he had seen of Helen and Johannes had been about half an hour before the Germans left. They were not in the flat, nor had he seen them leave. It was Schlaeffer's opinion that she had her own flat inside another building. He and his colleagues were 99 per cent certain that Helen and Johannes had gone to her flat. The door to the balcony was concealed behind a heavy curtain, which was partly opened from time to time to let out cigarette smoke, but he saw no one go out onto the balcony.

Robertson refers to an interview Schlaeffer had given in August 1980 in which Schlaeffer is reported to have said they searched the flat and balcony for Otten. 'Newspapers asked me very often . . . my answer and what they write down a big difference,' Schlaeffer replies. Robertson asks another question, Gill intervenes, pointing out that newspapers are subject to editorial control and are not reliable.

ROBERTSON: My concern is to qualify in a way which invites the witness to answer. If he accepts . . .

GILL: Do not indulge in cross-examination. Your task is to ascertain the facts. Your questions are getting close to cross-examination. Put your previous question in such a way that it ascertains information.

Robertson quotes from the report. '"*He just looked around the toilet, living room, kitchen.*" It was about two years ago that he made that statement. I'm reminding him and asking him if it is true.'

Schlaeffer did not look anywhere, nor did the others. Only Klaus Ritter had gone to the balcony windows and called out 'John, John' in a loud voice. Nor did anyone present – Mrs Arnot, Texier, Hayter – tell them that Otten was on the balcony. If anyone had said that, of course, they would have looked. It was the arrangement that the jeep should take Otten back to the harbour.

Sedley asks Schlaeffer if he knew why Tim Hayter sent Fleischer to see Harry Gutzeit. 'Talking about it, I don't think it was a misunderstanding. He only liked to see the bodies.'

Schlaeffer had been on his floating crane on the morning of the 20th. A telephone call had been made at 6.30 a.m. by either Fleischer or Hayter, leaving a message that an accident had happened. Hayter rang again at 7.30 a.m. telling him about the accident. Schlaeffer had been taken to the prison, where he shared a station cell with Ritter, Fleischer and Arnot. No one knew what had happened. Replying to Sir David Napley, Schlaeffer says he heard no noise of a sexual assault coming from the balcony in the period before he left. Nor had he heard any screams.

Harold Fowler rises. He refers Schlaeffer to the trouble they had with the company car (which was more like a Range Rover). The car had so much technology that Ritter set the lights flashing. Schlaeffer was concerned that the police might come along. He was only interested in what was happening inside the car, and did not look behind him at the flat or railings. He agrees that anyone on the balcony would have noticed the flashing lights of the jeep.

Lunch beckons. The morning has been somewhat slow. Fowler re-runs his finish – each German coming to the inquest voluntarily. 'Were you happy to come or were you reluctant?'

SCHLAEFFER: First there is [Fowler moves his hand around] absolutely nothing [Fowler produces a white piece of paper] to hide, second [it looks like a letter] in Germany things are coming out [Fowler has it out in his hand] through newspapers. Also there is Mr Smith.

Fowler holds up a letter. It is a letter purporting to have been written to Schlaeffer by Ron Smith. Fowler waves it, saying, 'Will you look at this letter? It is addressed to you from Mr Smith?'

Robertson stands, protesting, saying he has not attacked the witness at all, no charges have been levelled at him. Would the coroner accept that letter?

Ron Smith, seated, arm along the back of the bench, voice directed to his right in a low mumble, says, 'I am not accusing the German divers. I'm accusing Richard Arnot of murder and . . .'

There is muffled consternation throughout the court.

'What did he say?'

'Stan, did you catch that?'

'No.'

'Catch his last words?'

'Alan, you must have heard?'

'It could have been "Texier" – I'm not certain?'

'I'm not too sure.'

'Paul, did you hear it?'

'No, I didn't, I'm afraid.'

'Did you get what he said?'

'Sounded like "Texier" to me. What about you, Harry?'

'I can't be sure. Anyone got a tape?'

'Can't hear it Harry. Gary?'

'No.'

Gill half rises: 'Now is a suitable time for lunch adjournment.' In the press gallery a group of journalists are bending over the benches, ears on the tape being played back. (Gill has allowed tape-recorders in the court since the Monday, in the interests of accurate reporting.) Two other groups are forming and dissolving, journalists moving from tape to tape trying to pick up the last word.

At lunchtime a consensus emerges. It sounded like 'Texier'. It will be reported as Texier. We walk back into court.

Gill comes in. We wait for him to mention Ron Smith's

contempt, give us an indication of what was said. Nothing is said that afternoon.

Now on the witness bench are Dr Ian Keith, medical anaesthetist, and Mrs Lyn Kathleen Keith. They have journeyed specially from Canada to give evidence and Gill decides they must be next.

The Keiths lived in the flat beneath the Arnots. Dr Keith is small, active, bespectacled. Gill inquires into his relationship with the Arnots. 'Initially it was quite close, latterly somewhat distant – in nature, not in location.'

On the party night they heard no music or dancing or activity in the flat above. They watched television and went to bed at midnight. At 6.00 a.m. a junior surgeon knocked at the door, very agitated. He said there were two dead bodies outside and if Dr Keith had any booze he had better get rid of it. Dr Keith's strongest drink was grape juice, but he did have a copy of a banned book – *Crash 79*, largely about the Stock Exchange being manipulated by Arab interests.

Dr Keith went to the balcony, looked over and saw the two bodies. He did not hang around but he now gives the inquest a surprisingly detailed account of their position.

The railings were actually replaced by brickwork within twenty-four hours (which explains Dr Kheir's previous observation that there was builders' rubble – they had already started this work when he went to the scene at 9.00 a.m.).

The male body was just to the left of the lamp which had been knocked sideways to the right. Keith could see shorts, shirt, fair hair and the head pointing towards the street. A saw had to be borrowed from the hospital to cut him loose. The female body was lying to the left of the lamp in the gateway to the courtyard. She was lying curled up, her left arm stretched towards the lamp, briefs partially across her thigh, her dress bound up in her middle. She seemed to be 'just resting there'. He did not recognise her as Helen Smith. He was not really certain of the left arm position. It did not look as if the arm or shoulder was fractured.

Keith also mentions that the tiles on the balcony were slippery because of moisture from the humid heat. Gill homes in and asks if slippery tiles create a danger on the balcony. 'One could say that. I suppose one could slip on them,' Keith replies.

Robertson talks with Keith about flies, mosquitoes, the heat, the humidity. Keith agrees that they all make life unpleasant, which is why people seal their homes in Saudi Arabia – to make sure the air conditioning works.

No, you do not open doors, Keith adds – an interesting comment because Schlaeffer had that morning said the balcony doors were open a bit at the party to let the smoke out. Keith is obviously a man who would embrace somebody anywhere but the balcony – those insects, that heat.

Keith finally comments on the illegal immigrants employed by the hospital. Mainly Africans and Asians, they lived in 'cardboard shanty towns'.

Sedley has little to ask. Napley does not like Keith's description of Otten's head position. According to Napley's instructions, the head faced the buildings. Napley does not like Keith's description of Helen's head position either. Keith is emphatic that her head was on the outside tile of the gateway.

Napley shows him a model of the spikes, made by Richard Arnot. Dr Kheir was shown the same model. He thought the tips were sharper. So does Keith.

Mrs Keith moves into the witness box, a woman in her mid-thirties, with the only northern accent we will hear throughout the inquest apart from that of Ron Smith and the investigating West Yorkshire police officers. On the party night one of her children, James, was suffering from a bad attack of tonsillitis.

'He was awake most of the evening. He was in our bed most of the night. He was two then, he was born October '77. He almost constantly woke up. My husband is a heavy sleeper. I was awake with him. I had medicine and aspirin and a cold drink at the bedside,' she tells Gill, and then goes on to describe 'one very loud noise' she heard during the night: 'It was very difficult to describe. It was loud. There's a cabinet by the door with a glass front. It sounded as if it could have fallen over. It was a bang and a crash at the same time . . . It was a very loud noise. The air conditioning was on all the time. The noise was above it . . . It was the sound of breaking glass and a bang at the same time . . . It was just one noise.'

'Were you able to form a view of its location?' Gill asks.

Mrs Keith thought initially it came from the reception area of the flat or to the front of the building. Then she thought it was from the lift-shaft area of the flats. She was too scared to investigate. It could have been a lorry outside going over a pot-hole in the road. She estimated the time as 3.40 a.m.

To Robertson, Mrs Keith agrees that the bar height of the balcony was 'one of a catalogue of complaints about the building'. She was, of course, particularly concerned for her children.

Mrs Keith steps down from the witness box a few seconds later. We wait, expecting Gill to make a pronouncement on the event just before lunch. He is silent and the court adjourns.

Day Six

Thursday 25 November: '*Ron accuses Arnot and Texier of murder*' . . . '*I accuse!*' You cannot escape the headlines. They are on every newspaper front page. And there are huge pictures of the man himself, his face angry and contemptuous.

Gill enters. The tension is greater than it was on the first day. Promptly as Sir David Napley rises, Gill leans forward to him and listens:

'. . . My client is very concerned about that incident yesterday . . . One can well understand the reasons for

Mr Smith's allegations, but he made these allegations in full knowledge that they would achieve banner headlines. This amounts to a gross contempt of this court. I can understand his sense of frustration as the evidence fails to support his wild allegations . . .'

The court comprises some forty yards in length, some twenty-five across. It comprises eleven jurors, people in the public gallery, press. It comprises three and a half years. It comprises the distance from Leeds to Jeddah. It comprises millions of readers. It comprises the deaths of Helen and Johannes, yet all power at that moment is in the two yards separating Napley and Gill. Napley plays it . . .

'I know you are concerned to protect people such as my client, who have travelled thousands of miles to refute these allegations. I look to you to protect the reputation of these people and to deal with the matters with the powers you possess.'

Gill visibly shifts, looks down at his clenched hands. Ron Smith spoke a mumble at 12.55 the previous day. Gill had from 12.55 to 4.25 to punish him. He said nothing.

He speaks now. 'This has been a matter of great concern overnight . . . May I put to you, Sir David, my view? This is a great contempt of court . . . We all know that the proceedings must be extremely distressing and upsetting to Mr Smith. I am sure everyone here has a great deal of sympathy for him . . . Personally I have a desire to try and help Mr Smith and relieve him of his misgivings. On the other hand, I have a duty to those affected by this matter and the outburst yesterday produced very serious allegations . . . which in the event received a tremendous amount of publicity. Allegations were made about the calibre of Mr Texier. Mr Texier is not here.'

Geoffrey Robertson stands. He is going to have his work cut out to break into that two-yard stretch: 'Obviously, Mr Texier, Tim Hayter and Mrs Arnot, who were there when the events took place in the flat between 3 and 5.30 a.m. should be here. I fully endorse that . . . However, I do not accept Sir David Napley's accusation. Mr Smith's words fall into that catalogue of things said in court between people [e.g. exchanges between barristers]. Such things happen. They form no part of the court proceedings which are privileged by reporting. It is quite obvious his reaction yesterday was not in any sense an angry outburst but a statement of fact, something he said almost naturally, as a matter of making his position clear.'

Gill looks sideways, in the general direction of Robertson. He will not accept this. 'Everything that goes on in this court-room is part of the proceedings, whether or not it occurs as a result of what is given in the witness box, or any other behaviour of anybody else in the court, in whatever capacity.'

Robertson takes it on the jaw but does not flinch. 'Actually, no sir. This is a technical matter. How facts are reported is a matter for newspapers. I can produce cases to show that statements made and overheard are not part of the full record of the proceedings. If there be any question of action, it is an action which should be addressed to the press rather than to parties in this court . . . Statements made and overheard between people here are not part of the formal record. Mr Smith simply and naturally, and without any sort of aforethought, interjected, in a voice which was obviously overheard, to indicate what his view was in relation to any question of allegations against the German divers. There was no deliberate attempt to make headlines. He was simply making his position clear.'

Gill is adamant, however: 'I am considering how to react to Mr Smith's behaviour. I extend courtesy and expect it in return . . . [he calls Sir David, Sir David, continuously, only rarely calling the Smith barristers by name] I intend to consider this matter very carefully . . . this was an outburst in a loud voice, making allegations

about someone who is not here, made with the full knowledge that it would be heard and reported in the
press . . .'

Was it an outburst in a loud voice? Gill can hear the
tapes. And why was this 'great contempt' not dealt with
immediately after lunch the previous afternoon, or even
at the end of the day? If it is a 'great contempt' now, so it
was then. The only difference between then and now is
last night's television news and today's newspapers.

Gill asks Robertson if Mr Smith can substantiate his
claims or wishes to withdraw them, because he has to
notify Mr Texier about them: 'If it is not substantiated I
shall expect you to say so, publicly on his behalf, and if
in fact it is being withdrawn, I want to know the answer
before I take the next step, which is to endeavour to notify
Mr Texier.'

10.17 a.m.: Gill grants a short adjournment and retires
to his room. Helen Smith died. The inquest is supposed
to be about the truth concerning her death. Now it is
about Ron Smith. An onus of proof has entered the proceedings and from this moment on, that onus falls upon
him – all for an awkward, angry, frustrated comment that
never rose much above a mumble and tailed away un-
heard. Gill has said that everyone has 'a great deal of
sympathy' for Mr Smith. He personally has 'a desire to
try and help Mr Smith'. From his position of power, Gill
can afford to be sympathetic towards Ron Smith, but he
must be punished too for his human weakness.

The press gallery sits in silence, as does a woman at the
end of the witness gallery. She sits alone, legs crossed,
hands on legs, looking around. A few yards down the
bench sit Harry Gutzeit and Klaus Ritter. She is not with
them. She seems serene. She seems content.

Ron Smith walks across to her; she rises. They shake
hands, they talk, he smiles, walks away, she sits. Someone
whispers that her name is Agnes Johnstone, matron of the
hospital. At 10.31 a.m. Richard Arnot walks over to her.
She watches him, smiling, her large brown eyes open.

Between 10.31 and 10.38 a.m. they talk, Arnot leaning over that brown wooden wall which holds the witness bench within it. Matron Johnstone looks up at him, her eyes never leaving his face. A woman in her late thirties, her eyes on him, the geometry of her face alive. We sit watching, they oblivious of us. Arnot, a tall, gangling man, opens his jacket, his eyes on his hands as he pulls out his wallet, extracts his card and offers it to her. She takes it, still looking at him. He smiles, walks away. She watches him walk away. She smiles. She holds the card in her hand. She is a small woman, wearing a white shirt and black dress. She watches him that nine yards from her position to his bench, then she turns, opens her bag, places the card in it, closes it, looks up, her eyes serene, clear and still content.

At 10.56 a.m. the 'interested parties' fill into the well of the court. Arnot, Smith, Jeddah Embassy official Goron Kirby, their barristers, solicitors, advisers. The barristers are on the front row alongside Arnot's solicitor, Sir David Napley. Ron Smith sits on the second row, slightly to Gill's right. Richard Arnot alternates between the second and third rows, sometimes sitting alongside Kirby, other times next to his present wife (he has divorced Penny Arnot and remarried). No more than half a dozen people separate Arnot and Smith.

To the right of the coroner are the witness box and the witness bench. Above this, a public gallery, packed daily, as in every court much the same people coming daily. The inquest, a trial, has a life of its own. It occupies both day and night. Slowly life outside recedes. Opposite the witness box the jury sit. They are representatives from the world outside, here to deliver a verdict, here to bring their experiences to bear. The tragedy of the inquest is that no one knows anything about Saudi life, expatriate life, and the only education are the witnesses called. And the witnesses are implicated. The jury's ability to determine the truth through their own experiences has been usurped. They have no experiences to offer. Life outside the court is not the life in Jeddah.

The press are in a gallery at the back of the court, normally used as a public gallery. The gallery directly faces Gill.

10.59 a.m. Gill returns. He sits above the proceedings on a raised stage. From the press box, the door he enters is to the right of his desk, which is at the front of the stage, his chair in the centre of the desk, a black leather pad on the desk in front of the chair. He has a curious way of walking in. Physically, Gill is a small man, thin. When he approaches, from door to desk, he appears to scurry, and even though he seems to walk directly, so that we see him from the side, the impression he creates is of a man, through the movement of his body, approaching sideways in a circle. What heightens this is his speed of sitting. He sits fast, pulling the chair up, both hands on both its sides, into the desk, and it is only when he is sitting that he looks at the court. As he has not in his walk presented the gravity of his authority, the speed at which our perception decodes his movement leaves this image of him scurrying, since we are left with the question of how he got there.

Robertson stands. We perceive that he perceives the ground has been cut from under him. He informs Gill that Mr Smith's remarks were a spontaneous reaction to the evidence. Mr Smith has seen Texier's statement. He does not accept it as accurate. Mr Smith accepted the legal limitations of legal proceedings, but he wished questions to be asked tending to show that Mr Texier knew there was an unlawful killing, questions asking him to account convincingly for his movements.

GILL: Is there any evidence which you can produce which suggests that he was the murderer of Helen Smith, as was alleged yesterday?

ROBERTSON: I am prepared to provide you with a statement by Mr Smith tending to show that Mr Texier's account is not correct.

GILL: In other words, the answer to my question is that the allegations are being persisted with?

ROBERTSON: The allegations that Mr Texier knows that there was an unlawful killing, and questions, if he attends, that show his account, given in his statement of his movements and observations, is not correct, will certainly be pursued.

Sir David stands, his tone grievous. This conversation has only referred to Texier, not Arnot. Robertson replies, turning halfway to confront that two-yard circuit. 'Mr Arnot is here, and those are the ambit of the questions I am entitled to put and will put,' he states defiantly.

Gill responds, fingers beneath his chin. The manner in which the allegations were made was wholly unacceptable. 'I would be very remiss on behalf of the court if I did not indicate the court's displeasure. I have powers under the Contempt Act which can involve the loss of liberty of the offenders or monetary penalties of up to £200. I have very much regard for the distress which I am sure we all understand Mr Smith may be suffering and I take that into account. On the other hand, that sort of contempt cannot be tolerated, and I intend to impose a fine of £50.'

Is Gill prepared to accept arguments of legal doubts regarding the situation, Robertson asks. Coroner Gill replies: 'I impose the fine, and it will be a matter for you if you seek fit to question it.'

Sir David Napley now excuses himself, his job done. He has a heavy cold. His junior will ask the questions today.

First witness is then Harry Gutzeit, a plump man, dark, in his late thirties. He was Harms Salvage manager in Jeddah at the time. He received orders from Hamburg. Tim Hayter was his top diver, Manfred Schlaeffer the crane operator, Klaus Ritter the cook. Harry sat in the Manager's office. Harry fell asleep in the armchair at the party. Harry had the flat in town.

Harry now sits in the witness box with words to choose.

GILL: Did you see anything to indicate Johannes and Helen were attracted to each other?

GUTZEIT: I wouldn't call it being that, it was sort of . . . tender embrace . . . tender should be the word . . . nothing unusual if they did kiss. I would have noticed if they behaved in a manner which embarrassed me.

Harry went to the party in his own car and he fell asleep at 1.00 a.m.

GILL: The last you saw of them [Helen and Johannes] was when you dozed off at about that time?

GUTZEIT: Yes, I would say about that time.

GILL: At that time, did they seem to be in a happy mood, dancing together?

GUTZEIT: No arguments, nothing at all, it was just a happy, harmonious party. Not something could happen, not at that time. I would have said it was rather a boring party.

ROBERTSON (rising): Boring enough for you to fall asleep?

GUTZEIT: Yes . . . if I'm rather tired it doesn't matter if there are 10 or 100 people, I just fall asleep.

Harry left the party at 3.15. Someone woke him a bit earlier and said it was time to go. He worked out the time because his clock back at his flat showed 3.30 and the journey took fifteen minutes. As he left, he remembered a general remark being made about Otten's whereabouts because he had no transport back to the harbour, but Harry could not remember anybody looking for him. He did not look back to the flats as he walked across the road to his car and drove off.

Harry presents a stereotyped image.

FOWLER: Did you have a particularly heavy day that day?

GUTZEIT: I would say so.

FOWLER: What time did you start in the morning?

GUTZEIT: I started at 8.00 a.m. that day and went on until nine in the evening.

FOWLER: Yes, we all know about Germans working hard.

Harry was invited to the party by Tim Hayter. He should have gone somewhere else. But Tim Hayter was his diver and was about to go on leave for six weeks. Harry was due to leave for good in a fortnight. The chances were that they would never see each other again. At the party, Harry talked with the other Harms employees. Harry is a company man, loyal to his workmates.

Klaus Ritter takes the stand – a big, friendly-looking man in his early forties with black hair and trimmed black beard. He communicates with both words and feelings. He is the archetypal European working man – one can imagine him with a wife and children; a glass of beer; rolling dice and playing cards. He was the company cook at Harms Salvage.

When Klaus arrived at the party, Penelope Arnot showed him – and him alone – round the flat. It is a measure of the man that he introduced himself to her while the other three sat down. She pointed out the balcony to him and said it was a danger to the children.

Gill guides him through the party again – the party in two halves. Klaus remembers talking with Richard Arnot: 'It took a long time because my English not very good. I had to explain with hands and feet.'

Gill asks if he danced with Helen at all. Klaus grins: 'I cannot say that – I don't think she was the type of woman who would dance with me. I'm a bit too old.' He did, however, dance with the good hostess – Mrs Arnot.

Although Johannes Otten was not a company man, Klaus would feed him too. He regarded Otten as his

friend, knew his habits, knew he drank a lot, knew also
that he could take a lot of drink. Gill moves to the second
half of the party and asks Klaus what effect the drink had
on Helen and Otten. 'It is the normal effect, you become
more merry,' Klaus replies with a hint of surprise at such
a question.

'We have heard that the two [Helen and Otten] were
attracted to each other,' Gill asks.

'I had that feeling too,' Klaus says.

No, he did not see them leave, he had no idea when
they did so: 'I just didn't bother in particular with these
two.' When he himself left, he positioned himself in a
doorway and shouted, 'John, come along.' But he did not
think Otten was anywhere in particular; he just called out
for his friend. A few minutes later, Robertson mentions
that Schlaeffer told the inquest that Klaus went to the
balcony window curtains. 'Yes, I heard what Schlaeffer
said yesterday, but I did not go in that direction at all. In
any case, why should I have to?' the open Klaus contradicts the quieter, closed Schlaeffer.

Klaus also tells Robertson that Otten wore 'a shirt and
blue trousers – casual wear' for the party. He says Otten
carried his documents in a wallet, which he kept in his
trouser pocket, as they all did. Also that the controls at
the port gates were much sharper if you walk than if you
drive. You can get away in a car simply by holding your
pass to the car window. He also added that Otten would
become 'more and more quiet' when drunk.

Robertson asks if he and the others said goodbye to
Mrs Arnot and thanked her for the party. Not directly:
'We said, "Bye, that was nice, thank you."'' Klaus waves.
When they stepped into the street he saw nothing, heard
nothing and smelt nothing unusual. The first he heard
about the deaths was when Tim Hayter burst into the accommodation barge at 6.30 a.m. and told him to tell the
others. At first, Hayter offered no opinion as to what had
caused the tragedy. Later he said it was an accident.

Fowler asks Klaus a little more about his friendship

with Otten and he replies that Otten once visited him in
Germany from Holland. Fowler suggests that Otten may
have seen the flashing lights on the company jeep, but
Klaus says: 'He would never have left Helen for us.'

Klaus was sentenced to thirty lashes for taking alcohol,
reprieved by the Ramadan amnesty. He leaves the witness box, the last of the Germans to attend the inquest,
and leaving in the mind an interesting contrast between
himself and Schlaeffer. The latter told the inquest the
previous day that he did not drink at the party, he was
worried about all the company being away at once, and
he was concerned about smelling of alcohol as they passed
through the port gates on the way back. He barely knew
Otten, who was not a company man.

Ritter, on the other hand, drank whisky, had no qualms
about being away, circulated at the party (Mrs Arnot
showed him round and he talked to Mr Arnot with the
help of his hands and feet), and he knew the control at
the port gates was not so sharp as long as you were not
walking. Otten was his friend.

Schlaeffer came across as a worrier. He had wanted to
leave after Richard Arnot went to bed at 2.00 a.m., he
told the inquest. Perhaps the bed-bound Arnot was his
excuse for leaving. They were at an illegal drinks party.
And there was Otten, turning it into an illegal sex party
too. Ritter, however, is an adapter who makes the best of
everything.

Only twice did the Germans contradict each other
at the inquest: Schlaeffer regarding Fleischer's misunderstanding of Tim Hayter's instruction; Ritter regarding Schlaeffer's statement that he called out to the
balcony.

Klaus Ritter was just the right man to bring up the
rear.

At 3.15 p.m. Matron Agnes Johnstone takes the oath.
She answers, sitting back, looking up at Gill, voice firm,
in phrases, emphatic, with a Scottish accent. She had been
matron four years. She had responsibility for the nurses.

The hospital rule was an 8 p.m. curfew for each nurse. Later than that, the hospital book must be signed, stating your destination. Helen lived in a two-block apartment building on the opposite side of the hospital to the Arnots, three minutes' walk away.

Gill asks if Matron Johnstone was aware that Helen had gone to the Arnots' 'function' on 19/20 May. 'No.' Should Helen have been required to sign the book? 'She should have.'

Matron Johnstone's eyes flash, and not for the only time. She explains that the nurses' accommodation is guarded at night. The guard also acts as a general help and cleans. Even when they signed the book, nurses had to be back by 11.00 p.m., and if they were late they 'would have to get past the guard'.

What problems would arise then, Gill wonders. 'It depends on how often it happens. If it was once or twice, he would let her in. If repeatedly, he'd report it to the hospital administrator,' she says.

On the morning of 20 May, Agnes Johnstone's doorbell rang. It was around 6.00 a.m. It was a Malaysian member of staff. 'This was unusual, it is usually a porter,' she tells the inquest. Very agitated, he told her that a dreadful accident had occurred and surgery wanted her. In Casualty she met Mr Arnot, Dr Rahman and several junior staff: 'Mr Arnot came forward and became very distressed, crying. There had been a dreadful accident and Helen Smith was dead. She had been at his party the previous night. I took him by the hand and took him out of the hospital doors. We started to walk down the ambulance way ... I couldn't quite grasp the connection between the party and Helen Smith's death.' Her voice is controlled. She sits neither backwards nor forwards. She asked Arnot where the accident happened: 'At the bottom, Mr Arnot turned left and said to go towards my flat. I went to the scene and I had a look at Helen.'

She pauses. She saw Helen on the ground. She was lying between the building wall and street wall, at right-

angles, with her head towards the building. Her body was
clothed and covered with a sheet: 'I removed the sheet
and looked at her face . . . I removed the sheet to her
waist but no further.'

Gill, doubtless conscious that this description of
Helen's position contradicts the one given by Dr Keith
the previous day, asks if there were circumstances to suggest the body had been moved.

'No . . . I did think of moving her myself . . . I'd rather
have seen her in the hospital than outside but I did not
. . . she was wearing a loose dress, brown and white and a
brassiere in place.'

It is late in the day, but there is no sound of shuffling
as Matron Johnstone's vivid description unfolds.

Helen lay partially on her back, lying more to the right,
the right side of her face to the ground. Matron Johnstone
did not look at her legs. The left arm was raised, the right
arm she did not notice. The left arm was bent at the
elbow, her palm upwards.

GILL: Did you see any sign of injury?
JOHNSTONE: None at all.
GILL: Was there any blood?
JOHNSTONE: There was on the ground, but not from
    Helen.

Gill now asks about 'another body nearby', and she
replies that there was a man's body on the railings,
slightly to the right of her. The railings had penetrated
his groin. His head was on the building side, legs on the
other side of the railing. She looked at his face – she
wanted to see if he came from the hospital – but she did
not recognise him. The top half of him was naked. He
had no other severe injuries. His face was 'terribly discoloured'. She saw no damage to the wall, or ground surface. She did not particularly look. Her concern was for
Helen. She knelt down beside her, adjusted her hair. She
saw no marks, no bruises.

Did the absence of injury puzzle Matron Johnstone, Gill inquires. 'Yes . . . I probably expected to see bleeding from the ears. You look for it, as a nurse, in cases of head injury.' Gill presses the point but Matron Johnstone cuts the discussion short by declaring: 'I was relieved she was not a ghastly mess.'

She tells of seeing a passport lying in the middle of the pavement, more or less at Otten's feet. She was about to pick it up, but somebody warned her not to touch anything. She then went up to the Arnots' flat where she found the family – alone. 'I did walk out on the balcony and look over,' she adds.

Gill asks if she noticed anything on the balcony, and without further prompting she tells, as if it was only yesterday, of what she saw: 'There was a sunlounger up against the wall. It was damaged. It was against the outer wall of the balcony. It was against the balustrade.'

'Was it opened up for use?' Gill interjects.

'Yes.'

Her eyes flash towards Richard Arnot some nine yards away. The court is cut in half by it. He looks the other way. She stares, her gaze open, emphatic.

Gill asks if she can describe the damage. Her head moves back to him: 'The framework was bent. There were aluminium frames, canvas covering. The middle of the frame on the inner side was buckled.'

No, Matron Johnstone can not offer any explanation for the buckling and, no, she did not notice anything else on the balcony. Gill asks her what she thought about the safety of the balcony, and she replies: 'All balconies frighten me. It was low.' Gill asks her how high the sunlounger stood above the ground and she replies, 'Nine to twelve inches.' We wonder if Gill is thinking that Helen and Otten may have rolled off the sunlounger to their deaths while in tender embrace.

GILL: Why did you look at the balcony?

JOHNSTONE: I have no idea.

GILL: Where was the sunlounger in relation to the bodies?

JOHNSTONE: I would say it was above them.

GILL: Directly above?

JOHNSTONE: Yes.

Within minutes, the police arrived, as did Dr Bakhsh, the hospital owner. The police asked her to leave. She did not want to leave 'one of my girls'. She returned to the hospital and went into Administration. The police brought in Mrs Arnot and her children. Two gentlemen from the Embassy arrived.

Agnes Johnstone confirms that afterwards there was an 'enormous amount' of speculation and gossip and it was a 'very, very trying time for all'. It was very difficult to ensure that patients in the hospital were not harmed by doctors and nurses not paying attention to their work: 'If I was to believe every story I have been told I would have gone quite mad by now.'

The letter that Dr Deguara had confirmed the previous day, ordering employees not to release information, was issued, she says, to stop people talking to the press. The press were ringing every few minutes, but because of the publicity, the employees were given a free telephone call to reassure their relatives.

Robertson stands. She estimated her visit to the balcony as 6.15 a.m., she tells him. Yes, she noticed an indenture in Helen's head. There was blood underneath Otten but 'no puddles', and she felt that someone may have stood on the sunlounger. Yes, she remembered Mr Smith in Jeddah and her visit with him to the mortuary together with Geere from the Embassy. She could not recall Dr Bakhsh saying to him: 'There was no blood around Helen.'

ROBERTSON: There was some concern about Mr Smith's activities?

JOHNSTONE: I don't know about this.

ROBERTSON: On one occasion he had to be escorted off
the premises?

Gill steps in, stopping the questioning. The inquest
rules do say that proceedings and evidence are solely
directed to how, where and when the deceased came
to death. Robertson asks instead about parties in
Saudi Arabia. Gill looks as if he is going to intervene
again, but Matron Johnstone almost waves him away.
She is glad to have the chance to say something about
this. 'There are parties,' she says, each word hard,
'where there is alcohol served and there are little parties where there is Pepsi-Cola, orange juice and cakes
and this is normally the sort of parties Helen and I
would be at.'

Matron Johnstone is asked by Sedley of the last time
she and Helen were at a party together. It was a few days
before the accident. Again, it was a party with cakes,
Pepsi-Cola, orange juice. She leaves the witness box. She
will return to Jeddah. She takes her place in the witness
gallery looking around, serene. She will not be there a
few days later when Richard Arnot drops her in it.

'Mr Robertson,' Gill's words come out of the blue, 'I
am concerned, because you said to me that in your view
there was substantiating evidence in support of the allegations to which we referred this morning.'

Gill speaks, his head sideways from his neck, in
Robertson's direction, but not direct, rather to a point to
Robertson's right. 'It occurs to me that if this is so then
it places certain obligations on me [Gill looks up] to investigate the matter [his hands clasp together] and, if
substantiation is shown to be there, to draw it to the attention of the Director of Public Prosecutions.'

Gill continues, blue eyes behind his pale-framed glasses, 'At the moment I know of no such evidence and I
know of nothing which would tend to support any basis
for such an allegation. It may be that you are in possession of such information. I must ask that by Monday

morning I could be made aware of precisely what the nature of this evidence is so I can consider what action to take.'

Robertson waffles. He knows the noose has tightened. Monday it is.

4. *The British Embassy*

Days Seven and Eight

On Friday the Queen had visited Leeds. The court was closed. We returned on Monday 25 November. This and Tuesday were to be British Embassy days at the inquest, but first we had the matter of Thursday closing-time to settle. We waited on Gill's verdict. The jury were out, so the proceedings could not be reported. Then Gill called it back in and delivered his statement:

> These are very serious accusations and it was important that I should know whether or not these were accusations and allegations which would be substantiated by evidence which should be placed before you as an important and integral part of the evidence you should consider in the circumstances of Helen Smith's death.
>
> The situation is this. As far as Mr Texier is concerned, Mr Robertson urged on me that it would be highly desirable if he could attend as he could assist in explaining what happened in the circumstances surrounding Helen Smith's death.
>
> It is agreed by Mr Robertson that there is no question of a specific allegation being made against him [Texier] alleging that he was guilty of a crime such as murder. He doesn't take the matter further than saying that he was there and he would be in a position to assist and he would like him to be available to answer questions.

Gill did not consider that this was a substantial enough

reason to adjourn the inquest until Texier's attendance could be ensured.

Arnot was in a different position. As a British citizen, proceedings could be taken against him if it was alleged that he was involved in the violent death of another British citizen overseas. If such evidence was presented, Gill would have to refer it to the Director of Public Prosecutions: 'Mr Robertson has assured me there is no evidence to support that contention, other than evidence already given of some suspicion of the circumstances of death, and you have heard the evidence of the pathologists.'

Gill went on to say that Robertson had acknowledged that there was no allegation of murder being made against Arnot. As a result of hearing that assurance, he would continue with the inquest and in due time the jury would have to decide in what circumstances Helen Smith died.

So, to the diplomats.

Colonel Murray De Klee, getting on a bit, slim, grey hair, looking like a colonel, came on stage first. Defence attaché at the British Embassy in Jeddah in May 1979, he had met the Arnots back in England the year before. Bees were their common ground. Colonel De Klee had a swarm of them in his garden and wanted them no more. Arnot relieved him of them, and informed him that he was soon off to Jeddah himself.

So when De Klee mentioned that his wife was due to have an operation, Arnot told him that he would look after her as soon as he got to Jeddah.

The Arnot family duly arrived. A meal round at the De Klees was reciprocated at the Arnots. Who else should Richard Arnot turn to when the tragedy of 20 May occurred?

Colonel De Klee was awoken by the telephone some time between dawn and 6.30 a.m. You cannot really expect me to be more precise than that, his look to the inquest indicated. It was Richard Arnot asking advice. The old soldier in Colonel De Klee came out: ring the ambulance, the police and Michael Weston, the Counsellor at the Embassy.

What was the Embassy's role in situations like this, asked Coronor Gill. 'As a soldier, I don't know. I would imagine that you inform the next of kin.'

Colonel De Klee left the witness box as he entered it – looking bored and not quite sure why he was asked to come.

Enter Michael Weston, Counsellor at the British Embassy in Jeddah at the time. Did he have any previous knowledge of the deceased? 'Of Helen Linda Smith? None at all.'

Yes, Arnot telephoned him shortly before 6.30 a.m. He decided it would be wise to send someone round. So he tried to telephone Consul Francis Geere, but he was not answering. Next, he tried Vice-Consul Gordon Kirby. Alas, he had an out-of-date list; got the wrong number at first.

But Kirby was despatched eventually. As for Michael Weston: 'I did not visit the scene. Subsequently I became involved on several occasions as the problem of the detention of Mr and Mrs Arnot continued.' So perhaps Mr Weston would be so good as to tell the inquest what the British Embassy's role is in situations like this? 'We see the person detained and ask if we can give any help legally, or if they want us to get in touch with people in the UK. We see that he is being treated reasonably.'

It is common sense. The Embassy is not going to spring the Arnots. The delicate, skilled job of the diplomats came next: 'It was necessary to speak to the Saudi authorities at various levels, to see if there were any charges and when they might be released. Some approaches were made.'

Geoffrey Robertson stands up and politely asks him questions. Yes, Michael Weston agrees, the Embassy did send a telegram to the Foreign Office stating there had been an accident in which a British subject was killed. But did another report not state that there were suspicious matters as a result of interviews with hospital staff? Could he remember that one? 'Not clearly at all.'

What was the Embassy's attitude to Mr Smith when he arrived in Saudi Arabia? 'We were anxious to help in any way we could. We helped him in contacting the Saudi authorities.' Of course, and it was stated so confidently to the inquest. How else would you expect British Embassy staff to behave? Would they spy Ron Smith walking towards the Embassy and shout to each other: 'Watch out, Smithy's about. Stick sellotape over your lips'?

What then about a statement Penelope Arnot made to Vice-Consul Kirby a few hours after the deaths, Geoffrey Robertson continued. Michael Weston would not allow Ron Smith to see that, would he? 'Mr Kirby wrote a minute about a conversation with Mrs Arnot,' corrected Michael Weston. Embassy staff do not take statements in these situations. But agreed, Smith was not allowed to see it. The Embassy sent a telegram about the matter to the Foreign Secretary, and the reply was it would be 'wrong in principle to let it be shown'. Did Michael Weston tell Ron Smith, however, that the statement would not be produced unless the Saudi Minister of the Interior requested it? 'That I cannot remember.'

Michael Weston had subsequent dealings with the Arnots. Did he attend a meeting, in October or November 1979, with them and Timothy Hayter and a Saudi lawyer shortly after they were released from prison, but still unable to leave the country? Yes, he did. The meeting was because Penelope Arnot had said in prison that she committed adultery on the fateful night with Tim Hayter. She gave no account of the circumstances of Helen's death but said that she and Hayter had left the room while Helen was still alive to go to another room to commit adultery, Weston says. The penalty for a woman committing such an act is stoning to death. She, Richard and Tim were seeking advice from the lawyer.

This 'confession' was of great concern to the Saudi authorities, Ruth Bundey (Ron Smith's solicitor was standing in for Stephen Sedley that day) commented. 'Yes,' replied Michael Weston. Because there would be

great concern in Britain about Saudi Arabia if a stoning
to death took place? 'Yes.' It would embarrass relationships between the two countries? 'That's right.' Was
she originally aware of the penalties for adultery, Ruth
Bundey continued. 'I was under the impression she was not
aware.' Michael Weston and the Embassy decided, therefore, that they 'must continue the informal efforts to secure
permission for Mr and Mrs Arnot to leave the country'.

Meanwhile, Michael Weston was aware that the adultery confession contradicted the minute of Gordon Kirby
as to what Penelope Arnot did that night, a minute still
not to be shown to Ron Smith or the Saudi police. In the
end, Penelope Arnot retrieved the situation, at least as far
as being stoned to death was concerned, by retracting her
confession.

Michael Weston did not visit the scene of the tragedy,
but Michael Balmer did. He was Third Secretary in
Administration at the Embassy at the time and had only
been there two weeks.

Michael Balmer, an eager, younger man than the other
Embassy staff at the inquest, went to the scene with
Gordon Kirby at around 7.00 a.m. The police were there
and he noticed a European on the pavement who, from
television news reports of the inquest, he now thought
was Fleischer. He then went into the Bakhsh hospital to
pass on a request from Richard Arnot to Penelope to tell
her to drink plenty of water because she had been drinking alcohol. Richard Arnot had made this request surrep-
titiously. 'It was a very difficult situation, with members of
the British Embassy at the scene without prior authority,'
Michael Balmer explained. But, of course, it was a situation that he and Gordon Kirby would be able to handle.

He found Penelope and a little later, when Gordon
Kirby turned up too, she talked about the night. Gordon
Kirby took the notes, but Balmer remembered her saying
that she was awake all night and at about 4.00 a.m. she
woke up two guests who had stayed the night and
made coffee. They went out onto the balcony to watch

the sun rising and saw the two bodies below.

Geoffrey Robertson asked him whether there were any questions put to Mrs Arnot about whether it was possible to see the sun rise, given the direction in which the balcony was facing (which was due west). 'No. We were not in an investigative role,' Michael Balmer replied.

Interval of one night at the inquest. The following morning, enter Gordon Kirby, Vice-Consul at the Embassy in Jeddah at the time. He had not met the Arnots before, he told the inquest, although knew of them and had been on the same guest list as them at three functions in Jeddah. Had he been at the function of 19 May 1979? Coroner Gill asked. 'No, Sir.' Were any other Embassy staff present? 'None whatsoever, Sir.'

But he recognised the English doctor soon enough when he went to the scene with Michael Balmer and Richard Arnot came out of the hospital.

I said something like, 'Good morning, Dr Arnot', and introduced myself and Mr Balmer from the Embassy. He thanked me for coming so promptly and made remarks like, 'Oh God, what a mess' . . . He said he had been asleep in bed when he was woken by his wife. She had gone onto the balcony and seen two figures below. He said he came downstairs, checked they were dead, and then went to the hospital to telephone Dr Bakhsh . . .

Dr Bakhsh, who was standing with us, mentioned that it was terrible – the drinking and sex aspect . . . I could only presume he had been to the flat and seen the drink, and the sex came from the state of the dress of Helen Smith . . . At some point a police officer cautioned us to stop speaking to each other. It has happened before. Dr Arnot stood in front of me and to my left, and turned his head to one side and said: 'Can you go and see my wife in the hospital, tell her to drink as much water and coffee as she can and go to the toilet?' I presumed it was to offset the effects of the alcohol. Mr Balmer left the group and went to the hospital.

Later, Gordon Kirby followed Richard Arnot to the hospital, but he vanished into an office after asking for some multi-vitamin pills. Gordon Kirby then met up with Michael Balmer and the two of them then went back to see Penelope Arnot.

'We were offered coffee and in a relaxed atmosphere Mrs Arnot told me of the previous night's events . . . I certainly did not ask questions as if it was an interrogation,' Kirby told the inquest. Michael Balmer had already said that they found Mrs Arnot smoking, drinking coffee and eating a sandwich.

Unfortunately, Gordon Kirby only had a scrap of paper, so he jotted down what he could and later on that day he wrote down a number of 'one-liners' (diplomatic slang for making a first written record of conversations before you forget them. The points are jotted down briefly as a memory aid.) Later still, he drafted a twenty-four paragraph minute and addressed it to his boss, Francis Geere, the Consul.

This was the minute that Ron Smith had tried so hard to see. Coroner Gill asked if it would be normal to restrict it. Kirby replied that this would be the case 'where the document relates to an illegal activity, not in England, but in Saudi Arabia'.

Presumably it was felt that nobody any longer needed the protection of Her Majesty's Diplomatic Service, because, at the inquest, the minute *was* produced and read out in open court. Ron Smith was handed a copy – he almost grabbed it. For three and a half years he had wanted to see this.

In the main, it was an uneventful piece of writing. Penelope Arnot, 'composed, eating toasted cheese and sandwiches', gave her original story. She told who was at the party: Tim Hayter (New Zealander), Jacques Texier (French), Helen Smith (UK), John? (Dutch – actually Johannes Otten), Alan Kirwen (UK) and some German diver guests whose names she did not know (and who Kirby mistakenly put down as being Dutch in his minute). Alan Kirwen had supplied the booze and the Germans were wild and seemed intent on drinking as much as possible. At some point she saw Helen Smith and John go out onto the balcony.

Around 2.00 a.m. she showed the Germans to the door. Tim Hayter and Jacques Texier were staying the night. She began clearing up the mess, then made coffee and listened to music until daylight, when she stepped onto the balcony and saw the bodies below.

There was no hint of her later story in this conversation – that she committed adultery with Tim Hayter during those fateful hours – but at the end of the minute, Kirby put down his own thoughts. He was puzzled. Penelope Arnot told him that Helen was the only other female there. Why were not others from the hospital there, at a party thrown by the senior doctor? Or were there? And secondly, Mrs Arnot was a working mother (she worked for a merchant in town). Gordon Kirby found it hard to believe that she had been sitting around, drinking coffee and clearing away the debris in the early hours when she had probably been awake since 6.30 a.m. the previous day and had to be at work again early in the morning.

So that was it – not even the status of a statement. It was a 'minute' of a conversation made partly from memory, partly from notes on a scrap of paper, with the queries of an amateur detective at the end; an imprecise document that you could read into what you wished.

And the reason it was restricted, according to Gordon Kirby, was that Alan Kirwen was a British national and had supplied the booze. This would mean two years in jail and 200 strokes of the cane if found out.

Coroner Gill understood: 'This was a serious matter which you would not wish to precipitate.'

Ruth Bundey understood too. A few days later, Ron Smith arrived in Jeddah. Alan Kirwen, Ron Smith – both British subjects. One incriminated in a minute the other wants to see. Was there not the possibility of a conflicting situation, she asked. 'Yes, it was possible,' replied Gordon Kirby. After his conversation with Penelope Arnot, Kirby took hers and Richard's passports and returned to the scene. He and Michael Balmer decided to leave, but as they were getting into their car, Dr Bakhsh came up and demanded Richard Arnot's passport.

'Is it right that passports are normally retained by the employer?' Gill asked.

'It's certainly a Saudi custom. It may be a Saudi law – I don't know,' replied Kirby, but in any case he decided to defend his country's pride and property: 'I said "no", it belongs to Her Majesty's Government.' Dr Bakhsh was unsympathetic to this attitude. He put his leg into the car and called a policeman. 'I saw that the situation was getting grossly out of hand, so I gave him Dr Arnot's passport,' said Kirby.

A few days later, two people who worked at the Bakhsh hospital visited the British Embassy because they wanted to get married. Gordon Kirby saw them and the subject of the deaths arose. According to Gordon Kirby, they told him of rumours going around the hospital to the effect that Helen Smith had been murdered. He made a note of these rumours. They also told him they had heard a bump in the night and it was strange that Penelope Arnot had not heard it too.

Last of the Embassy witnesses to be called to the inquest was Francis George Geere, Second Secretary and Consul at the time. His position in the hierarchy was between Gordon Kirby and Michael Weston. His evidence was mainly of the 'asked nothing, heard nothing, cannot remember' variety. After being informed of the deaths by Gordon Kirby at the Embassy on the morning of 20 May 1979, he went in the afternoon to the police station where he spoke to Richard Arnot.

Did he recall what was said? asked Coroner Gill.

'Nothing at all. It was very difficult. The Saudis are keen to have uninfluenced statements.'

Did he ask about the circumstances of the deaths?

'No, not my function.'

Was he satisfied that no Embassy staff were present at the party?

'None to my knowledge.'

Did he remember a later meeting in a lawyer's office, attended by Richard and Penelope Arnot and Tim Hayter?

'I remember accompanying the Counsellor to a lawyer's office. I have no great recollection of what was said.'

Did the Saudi authorities do a thorough investigation?

'I have no opinion on whether they discharged their duties or not.'

Did he know that the Saudi authorities were considering foul play as a possibility? asked Geoffrey Robertson.

'I did not know.'

Could he recall taking any action on the basis of Kirby's minute?

'I don't think I did. It might have formed the basis of a telegram to the Foreign Office.'

The minute was potentially embarrassing?

'Yes.'

Kirby expressed doubts about what Mrs Arnot had told him?

'My attitude was that it was a question for the Saudi police.'

When Ron Smith arrived a few days later, he accompanied Francis Geere to the police station. Robertson asked Geere whether the conversation Ron Smith then had with Richard Arnot in the police station yard was within his hearing? Did he hear mention of the words 'sun rise'?

'At the beginning it was, but I retired to a respectful distance. I remember hearing the phrase "sunrise", meaning sunrise – the dawn.'

He also went with Ron Smith to the mortuary to identify Helen. Did he notice an indentation on her body above the left eye? asked Ruth Bundey.

'I did.'

Was there a conversation about it?

'There may have been.'

When Ron Smith examined the body further?

'I retired to a respectful distance.'

Obviously no astounding revelations came from Francis Geere. There were, however, one or two occasions when he could be more precise: 'I remember a Saudi police official telling me that as far as they were concerned the deaths were accidental.' And: 'No, never,' there was never any other view than that the deaths were accidental.

These answers were to questions put by Coroner Gill. Questioned further on them by Geoffrey Robertson, Francis Geere fell into his old ways.

Who of the Saudi police told him the deaths were accidental? Robertson asked.

'Probably the officer in charge of the case.'

Could he be more precise?

'No, I cannot be more precise.'

'It was something a policeman said, no more weight than that,' Robertson commented but Geere would not be drawn.

Francis Geere left the witness box as Colonel Murray De Klee had entered it: aloof and with a slightly patronising air.

Days seven and eight of the inquest belonged to the British Embassy. Anybody who expected to hear astounding revelations of cover-up was to be disappointed. Coroner Gill kept closely to the rules of the inquest: no cross-examination and only questions relevant to how, when and where Helen Smith died. 'I am not getting the co-operation I am looking for,' he told Ruth Bundey at one point, after repeated interruptions by him of her questioning. The assumption at the inquest was that the Embassy witnesses were cooperating to the hilt and we should all be grateful to them for deigning to come.

Maybe they were cooperating; maybe they were not. The inquest certainly did not make it clear.

Sandwiched between the Embassy staff on these days were two other witnesses – fellow employees of Helen Smith at the Bakhsh hospital, who had little bits and pieces to fill in on her character.

Christine Germaine Loughwed shared a flat with Helen at the Bakhsh hospital: 'I knew her quite well but was not a close friend.' She knew that Helen would babysit for the Arnots and they would sometimes go with her to the Red Sea. Helen had been going steady with a Malaysian called Guru who worked in the kitchens, but without warning, he was told one day to leave the country. Helen was most upset and the whole staff were up in arms. 'It seemed unfair,' Christine Loughwed told the inquest. After that, Helen saw a Dr Sachel, the hospital paediatrician.

After Helen's death, said Christine Loughwed, a notice appeared on the hospital board. New, stricter regulations were introduced regarding the curfew times and no members of staff were allowed to babysit.

William Teague shared a flat with Helen's Malaysian boyfriend. He agreed with Geoffrey Robertson that Helen had resigned after her boyfriend was expelled (she was working her notice at the time of the party). He also said that Timothy Hayter was a friend of Helen and he would sometimes call for her. Asked by Coroner Gill if Helen had a 'wide circle of friends', he replied, 'Yes.'

Helen, in fact, passed William Teague on her way to the party on 19 May 1979 and asked him if he wanted to come along, but he declined the offer. At that time, she seemed perfectly happy and normal.

Teague also told Geoffrey Robertson that he 'chose not to be' in Helen's company. Expanding the point to Sir David Napley, he said: 'She was up and down. She could be stroppy and abusive. She had a temper which would come on suddenly.'

Christine Loughwed and William Teague spent very

little time in the witness box. But the popular press loved it. *The men in Helen's life* headlines were in profusion.

At the end of day eight, the police report of an interview with Richard and Penelope Arnot shortly after they returned to Britain in August 1980 was read out. Much of it was covered by Richard Arnot's own evidence to the inquest two days later, but Penelope had written saying she could not attend because she did not want to be away from her children any more. Some of her statements were interesting, particularly in view of what she had said in Saudi Arabia.

After her conversation with Gordon Kirby on the morning of the deaths, she was taken into custody with the others but, being a woman, soon found herself apart from them in the women's prison. There she admitted committing adultery with Tim Hayter on the fateful night.

When she was let out of prison on bail a few months later, she went with Richard and Tim Hayter to a Saudi lawyer as the possible consequences of her admission sank in. Stoning to death is the penalty for a woman committing adultery in Saudi Arabia.

This was the meeting that Michael Weston from the Embassy, and possibly Consul Francis Geere, attended. Shortly afterwards she retracted her adultery confession in front of a Saudi judge.

The West Yorkshire police report made it clear that she continued her adultery denial once back in England, which was interesting since she no longer faced stoning to death.

She also gave details to the police that she saw Helen and Johannes go onto the balcony about half an hour after her husband went to bed at 2.00 a.m. and later she pulled aside the curtains momentarily and saw them standing there, 'silhouetted against the lights of Jeddah'. After the Germans left, she was sitting in the room with the two remaining guests, Jacques Texier and Tim Hayter: 'It struck one of us we had not seen Helen and Otten leave.

Therefore, I looked out of the balcony door down to the front balcony. They weren't there. I checked the other balcony. They weren't there either. We all presumed they must have slipped quietly out together, out of the back door of the balcony and through into the hall, not wishing to say goodbye.'

5. *Ron Smith Goes to Jeddah*

Day Nine

Wednesday 1 December: Coroner Gill opened with some bad news, although good from the point of view of the inquest. Jacques Texier's elderly mother in France had suffered a stroke when she read the allegations about him in the French press and was seriously ill. Texier was leaving Saudi Arabia immediately to see her and had indicated he might be able to be in Leeds in the next day or so if the inquest could wait to hear his evidence. 'We owe it to him to be able to do so,' said Coroner Gill with just the right degree of regret tingeing his voice. Everyone looked sadly back at him.

Gill had said earlier in the week that he was still hoping that Timothy Hayter might be able to come, but now the news was not so good. He would not be available until at least 15 December. Gill had, however, subpoenaed a recent interview Hayter had given to Thames Television's *TV Eye*. Given Hayter's previous track record with requests to attend the inquest, Gill thought he would rather now admit the film as evidence and show that to the court.

Geoffrey Robertson suggested that a letter requesting Hayter's attendance was not all it might have been, but had to accept the film as second best.

Then Gill suggested they might have Ron Smith in the witness box today, followed tomorrow by Richard Arnot. Sir David Napley stood up and had a polite discussion with Gill as to the exact position of his client in the witness order. He would rather, of course, Richard Arnot was last – after Jacques Texier. Gill replied that the difficulty was that he did not know exactly when Texier would be able to attend. He wanted to be totally fair to him.

'Sir, my concern is to be totally fair to Mr Smith,' interrupted Geoffrey Robertson. Ron Smith was definitely in the dog-house that morning over Texier's mother and barely a glance had been passed in his direction.

Robertson would rather have him in the witness box after Richard Arnot and there had been no previous indication that he would be called that morning. Failing that, it was suggested that Ron Smith give part of his evidence and then resume after Richard Arnot had given his.

Behind all this, of course, was a subtle, unspoken jockeying for position between Gill and those representing the various parties. Witness orders have been known to affect the outcome of trials.

But Gill would hear none of it. 'I am anxious not to have Mr Smith in two parts. I think it should come before Mr Arnot's evidence.'

Ron Smith did have half an hour's grace, however, as Detective Sergeant Hemsley of the West Yorkshire police gave some incidental details of the August 1980 interview with Richard and Penelope Arnot – just three weeks after they returned to Britain. Then he went into the box.

Coroner Gill nervously began on the preliminaries – where was Ron Smith on 20 May 1979, etc. 'May I ask permission to make a statement which I promise will not be controversial?' Ron Smith interrupted.

'No, Mr Smith, if you are going to give evidence at all . . .'

'I am prepared to give evidence on every matter relative to this affair, no matter how long it takes, except on everything that occurred during the hours between 2.30 and 5.30 a.m., on what I call the anatomy of double murder. I will not comment on these until after Richard Arnot is put in the dock.'

He had got the statement in after all, and Gill struggled to regain control of his court. He wanted simple answers to simple questions. Why had Mr Smith gone to Saudi Arabia after the deaths? he asked hastily.

'The purpose of the exercise was to see the body of my daughter for the last time, also because of a bureaucratic foul-up at the Foreign Office. I was very concerned about information given to me and to my son who went to the Foreign Office.'

Coroner Gill again interrupted, Ron Smith's complaints about the Foreign Office had nothing to do with how, when and where Helen Smith died.

'I went to see my daughter's body, pay my last respects, and because of my feelings of a bureaucratic foul-up,' Smith repeated, and added: 'I had no intention to search for crime.'

Coroner Gill, now more relaxed, asked what happened when he arrived in Saudi Arabia on Friday 25 May 1979.

I was met at 4.30 p.m. on the Saturday afternoon by the consulate [Francis Geere]. Within forty minutes I was talking to Richard Arnot. I managed to obtain permission from the police. I went into the prison courtyard. Incidentally I had a tape recorder in my pocket. There was nothing in this – I always carried one.

Richard Arnot said it was a *super* party, Helen was a *super* girl and a *super* character. On the Saturday afternoon, Timothy Hayter had received termination of notice and was leaving next day. Arnot was therefore throwing a farewell party. Because of the lateness, Helen was not aware of this, but as he was walking through Casualty that evening he saw her and asked her.

In the event, there was a cardiac arrest that night and Helen did not get away from duty until around 9.20. 'Helen got changed and arrived in my flat around 9.45 p.m.,' Arnot said. And then he went on about how he couldn't understand, how it was a dreadful accident. He reiterated on many occasions that Helen was a *super* girl and it had been a *super* party.

He said that shortly after Helen arrived, he left the party and then he went on to say that shortly before midnight he went to bed because he was the duty doctor that night and also had major surgery to perform at 8.00 a.m.

He said that at sunrise, two divers (yes, he called them divers) and his wife, Penny, had gone onto the balcony to see the sun rise. At this point we had an altercation. I said this was improbable as the balcony in question faced west. Francis Geere had taken me very quickly past the flat and I had a geographical layout in any case.

We were surrounded by police officers with tommy guns – everything. They became a little agitated.

He said, and kept repeating many times, that it had been a *super* party and I asked him how many people had been at this party. He said, eleven.

I said that I understood only two women were at this party, so that meant only two women and nine men. I was querying his morality as to how this man could allow two women and nine men to be at his party and he goes to bed leaving his wife and my daughter in the company of these people. I was making a downright condemnation of his moral outlook.

He could not look me in the eye. He blushed and hung his head down. I don't think he replied.

I asked about booze. He said, yes, there was a bottle of whisky – his – and a few bottles of 'hooch' supplied by a grateful patient. I now know this to be the local illegal drink, sadikki.

Sir David Napley rose at this point to ask whether he would be able to be provided with a copy of Ron Smith's written statement to the police, so that he could compare it with what Mr Smith was saying now.

Coroner Gill said no. This would be equivalent to cross-examining Smith. 'I would like it known, therefore, how unsuitable the procedures in this court are for in-

vestigating matters of this nature,' were Sir David's last
words on the subject.

Ron Smith continued: 'He said a few more things that I
have not repeated and will not do until after I have heard
Arnot's evidence. The meeting lasted 10–12 minutes.'

'Did he ask you anything further?' asked Gill.

'No. He did say he was in the process of writing to
Helen's mother in the USA.'

Coroner Gill asked him what happened next.

'We went to the Bakhsh hospital to see Dr Bakhsh and
Matron Agnes Johnstone and then to the mortuary. There
I saw Helen's body – yes. I must say here that I took no
photos of Helen's body in 1979 because I was not allowed
to do so.'

'When you saw Helen's body, some things perplexed
you?' asked Gill.

Yes. In practice the hospital mortician only opens
the shawl just wide enough to expose the face. The
only reason for me being there was for me to ascertain
that it was my daughter.

The first thing I noticed was an indentation, like a
mosquito bite in reverse. [*Ron Smith at this point indicated the position with his finger above the left eyebrow.*]
It was whitish. I thought it was indicative of a hit with
the blunt end of a pencil. Some people have suggested
that it could be a stone on a person's ring. It was between the left eyelash and the hair line. There was no
break of the skin, but it was quite deep.

Coinciding with this, I also noticed that her face was
as if Helen required a good wash. She seemed to be
dirty all around her face.

These were the precipitating factors that removed the
emotional content and have left me a factual machine
ever since.

Because of the darkness on her face, I thought
she might have been strangled. I insisted on them
taking the shroud off – to see her throat. Her body was

perfect in every shape and form – I am talking about the contours on her body. It was as if she was laying on the slab asleep. There were no autopsy marks.

I insisted on examining Helen's body. I started on the back where there was hypostasis [blood under the skin] which indicated to me that she had died on her back [because the blood runs to the lowest point of the body when someone dies]. Helen's left arm was in a *rigor mortis* position above her body [*Ron Smith indicated that the left arm looked as if it might be protecting her body*]. I noticed that the left elbow was also up.

Helen's body throughout, with the exception of what I am going to indicate in a moment, was a perfect flesh tint. On the inside of her thighs – *not* on the outside or top – were bruising marks. They were not abrasion marks. These indicated a certain thing to me as an ex-police officer. Her right abdomen on the top side was obviously full of blood but there was not a bruising.

I did not have X-ray eyes, of course, and I did not see any fractures. I had a feel and I did not feel any. Subsequently, I was told there were, of course.

I examined her pubic parts . . . [*Ron Smith paused*]. Forgive me one minute . . . [*Coroner Gill tried to interrupt as Ron Smith fought back his obvious emotion*]. It's all right . . . Don't bother . . . I examined her vagina and could not see anything at all. I did notice that her pubic hairs were very short.

I think that is all I can tell you.

Coroner Gill asked if there were signs of any marks on her face. 'Yes. It was certainly obvious to me that the blue marks on her face the fact that she was dirty, that these were bruised blood capillaries under the surface, but I'm not a medical man.'

'When you saw the condition of the body, did it make you doubt what you had been told?' continued Gill.

'I went with a great feeling of trauma. The body was perfect, as if Helen was just lying down. There was no way my daughter had fallen any considerable distance onto a solid, marble floor.'

Coroner Gill now asked him if he visited the block of flats where the deaths of Helen and Johannes occurred. 'I have received every cooperation from the Saudi police. I got no cooperation from Dr Bakhsh and therefore I did not go into the Arnot flat until I returned to Jeddah in June 1980.'

Of the height, Ron Smith said there were six floors up to the Arnot flat, no matter how they were counted. From the entrance doorway to the first flats there was a total of eight steps – about ten feet. He had estimated the height from the balcony to the ground as seventy feet and had been told the same by other doctors at the hospital. The wall that had replaced the railings was about 6 feet 8 inches high.

Ron Smith said he was handed Helen's personal belongings – a brown envelope containing a chain and pendant, and a Dutch contraceptive cap. This later surprised him as the Saudi pathology report said that she was fitted with an IUD.

The following week, on Wednesday 30 May, Ron Smith visited the mortuary again. He was accompanied by Francis Geere, Agnes Johnstone, Joe Deguara (the consultant pathologist at the Bakhsh hospital), the mortician and some other staff. He said that they wished to see Helen's body again because they were convinced she had been murdered. 'These people are medical experts, and one is a pathologist,' he added. Joe Deguara certainly felt there were grounds for suspicion because of the slight injuries, although he said nothing to Ron Smith at the time.

Coroner Gill then tried to get Ron Smith to tell the inquest what other evidence he had of what had happened at the party. But Ron Smith stood firmly by his opening statement. 'You're not going to get it from me until Richard Arnot has been in the box.'

Sir David Napley had nothing to ask at all. Stephen Sedley then got up and referred to a conversation Ron

Smith had had with Dr Bakhsh while in Jeddah. Ron Smith said he had it on tape: 'There was no blood, Mr Smith, there was no blood.'

Sedley asked about the first-floor balcony to the block of flats. Ron Smith insisted that this did not project as far out as the others. As he understood Helen's body to be partly in this recess, he did not see how she could have got there by falling from the sixth floor.

Ron Smith then told Robertson that although Helen was wearing a dress when he first saw her, there were no knickers on her. And all previous references over the past three and a half years in reports had been to knickers. Only in this court, during the pathologists' evidence, had the term 'pantie-girdle' been used.

And, yes, he had later been handed other belongings, besides those previously mentioned: Helen's handbag, containing her diary, address book, camera minus film, and keys.

Robertson asked if Helen had had any self-defence training, and Ron Smith replied that she almost joined the police. 'She could defend herself against any one man,' he said.

Ron Smith told the inquest that the street outside the block of flats was well lit with overhead sodium-type lamps which were down both sides, and finished his ninety-minute stint by describing what happened after he went to see Dr Bakhsh a second time on Sunday 27 May. 'I was approached by two nurses. Would I go to the doctors' quarters where many medical staff were assembled to tell me how Helen was murdered?'

Gill intervened to state that none of the people at this meeting was in a position to give anything other than rumour and speculation, and that was that. Ron Smith walked back to his seat and the press gallery all but emptied.

Coroner Gill now started on the written statements of the various witnesses who could not attend the inquest.

Dieter Chapuis, one of the German Harms Salvage workers, was first. His statement largely confirmed the evidence given by the others. It was a friendly party, he fell asleep, he did not see anyone on the balcony and he left with the others at around 2.30–3.00 a.m. Mrs Arnot ensured that bottles of whisky were always on the table. They got lost on the way back to the port, however, and it took them an hour. None of the other Germans had mentioned this.

He added that he thought he would have seen the bodies if they had been there when he left by the main entrance, and Timothy Hayter had told him in jail that he had had sex with Penelope Arnot that night. There had also been a rumour that Tim Hayter and Penny Arnot had thrown away Otten's clothes.

The session broke up for lunch. The press were waiting outside in droves for Ron Smith. The morning had started with contempt for him for having caused Texier's mother to have a stroke. It ended with at least the recognition that he was suffering too – it was, after all, his daughter who was dead.

The statement of Dr Saud Abdul Rahman was read first after lunch. He had been interviewed by Interpol and at the time of the deaths lived in the same block of flats as the Arnots, on the first floor. He explained that the building had six floors and there were two flats on each floor.

On Sunday 20 May he was informed at about 5.30 a.m. by the building porter that there were two bodies outside. The porter had been on his way to morning prayers.

Yes, he did see the bodies *in situ*. The man was 'hanged upside down on the railings' and naked apart from around the lower abdomen. The man had clear bruises on his face and there was blood around him. The girl was lying about one metre from the wall.

Dr Rahman then decided to inform all the residents. He went up to the sixth floor. He heard a lot of noise coming from the Arnot flat and when Arnot opened the door there was a small man with a white beard standing behind him. He could smell wine.

Arnot told him: 'If you mean the event down the building, I know about that. I will deal with it.'

Dr Suktian, the orthopaedic surgeon at the Bakhsh hospital, was interviewed by the West Yorkshire police in September 1980. He lived on the sixth floor, opposite the Arnots. He told them that he was advised of the deaths just after 5.30 a.m. He went down and recognised Helen Smith. He was alone at the time.

The man was impaled on the railings with his head to the inside. He was wearing underpants and a watch. The underpants were around his thigh. Dr Suktian understood that the watch had stopped at 3.00 a.m.

Helen's head was towards the ground-floor balcony and her left arm was up in front of her head. Her pants were pulled down to the knee region, she was wearing a blue dress and there was no bleeding from her body.

On his first visit, Dr Suktian could not recall seeing any documents, but later he saw a passport. At some stage during the initial discovery of the bodies he saw two men – one elderly, the other younger – leaving the Arnot flat. A little later, in the hospital casualty department with Arnot, he spoke to Dr Bakhsh on the telephone and phoned the police.

He heard no disturbance at the Arnot flat that night. It was very difficult to hear anything because of the air conditioning. The Saudi police never interviewed him.

Although a common visitor to England, Dr Abdul Al-Rahman Taha Bakhsh refused to attend the inquest. He was, however, interviewed by West Yorkshire police on 26 August 1982. He confirmed that he is the owner of the Bakhsh hospital and said that Dr Suktian telephoned him about the deaths.

He contacted a friend who was a chief of police and went to the scene. There was no blood around Helen

Smith, and he remembered telling her father this. Only one leg was in her pants.

There was much blood around the impaled Dutchman, however. He was naked apart from underpants or shorts which were in position. Dr Bakhsh saw several documents in the road and he placed these near Otten.

He recalled later having an altercation with Gordon Kirby over the Arnot passports and having a poster put up in the hospital warning staff not to speak of the incident. This was because of press inquiries. He did, however, allow all staff to make a telephone call home.

Yes, he did pay for the repatriation of Helen Smith's body to England. He recalled asking Ron Smith not to mention his name, but this was not a condition of paying for the repatriation.

6. *Arnot, Hayter and Texier*

Day Ten

Thursday 2 December, 11.23 a.m.: Richard Arnot enters the witness box. He is cool and relaxed. He speaks so forcefully into the microphone that his solicitor tells him to hold his head back. Arnot remains in the witness box for the next eight court hours. The first day is gentle, the second day a brawl.

Each of us, in the press, in the court well, expected an event. What we expected it to be depended on whether we believed Helen was murdered or died through an accident. Arnot's appearance, over two days, was a non-event.

11.26 a.m.

GILL: To my knowledge, the only means of access to the building was the front door.
ARNOT: I don't recall any side entrance to the building.

11.27 a.m.

GILL: On coming in through the entrance, there was a stairway?
ARNOT: There was a central lift with stairs spiralling around the periphery of it, all contained within the black-fronted part of the building.

11.29 a.m.

GILL: Could you tell us about the specific events, the circumstances about this party?

ARNOT: I have thought about it for three and a half
   years ... I'm still not absolutely sure whether my
   wife or I asked Tim Hayter, or whether Tim Hayter
   asked if we would arrange it. It was either.

Helen Smith had introduced Hayter to the Arnots and
the four went scuba diving. Tim Hayter resembled
Helen's brother. Hayter could teach them diving. Helen
had been the children's favourite babysitter, and had sat
for them since December 1978, more frequently at the
beginning, less frequently in the period up to the party.
The party had been loosely arranged over the preceding
days. Arnot is asked who invited Helen. 'I think I did
...,' he replies. 'Helen might have extended a general
invitation. There would have been nothing exceptional in
them coming. We'd made our flat available for staff
meetings. There was a lot of unhappiness and resentment
between British staff and employers.'
   This unhappiness was never explored at the inquest.
Gill had been given a list of sixty-three witnesses by Ron
Smith. He called six. Many of those on the list were
former employees at the hospital. Much of the unhappiness and resentment came from the sudden de-
portation of Helen's fiancé, Guru, a Malaysian, who,
without notice, was deported to Malaysia. The hospital
staff were up in arms and Helen was so angry she handed
in her notice.
   After finishing his duty around 9.20 p.m., Arnot met
Helen in the hospital corridors. She was on her way to
change her clothing for the party. Arnot, arriving at the
flat, discovered there was no ice, so he returned to the
hospital and filled a bucket from the kitchen. He met
Helen going up to the flat and they entered it together at
9.45 p.m.

GILL: Was Alan Kirwen there when you entered the
   flat?
ARNOT: My recollection was that until Kirwen got there

the drink was in short supply . . . I couldn't recall
exactly who was there . . . it's all done in retrospect.
I recall the only persons there who I'd not met before
were Otten, and the other was a German national
who stayed just a brief period. I think he was referred
to as Peter, but I do recollect a German national . . .
Alan, Alan Kirwen, he arrived shortly after I
returned with the ice. My recollection was that the
arrangement was that he should bring it [the whisky].
My recollection was that he brought it with him.
Texier arrived uninvited. Kirwen arrived around ten
o'clock.

It is his first contradiction of another witness. Kirwen
said he took the whisky around lunchtime. There is a
sudden stir, a few whispers. If there was no drink before
Kirwen, then what was the speed of the alcohol consumption? If there was drink, what was the state of the
guests when Helen arrived?

Arnot says there was nothing unusual in having alcohol in Jeddah: 'It was readily available on the Saudi
black market. Provided consumption remained a private
affair it was acceptable because the police did not raid
people's homes or enter residences without specific invitation.'

GILL: Was there any refreshment?
ARNOT: There was, some . . . a tray of something to eat
    on the table . . . nuts, crisps, small things to eat, soft
    drinks available . . . orange juice . . . on a circular
    table in the corner.
GILL: Can you remember which rooms were in use?
ARNOT: Yes, the sitting room, and you could use the
    hallway and dining area to dance in. Two rectangular
    things were there, flat, foam-covered things which
    people sit on.
GILL: It was held in the two rooms?
ARNOT: Yes, we used the sitting room . . . food was in

the hall, ice in fridge in kitchen, orange juice. The children, aged five and seven, were in bedroom number two, which I've indicated.

GILL: Were drinks served?

ARNOT: One, at the most two bottles – on the rectangular table in the sitting room. It was a low table. I don't recall giving anyone anything to drink, people just helped themselves.

GILL: What were the events from the time you arrived until the time you left?

ARNOT: It was a quiet party. We had a hi-fi tape playing from the beginning. What it played I couldn't tell you. We were sitting around the sitting room area and there may have been dancing, a quiet, convivial evening much as when one has friends around in this country.

GILL: There was dancing?

ARNOT: Yes, in the dining room area. Underneath the window there were foam-covered things one could sit on. In a Saudi house, guests could sit on these and wait before being invited through.

GILL: As the evening wore on, can you remember anything about the behaviour and demeanour of the guests?

ARNOT: As the evening wore on, everybody was certainly drinking alcohol, but no drunkenness was evident at any stage. Between 11.30 and 12.30 I left to see some patients. I normally leave at nine, but in view of the party I went later. Prior to my departure, the people we have heard about were there plus Peter plus Kirwen. I don't remember Jimmy Yeong being there and I don't remember seeing anyone else. I can't remember Peter and Kirwen being there when I got back . . . On my way back from the hospital I knocked on the door of Matron Agnes Johnstone's flat. I had not invited her but I thought she might like to come along. There was no reply so I went on. I got back about 12.30.

More eyebrows raise in the court. Agnes Johnstone had taken great pains to establish the sort of parties she normally went to.

Gill and Arnot now discuss Helen and Johannes.

GILL: Did you form any view of their relationship?

ARNOT: I don't recall observing or watching or taking an active interest ... When I said goodbye to them at 2.00 a.m., they were in the middle of the room dancing, both perspiring profusely. They seemed OK.

GILL: Helen has been described as happy.

ARNOT: The prevailing mood was jovial, a very relaxed and pleasant evening.

He leans back as he says this, legs crossed, the right half of his body slanting right, his left elbow up by his ribs, his right arm touching his left kneecap, his head to the right, a long lean face, with prominent eyebrows, brown eyes darker with distance. Streaks of grey run through his hair.

GILL: You retired to bed?

ARNOT: I was operating at nine o'clock the next morning. I'd prearranged the alarm clock for two o'clock and when two o'clock came I went to bed. I said goodbye to everyone and went to bed. I was asleep within seconds. What happened from then on until I was awoken between 5.30 and 5.35 would be hearsay.

GILL: It was very much Tim Hayter's party?

ARNOT: I always regarded it as such. There were two I'd never met before. I'd only had brief acquaintance with most of the others. I'd been there [at the harbour] the day before. I didn't really know them. I think he asked me to extend a general invitation to any of the nurses but I cannot be specific.

It was a question which had been asked often in those long hours around the inquest. Why only two women? Gordon Kirby had asked it in the original Embassy minute. If Hayter had asked Arnot to extend a general invitation, then why had not Arnot done so? Why did he go to Agnes Johnstone, the matron, a woman who would not be known to most of the other guests, who would spend most of her time with either him or the English-speaking guests?

The photographs come out. Three sets of photographs taken inside the curtained flat at the party by the guests have gone. Presented continually to the inquest are either photographs of the outside of the building or the interior of Dr Keith's flat on the floor below. (Keith had supplied the photographs to Dr Green when Green made his autopsy.) The photographs are given to Arnot.

Arnot leans forward. He took a degree in medicine and chemistry at St Andrew's University. He became a Master Surgeon in Capetown. He has spent years in lecture rooms. He extends himself to cover the witness box, left arm holding the photographs above the witness box wall, the right finger-tips indicating what he is referring to as he speaks. His body is open to the court so that we are drawn into the photographs, his moving fingers, his voice, words. There is a slight nasal echo in his voice as he relaxes. Uptight, pressed, he becomes plummier, the richness, though, flattened. Gill asks him about the positions of the flat's two balconies.

ARNOT: These two lines [he fingers the balconies on the photos] . . . The constitution of all the balconies was the same. In addition there was a balcony in the rear of the building. The larger picture shows the front balcony before the addition of the rail. The two later show the balcony after the rail was put on . . . The height was 90 centimetres to the top of the rail before addition. My wife was half an inch shorter than Helen. Helen was slightly taller . . . We regarded it as a very dangerous balcony. We were never happy anywhere in the vicinity. We never let the children out in that area . . . The front balcony of the flat was the last place I gather Helen and Johannes were seen alive . . . The front of the flat faced due west, the back due east, out towards Mecca and Jeddah airport a quarter of a mile distant.

GILL: There were two access doors . . .?

ARNOT: Yes, if you compare, see both doors, photograph 41, see the double doors. Those leading to the front. From dining room to the balcony was a side door with an air conditioner directly above that door.

GILL: With regard to those two doors, were they opened or closed?

ARNOT: The practice was to keep them closed because of the heat. We were never able to keep them open for more than a few minutes because the temperature and humidity were quite fierce. The inferior air conditioner made a terrible racket. It was difficult to sleep because of the racket . . . I would say, as photos show, certainly sheer gauze curtains with the thicker on the room side . . . Certainly at night they were kept drawn. If people could look in and saw people dancing . . . that's a natural precaution we took.

GILL: Were other things in the room? Plants?

ARNOT: We had a few hanging plants in the main room, hanging diametrically opposite. We had some on the ground.

GILL: Was the sitting room doorway kept closed, or was it possible for them to be opened?

ARNOT: Both were used from time to time. I don't know if they were ever kept locked. Both had lock and keys. The children knew they were not allowed out, both were old enough to have unlocked themselves.

GILL: And the doorway from the dining area?

ARNOT: I don't recall it ever being locked. We could use it from time to time.

GILL: The balcony, what was on it?

ARNOT: A sunlounger. It was kept there for storage. It was bought when we first moved in, some time in December. It was a very pleasant climate then, by no means too hot to sunbathe. We bought it so my wife could sunbathe on the roof. It was a cheap Korean affair with a tubular steel frame. The central part of it tended to flap down for the legs and head. It was more something you could sit up in with it at your back. It had a lightweight canvas attached to the outside framework and was lightly sprung. Within days the springs started to break. By the time of the party it was pretty unserviceable. One person could not lie on it, let alone two. At points around the periphery the springs pulled away. One lay on it at one's peril if one lay to one's side.

GILL: Was it opened up?

ARNOT: My recollection was that it was not opened out. My recollection was that it was tucked away between the balcony side and the end wall.

Arnot went on to say that he had only noticed it was there after the party, when he had returned to the flat and the police drew his attention to it. He could not honestly remember the last time he had seen it. In the months prior to the party, it had been kept up on the roof, which had led to the deterioration of the canvas.

GILL: When it was fully extended, would it have projected into the area of the doorway?

ARNOT: I honestly couldn't say. It was too short for me to lie on, that I can remember.

GILL: Wasn't it a curious way to leave it?

ARNOT: I cannot recall anyone using it for months. I intended mending it at some stage. By the time of the party we hadn't used it since January, February . . . my wife wouldn't use it because of the flats which overlooked the roof.

The police had referred to the sexual aspect of the whole scene when they had entered the flat with Arnot. Coroner Gill points out to him that Miss Johnstone had said the sunlounger was open when she went up to the flat. Arnot cannot recollect that. He remembers that, as Miss Johnstone had said, the framework was buckled. It was put aside then to be mended.

The two men discuss the light on the balcony. There was a balcony lamp. Arnot could not recollect if it was ever used, as it tended to attract insects. The light it emitted was diffused through the thick curtains. The street lamps threw a yellow light which, in Arnot's awareness, did not reach the level of the balcony. 'One would be pretty well invisible.' The Arnots sat out having drinks after dark, invisible on the balcony from the positions below.

Humidity and moisture were particular problems. Anything taken out from inside instantly condensed. 'A very heavy dew,' Arnot emphasised. The balcony floor was highly polished, and the girl employed to clean and tidy had cleaned the balcony floor tiles only a few weeks before the party. The surface was extremely slippery. If anyone was perspiring in any way, any moisture at all could be extremely treacherous.

After the lunch break, Arnot reruns where he left off. He went to bed at 2 a.m. and fell straight to sleep. 'It had been a long day and I was operating the next day,' he says. 'I was asleep within seconds and the next thing I knew I was being awoken by my wife at 5.30 to 5.35 a.m. Hayter and Texier were standing behind her. She said, "Richard, wake up, something horrible has happened. I think Helen has fallen off the balcony." '

He 'leapt' from his bed, 'covered myself with a towel or some garment, ran down the corridor, through the dining room, on through the living room, and onto the balcony.' He held both his hands on the balcony rail and looked down. He saw the body of Helen Smith lying below, 'in a perfectly natural position, on her right side, as though she was asleep'. He heard later that his wife had made a similar comment when she first discovered the bodies. 'Good God, what's Helen doing there?' she apparently asked herself. As far as he could see, she was wearing her dress. He ran back into the flat, grabbed a shirt, trousers and shoes but apparently did not have time to get his socks – 'a day without socks. I couldn't remember if I had my stethoscope,' and raced down the stairs.

He decided that Helen had been dead for at least 'an hour or two'. Her dress had ridden up, her pubic area and buttocks exposed. 'I felt for her pulse on her left wrist and as I touched her there were two clear impressions. Her skin was cool to the touch and her arms were stiff. I then felt for another pulse, which was more easy to feel, and there was no sign of any pulse or any form of life.'

Arnot tells the inquest he thinks he did take his stethoscope with him, thinks he listened for a heartbeat. He recorded the time as 5.35 a.m. 'I know I made a mental note of it because it is a standard medical procedure. When one certifies a dead body, one records the time to the nearest minute.'

On her forehead he noticed the same indentation that Ron Smith noticed. This, without bruising or bleeding around it, must have occurred at the moment of death. He thought it could have been caused either by hitting the building while falling or catching a button on Otten's clothing. He noticed no other marks on her face, neck or upper chest. He was at her body for a minute, then stood up. Otten's body was in the middle of the wall section between two lamps, lying across railings.

'In relation to what was published subsequently,' he tells the court, 'the two bodies were no more than three feet apart when looked at from above. I recall as I stood up his body was right next to where I was when I'd stepped over her legs and examined her from her right side. He was pierced by three of the railings, they'd gone through the pelvic groin, whether completely couldn't be

seen. He was lying with torso and head inside of the railing on the building side. His legs were hanging over on
the pavement side. There was a little puddle of congealed
blood two to three inches in diameter directly below his
head. Two or three ants were paying an interest in this.'
Blood had dripped from Otten's head to form this
puddle.

Helen was wearing a floral-patterned dress, pinkish or
brownish in colour, sleeveless, the lower part ridden up.
Arnot could not recall noticing where her panties were.
The pubic area and buttocks were evident when one
looked at her. He did not think she was wearing jewels
nor could he recall a wrist-watch.

There may well have been people on the street. Otten's
shirt was completely unbuttoned, hanging off his shoulders, 'so much so I could move the shirt to one side to
look at his face'. Otten was wearing a watch with a
stainless-steel strap, but Arnot did not look at the watch
either to see the time or to see if it had stopped.

Otten was evidently dead. 'I only went through the
motions.' There was no pulse, his skin was discoloured,
his arms were stiff. Arnot's only movement of the bodies
was to lift Helen's arm. Helen was lying with her feet
towards the wall, head towards the building, in a sleeping
position, her head to the right. He stepped over her legs
and went onto the pavement.

'The most distinctive feature of Johannes, my distinct
impression,' he continues, 'was Johannes' underpants
were not in their normal place – they were down in the
mid-thigh region. His genitals fully exposed to view, he
was in a state of some sexual excitement. It was really
quite a grotesque appearance from the road.'

Coroner Gill, somewhat surprised, not having been
presented with this evidence before, asks him how erec-
tions occur in deceased males.

'It can occur in hanging,' Arnot replies. 'It was extremely evident in the overall scene.'

Arnot raced back upstairs. He told his wife and the two

men present, Hayter and Texier, that the bodies were Helen and Johannes, and both were dead. He asked his wife, 'What on earth happened?' She replied that after he had gone to bed, she had observed Helen and Johannes go through the balcony doors and out onto the balcony. Later, either when the guests were departing or shortly after their departure, she realised Helen and Johannes had not been with them. She had checked the balcony to see if they were still there. Finding no sign of them, she assumed they had gone through the balcony's dining room door, through the flat's dining area, and back to Helen's flat.

Arnot cannot now remember the precise moment Penny told him this. 'The one thought uppermost in all our minds was that the police would be in the flat and there was a considerable amount of alcohol in the flat, and it would be wise to get rid of it. I recall before going back to the hospital, my wife was pouring whisky down the kitchen sink. Texier, Hayter and myself picked up a large container of partly fermented wine in the second lavatory in the flat and emptied it in the bathroom.' They could not dispose easily of the empty bottles, however, and these were deposited in a hold-all in the cupboard.

There was a knock at the door. 'A Sudanese gynaecologist and a black porter stood outside the door. They asked me if I knew about the two bodies. Various versions of this conversation have been described. I cannot recall the exact words. It was something on the lines that I knew about it, and would take the necessary steps.'

His only recollection was of opening the door. He is unable to say whether he was ready to go out, or happened to be next to the door when they knocked. In the event, after this brief conversation, he dashed down the stairs, went around the bodies, ran into the Casualty Department and asked the male duty nurse to telephone Dr Bakhsh, the hospital owner.

He told Bakhsh what had happened. Dr Suktian

arrived. Suktian and Bakhsh spoke together in Arabic some minutes and then, after they had finished, Arnot asked Suktian to ring the police on his behalf since, 'It was widely known the police hardly ever, if, did speak English.'

Matron Agnes Johnstone arrived with Suktian on the telephone. He told her what had happened. Arnot thought they briefly went outside the Casualty Department. He did not see the bodies again then. He told her where they were and went back into the office. He rang the only person he knew at the Embassy, Colonel De Klee, the military attaché. Whether De Klee told him to ring the Embassy, or whether De Klee said he would do it himself, Arnot cannot remember.

He returned to the flat. He remembers Agnes Johnstone being either at the flat or still looking at the bodies. Shortly after, Dr Bakhsh arrived. Arnot was by now in the flat. He went down and spoke briefly to Bakhsh. He cannot recall clearly what he did at this stage.

At this point Arnot, throughout the day composed, his narrative well textured, seems uncertain. He has been measured, coherent, a style of delivery difficult to shake since it counterposes Arnot in the flesh – Arnot a tall gangling man, his voice modulated.

Arnot had exchanged photographs with Gill, speaking as a medical man, either leaning back, legs crossed, tapping his ankle, or leaning forward, body across the witness box, face on to the court. Now, leaning back, he tries to place Hayter and Texier in the flat between his periods of movement. 'After getting back to the flat, Texier and Hayter stood in the flat . . . they left the flat soon after I returned to it . . . a bit after six . . .' (he pauses, fingers towards his chin, comes forward), 'they left after I rang the police . . .' (his hand comes onto the desk inside the witness-box wall, fingers tap) 'it certainly doesn't tie up' (his head lowers so that his shoulders are more over the box).

GILL: You left the flat and went back to the hospital. What did you do then? Did you come back?

ARNOT: Yes, let me get this right, whilst Suktian was talking to the police I spoke to Agnes, then I rang De Klee . . . at some stage whether she went back to the hospital and returned . . . at some stage I went to the flat, saw Texier and Hayter. Texier went to the French Embassy, Hayter then took a taxi back to the port.

GILL: Were you at the flat when they left?

ARNOT: I don't know if I was or not. I can't be sure of that. Whether they left then or after I returned the second time I can't be sure . . . They were not there when Agnes came to the flat . . . Was she around when Bakhsh came to the flat? I'm not certain . . . At 6.15 when Bakhsh arrived I went down and had a few words. Texier was very friendly with the French cultural attaché . . . as far as I knew Hayter took a taxi back to the port . . . it may have been whilst I was 'phoning. I'm not absolutely clear.

Arnot went down to the pavement. Dr Bakhsh was there. He informed the hospital owner that people had been drinking alcohol at the party. Bakhsh told him not to worry. Arnot decided then to be frank with the police. Around this time, fifteen yards away, he saw a passport in the road and placed it beneath Otten's legs.

Otten's trousers? 'Aha, problem number one as far as we're concerned.' There were no trousers on the body, no trousers in the flat. 'That was one of the things which puzzled the police . . . this has remained a great mystery . . . the police went to great lengths to find out.'

GILL: There was no question of them being disposed of?

ARNOT: Absolutely not . . . at no stage has any light been shone on that point.

GILL: Presumably they'd fallen on the road?

ARNOT: A passer-by had either spotted them or taken them. If we could have produced them, we would have done so. It was, and is, a great mystery. None of us had any knowledge . . . no one has ever given a good account.

GILL: Unless the trousers were in the road, it's difficult to see how the passport would have got there?

ARNOT: Our hypothesis was that since Otten always carried a large amount of money, somebody stole the trousers and the wallet and the papers fell out.

By this time a crowd had gathered around the bodies. Arnot noticed a certain amount of hilarity among the onlookers. He asked an Arabic member of staff to translate what was being said. The translator told him the crowd were discussing what the bodies had been doing whilst falling: 'Who is riding who? . . . I recall feeling very nauseated about this discussion at a time like this,' Arnot says.

Gill makes a comment about Arnot being offended by their indifference. Arnot replies, 'They were joking among themselves. One could have laughed or cried, I certainly wasn't laughing. I was most upset this sort of thing should be said.'

He leans back, his long arms over the desk, a finger pointed on the desk top, his head down towards his chest, a characteristic pose. Blue suit, hair turning grey.

The police arrived. He told them Helen and Johannes had been seen going onto the balcony. They asked a few questions. Fleischer arrived. Arnot knew the guests only by their Christian names, if he knew their names at all. Fleischer and he wrote out the list of guests, omitting Kirwen for obvious reasons, omitting Peter, the German national, because Arnot did not know him at all, and 'he hadn't really been part of the party'.

There was no question of being arrested, he was told. He escorted his wife and children to the hospital. The children were obviously shocked. (During the inquest,

Arnot never mentions the children by their names. It is always 'the children', just as it is always 'one did this' or 'one did that'.) Kirby and Balmer arrived from the Embassy. Arnot held a hurried conversation with Kirby and asked Kirby to remind his wife to drink a lot of fluid and get something to eat.

The police disturbed the snatched conversation. It was now around 8.00 a.m. They took him up to the flat. A cursory (his word) search was made for the trousers: 'A fairly superficial search.' They asked him why the flat was so tidy. 'It was tidy when I got up,' he replied. As Penny said, she had spent the night washing glasses, tidying up. He kept a stockpile of bottles for wine-making. There had been insufficient time to remove these and they had been placed in a hold-all and deposited in a cupboard. The flat was never searched.

Remembering the indentation on Helen's forehead, he went out on the balcony and examined the outside of the wall for damage. The police warned him to move away because of fingerprints. (A few days later, he returned to the flat with the police. It was covered with fingerprint dust but their fingerprints were never taken. The main concern of the police was how tidy the place was.)

He showed them the possessions of Helen and Johannes in the flat: her handbag, her abeya (shawl), Otten's glasses. The senior officer pointed at the sunlounger. 'It excited some comment because of the appearance of the bodies.'

It was his first recollection that it was on the balcony. He went back down with the police. At some point, he went to the hospital, took several multiple vitamins, and left for the police station at 10.30 a.m.

The Arnots' Ethiopian maid arrived, an illegal immigrant. She was stopped by the police. She said she was visiting someone and moved away. Arnot never saw her again. The Arnots were escorted to the police station and kept in the station yard. At 4 a.m. the next morning he went with Penny to the women's prison where she was detained. From then on, she was always separate.

During the following days, they were questioned and questioned. He shared the station cell with Ritter, Schlaeffer and Fleischer. They talked endlessly. The Germans gave him their story. They had left, had not seen anything. The only person who had seen anything had been Penelope. His wife's adultery is now raised at the inquest, Gill handling it delicately, as do all the lawyers.

'She had made a statement in all innocence,' Arnot tells him, about having sexual intercourse with Hayter, without, 'realising the possible penalty.' He had no doubt she made the statement. It had been a joint statement together with Hayter, with 'full physical details'. They had been assured of complete confidentiality. Within a day or two, it was all over Jeddah. 'Even' the woman looking after their children knew.

'Even' – it was a telling remark. It indicated an enormous gulf between one world and the next, both existing simultaneously in the court. His court appearance was concerned with alcohol. The police assured him that, despite Mr Smith's allegations, they were perfectly satisfied that the deaths were accidental.

Arnot and Gill talk together.

It approaches 4.00 p.m. Arnot says that if there had been any hint of murder or violence he would still be in Jeddah: 'Assault is regarded with extreme gravity.'

Gill runs through the account given by Hayter and Penny. His wife was tidying up. Hayter was asleep. She woke up Hayter. 'One thing led to another,' Arnot explains, leaning back, his right hand raised to a point below his chest, moving slightly from side to side. 'Whatever happened, happened. Texier then woke up ... I understand Texier was present and asleep.'

Gill asks a question. Arnot gives the finale ... 'Whilst I was at the party there was no sign of violence, aggression, show of temper or anything else other than a perfectly relaxed and enjoyable occasion. There was no jealousy or fighting over the two women present. The two girls simply danced with the guests in turn. What we saw the next day was just so awful. The contrast between the thoroughly pleasant evening and the awful things that happened then, and in the next three and half years, have been appalling.'

Day Eleven

Friday 3 December. An accident needs an observer. An event needs perception to observe it. Every event from then on becomes an image in a labyrinth. Ron Smith had chased down the labyrinth. Day eleven had been billed as the day when possibly the curtains would reveal a chink.

Arnot is in the witness box; Smith's barristers are questioning. Flyposters in Professor Dalgaard's home town of Arhus carry the banner: ARNOT IN TODAY. READ TOMORROW.

It is a scrappy, gruelling day. Eighteen interruptions are made by Gill, Napley and, once, Arnot. The court as a language, the proceedings as the narrative, disintegrates. The day resembles a public-house crawl, a fight outside every pub. Eventually, in the knowledge that the interruptions will never cease, lethargy and boredom set in among the onlookers. Before lunch people get up and leave. People give up, sprawling. The interruptions effectively block any flow in the links between the various components of the party – the alcohol, the sex, the guests. No overall picture can be gleaned.

The first interruption comes at 10.30 a.m. At 10.16 Gill had asked Arnot for his professional opinion regarding the fractured sternum. Arnot thought it was a mystery. At 10.23 Robertson began asking questions. The Arnots gave a series of newspaper interviews to the *Daily Mail* in the autumn of 1980. They had only recently been allowed to leave Saudi Arabia, and returned to 'horrendous debts, well over £10,000'. Initially they were not inclined to be interviewed, but they felt they had to give their side of the story. Journalists were pursuing them. The interviews, Arnot agrees with Robertson, were largely accurate.

ROBERTSON: Were you paid?
ARNOT: Yes, I was paid.
ROBERTSON: What was the payment?
ARNOT: That does not concern this court.
GILL: I certainly agree with that.

Interruption number two comes only a few minutes later. The photographs of the flats are out. Arnot and Robertson discuss whether the first-floor balcony was set back. Some witnesses have said it was. Ron Smith has said it was. The point is important because Ron Smith believes Helen was found partly in the recess caused by the setting back and therefore reasons she could have been dropped from no higher than the first-floor balcony. This balcony is also about ten feet from the ground and Professor Dalgaard has said her injuries are consistent with a fall from this height.

Without warning, sitting at his desk, the photographs beneath him on the leather pad, Gill interjects into the two men's conversation: 'If there was any setting back. Look at photograph 34.'

Arnot and Robertson then discuss Helen's position, Arnot's action and reactions.

'A number of things went through your mind?' prompts Robertson.

'My first thought was whether she was dead or not,' replies Arnot. 'She was not only dead but had been dead for some time. I was checking her pulse for a full minute ... I remember seeing a little mark on her forehead but was not aware of anything else ... My further thought was that we were in a bit of a fix because we had been drinking alcohol the previous night.'

Robertson refers to the *Daily Mail* articles again. Arnot

is quoted as mentioning that he realised they were in a
'hell of a fix' over the alcohol, and as he raced back up
the stairs he thought he had better get rid of it. Arnot
replies that he may have said something like 'gosh'.
Robertson asks him if he was worried about the alcohol.
Arnot replies it was a question of what seemed the most
important. There was nothing to worry about over two
accidental deaths but something had to be done about the
alcohol on the premises.

ROBERTSON: You were far more worried about the alcohol?
ARNOT: From a legal angle, yes.
ROBERTSON: You were worried until Dr Bakhsh gave
you an assurance?

Napley stands and complains that Robertson is cross-
examining his client. Gill says, 'I am of the same opinion
as you, Sir David,' and informs Robertson he must stop
cross-examining.

Three minutes later Robertson refers again to the assurance given by Bakhsh. Arnot replies that one learns to
take these assurances with a pinch of salt. He told his
children that he might be 'going to prison for a while'.

ROBERTSON: You were more concerned about the alcohol rather than anything else?
NAPLEY: My colleague has this snide habit of putting
words not said by witnesses into their mouths.

Napley threatens to report Robertson to the bar for
professional misconduct. Robertson replies that he only
put what could be inferred from Arnot's previous replies
'Put your question, get his answer and pass on,' says
Gill.
They discuss the empty bottles. Robertson asks if
Arnot put them in the hold-all and deposited them in the
cupboard 'for the police to find'. 'Mr Robertson,' says
Gill, 'this is another example of putting words into the

witness's mouth. I must ask you to stop from cross-examining.'

Arnot does not know where Helen's abeya had originally been found in the flat. The shoes – both bodies were barefooted – had been found. The trousers?

ROBERTSON: The only explanation you gave yesterday was that a passer-by took them?

ARNOT: A fairly gruesome thought.

ROBERTSON: Are you aware of the law of theft in Saudi Arabia? [This is that a thief's hand is cut off if he is caught.]

ARNOT: I think that just walking past a dead body and not reporting it carries a greater punishment.

GILL: I don't want us to get into conjecture. The fact is that the passport was in the road.

They move onto the payment for the alcohol.

ARNOT: I have no clear recollection as to whether Hayter asked us (to host his party) or we suggested it.

ROBERTSON: In the event, you were hosting his farewell party?

ARNOT: It was his party. When Kirwen came in with the booze . . . [Arnot smiles, leans back, finger on the witness-box desk, before continuing.] Yes, the whisky. Hayter actually produced a roll and Penny said, 'It's all right, we'll pay for it. It's quite a bit of money.' [He laughs.] In my mind, it was not really our party. Two were there whom I only knew slightly.

Arnot then said that he had told the Saudi authorities the alcohol had been supplied by 'a grateful patient'.

The main evidence throughout the day, put together from fractured moments and breaks in narrative, concerns the nexus of the Arnots and Hayter. Arnot says that he was quite satisfied that Penelope and Hayter told the truth when they said they made love that night. He could not believe they invented it as an 'alibi for murder', as a *Daily Mail* headline put it. Mrs Arnot had changed her story in Saudi Arabia, first admitting the adultery, then denying it, and this denial continued both when the Arnots replied to questions put by the West Yorkshire police and in the interviews to the *Daily Mail*.

Robertson points out the *Daily Mail* article entitled, 'The love alibi that held a fatal flaw they never suspected'. He goes on to suggest that the story told to Mr Arnot by his wife and Hayter might not be true after all. Arnot says: 'It was a sort of double-double-double-double bluff? I don't agree. The Saudi police were hammering away at Penny and Hayter. They kept saying, "We know you are hiding something. We know you are not telling the truth."' After Ron Smith had arrived, the hammering increased.

Eventually Penny cracked. She was 'physically in a dreadful state'. She had been taking anti-depressants. In jail she had not been able to receive her medicine. Arnot says: 'She had not intended to tell the police about this love-making business . . .' She told them, however. They called in Hayter. He confirmed it. 'They signed a joint statement. There is no doubt in my mind that they were telling the truth. When I saw her later in the jail, Penelope claimed she did not know of the significance of the admission when she made it. She did not know she was committing a capital offence. She was terrified.'

Penelope continued the denial in the *Daily Mail* articles because, Arnot says: 'My wife was very very embarrassed and ashamed of the whole episode. In her description of it to me she described it as a spur of the moment thing with no commitment either way. She was horrified that because of press interest in this matter, suddenly it was the focal point of the whole issue. She really did not want to talk about it with anyone.'

Arnot tells the inquest of the night when Hayter told him of the 'encounter'. They had been transferred from the police station to the jail. It was their first night in the jail. Twenty-six people were jammed into a room fifteen feet square. It was, says Arnot, '. . . an incredible mass of humanity. He and I were lying adjacent to one another and he said, "Look, there is something I had better tell you. Penelope and I had sex that night at the party."' Hayter did not tell him at this time whether he had mentioned it to the police.

Arnot then says: 'As far as I know, the first time I realised this formed part of the police interest was when he and Penelope signed a joint statement referring to both of them.' At the time he did not realise the implications. The next time Arnot saw Penelope in jail – he was allowed to visit her two or three times a week – she told him that Hayter was telling the truth. They had the naive belief that they would not be treated with the 'full rigour' of Saudi law. Later, Consul Francis Geere put the 'fear of God' into Penelope by telling her they would be treated under the full law. She realised she was facing the death penalty.

'The way the law works out there,' Arnot explains, 'is if you admit to something twice in the presence of a judge, then that constitutes a conviction.' At the time, the siege of the Great Mosque at Mecca was in the minds of the Saudi authorities. The Arnots believed they would act puritanically. There was a very real risk that Penelope and Hayter faced the death penalty, so they 'both decided that perjury was better than capital punishment'.

Arnot is now questioned about the bodies. He, as far as he was aware, was the first person to go and look at them. He and Robertson discuss the signs of death. Arnot made no attempt at resuscitation.

ROBERTSON: You took the view there was no purpose in it.

ARNOT: Yes.

ROBERTSON: Might not other doctors take a different view?

GILL: He told you his view. What others do he cannot answer.

Arnot adds that because of the position of her body (partially on her front), resuscitation would have been difficult (she would need to be on her back). Her skin was cold, there was no pulse. There was no bruising on Helen's body. The indentation on her forehead did not puzzle him. He cannot say how deep it was, but it was deep enough to be evident.

He says that during the party he had drunk five glasses of whisky but was still surprised when a blood test the following day for the presence of alcohol proved positive: 'I did not think I had drunk nearly enough.' Eight bottles had been drunk in all, and everybody who was rounded up proved positive except his wife.

The balcony was overlooked by an adjoining building one or two floors higher. The occupants there could see down onto the balcony. He could not remember the cockroaches, as stated by other occupants of the building, being on the balcony. The sunlounger was not serviceable. It had been folded up and placed in the corner awaiting repair.

It was his understanding that Penny had seen the bodies first. He is asked about Penny seeing Helen and Johannes go out through the doors onto the balcony. He states that it was the double doors (from the sitting room). He adds that not only had Penny seen them go through, peering through the curtains a short while later, she had seen them there, silhouetted against the Jeddah lights. Later still, after the Germans had left, she had gone out onto the balcony to look for them but there was nobody there.

ROBERTSON: Was anything said by the Germans to you in jail about why nothing was said to them of the whereabouts of Helen and Johannes in the flat?

ARNOT: I think that has already been covered in their evidence.

ROBERTSON: Did anyone say anything to you?

ARNOT: I was not there.

GILL: Ask questions Mr Arnot can answer, that are
within his knowledge.

Sedley takes over. He quickly establishes that Helen
and Johannes were fully clothed and had no bruises when
Arnot last saw them, and that the latter was carrying his
papers.

SEDLEY: Will you accept that by the time Helen died
she had received damage to her head and throat?
ARNOT: I don't accept that.
GILL: These are matters for the jury to decide.

Sedley has been on his feet less than five minutes. There
is a fracas. Gill quotes Dr Kheir, who saw no evidence.
Sedley points out that Kheir did see head bruises and the
other pathologists' evidence went one way – bruising
before death. Gill reiterates that it is a matter for the jury
to decide.

Arnot, without prompting, states that in his recollection, when he saw the body there were no marks on her
face except the indenture. Agnes Johnstone saw no marks.
Dr Suktian saw no marks, nor did Dr Kheir, nor, for that
matter, did Mr Smith except for a 'dirty discolouration
of the skin'.

Sedley rounds on him: 'Why have you volunteered
that?'

'I think you were trying to infer that the injuries
occurred in life, before death. My understanding of the
evidence is that these lesions and bruises came in a post-
mortem examination nineteen months after death. The
evidence does not indicate bruising before death.'

They discuss the fall, the speed of bodies falling (which
they agree to be 46 and 48 m.p.h.), and then . . .

SEDLEY: You went to bed leaving Helen and your wife
with seven men?
ARNOT: Fair to say, yes, eight men in the room.

SEDLEY: Are you aware that Mr Texier in his statement
indicates all of them were drunk?
ARNOT: I haven't read it.

The danger of the balcony was common knowledge.
Helen, he could well imagine, would have been told about
it (she did, after all, look after the Arnot children from
time to time). It was common for people to dance bare-
foot. He did not find the key to Dr Sachel's first-floor
flat in her handbag. They discuss Penny's belief that, after
the Germans had departed, Helen and Johannes had
returned to Helen's flat.

Arnot agrees that the front entrance to the nurses'
quarters was under guard. The apartment Helen lived in
contained three bedrooms. He thought she had her own
bedroom. He had visited her there in a professional capacity. Only the front entrance to the quarters was guarded,
and there was a back entrance through a kitchen window
of a ground floor apartment (not Helen's).

Sedley asks if his wife seriously thought Helen would
have gone through this rigmarole to get a man back to
her shared apartment. Gill interrupts, saying it is impossible for Arnot to know what his wife thought. Sedley
tries to argue and Gill points out that the jury must decide
on the rationality of the situation.

Sedley and Arnot discuss Hayter's knowledge of first
aid.

SEDLEY: Hayter, as a diving instructor, should have
some knowledge of first aid?
ARNOT: He called himself a diving instructor . . . I don't
think he had.
SEDLEY: He should?
ARNOT: Yes.

Texier is discussed. He had been kept separate, detained
in another section of the jail. Arnot occasionally met him
in the prison library.

The Arnots had separate beds. He never had reason to doubt the truth of his wife's adultery. He gathered the impression that her 'brief encounter' with Hayter took place after the Germans had left, Texier had bedded down and the two were on their own.

They discuss Otten's watch. Arnot recollects that Otten was wearing it when he saw him on the railings. He did not look at it then, but the police later told him it had stopped and the time on it (3.10 a.m.) established the time of Otten's death. Sedley suggests the watch could have broken at any time, not necessarily when Otten fell. Napley objects.

It is 2.59 p.m. There is a three-minute altercation between Sedley and Napley. None of the lawyers is allowed to address the jury at the end of the inquest, so Sedley is trying to make his case by the questions he puts to Arnot, Napley claims. Various cases are referred to. Sedley quotes the Lord Chief Justice, who has made a judgement that such questions should be able to be put. Gill disagrees, stating that Sedley is going further than is allowed, drawing conclusions. Sedley complains angrily that both he and Geoffrey Robertson have been constantly interrupted by Sir David and it has been impossible to achieve any flow in questions and answers. Gill states that he appreciates the difficulties but some questions are allowed and others are not. Sedley must resume.

Sedley establishes that Arnot slept from 2.00 a.m. to 5.30 a.m. He did not hear anything. If violence had occurred, he would not have heard it.

SEDLEY: You had learnt to sleep with that air conditioner on?

ARNOT: I'd had a long day and some glasses of whisky before going to bed. I was tired.

Otten's glasses were found by Arnot on top of the hi-fi. He noticed them when he went back to the flat after his telephone calls. He recognised them as belonging to Otten since no one else wore glasses. He could not remember if he handed them to the police. The relevance of Otten's trousers and glasses 'concerned us then and still does'.

Sedley points out that Chapuis said in his statement there was a rumour that Otten's clothing had been thrown away by Penelope and Tim Hayter. He asks Arnot if Chapuis had any way of learning that in jail. Arnot replies that he had no certain knowledge, but it could well have been a police tactic, suggesting to one prisoner what another prisoner had said in order to gain information.

'Can we discount the possibility of the trousers being stolen while Otten was impaled?' asks Sedley. 'Apart from the grizzly aspects: one, if the trousers were in the proper position then they would be impaled too, and two, you can steal a man's wallet without stealing his trousers.'

Arnot is not so sure that he wants to discount the possibility, so Sedley approaches the subject of Otten's trousers from a different angle. Arnot agrees with him that if Helen and Johannes went onto the balcony it was for a sexual purpose. Helen leaves her abeya in the flat together with her shoes. Otten leaves his glasses neatly on the hi-fi. Arnot states he has lost the drift of Sedley's argument. Sedley evidently believes that if Otten had taken the trouble to remove his glasses and neatly put them to one side, he would have removed his trousers too.

ARNOT: We don't know.
SEDLEY: If the trousers were not on him when he fell, they were in the flat?
ARNOT: Yes.
SEDLEY: Then someone must have got rid of them?

Gill interrupts and says, 'Speculation.' Sedley repeats his reasoning to the coroner. It is self-evident, surely? If nobody took the trousers and Otten was found without them, then they must have been in the flat and somebody removed them from there. Gill suggests that a police officer may have removed them, so Sedley then establishes with Arnot that they looked for the trousers, without any luck, before the police came.

Arnot leans back, frowning. He and Sedley discuss Otten's papers. Sedley says they must have been in Otten's trouser pocket and Arnot replies they could have been in his shirt pocket. Sedley says that, at any rate, they were not found on his person but in the street. 'Do you know why anybody might have thrown them out into the street,' he asks. Arnot says that they may have fallen out of his trouser pocket while in the street or they may have been thrown out.

They turn to the position of Helen's body and then to Otten's erection. This is apparently a well-known post-mortem phenomenon and Sedley asks Arnot to accept that any erection Otten may have had before he fell, if he fell, would have vanished because of the fall. Therefore any erection before death would have nothing to do with an erection after death.

ARNOT: No, I wouldn't accept it.
SEDLEY: Do you know one way or the other?
GILL: He is simply saying it could be either way.

Sedley tells Gill that it is a pity this erection business has come up so late in the inquest. None of the pathologist witnesses were asked about it.

It is getting late in the day and Sedley informs Gill that he and the other lawyers have come up with an agreed height above ground for the Arnot flat from studying the photographs – sixty-five feet. Sedley then asks Arnot to agree that if Helen Smith fell separately from Otten, it could not have been an accident. 'This is not a proper question for the witness,' states Gill. 'It is for the jury to decide.'

Unperturbed, Sedley turns back to Arnot: 'You said to the coroner yesterday that you know of nothing to suggest that Helen and Otten had left the flat?'

'No.'

'Overall, if Helen's injuries are not consistent with a sixty-five-foot fall, she must have left the flat?'

'If not consistent, I must agree.'

Sedley winds up a few minutes later. Did anybody say anything that gave Arnot reason to think that Helen had become unconscious in his flat? 'No.' Was there anything to suggest that somebody had tried cardiac massage? 'It was the first I heard of it at this inquest.'

Sir David Napley has nothing to ask. He looks proud of his client.

Day Twelve

Monday 6 December. Tim Hayter had sent a message informing Coroner Gill that he could not attend the inquest before 15 December. Negotiations with Hayter had proceeded for two months prior to the inquest. Massive inducements had been offered – his expenses for travel, hotel, food, daily allowance, wages, all would be paid. Wages for a work replacement would be paid. Hayter had said, 'yes', 'no', 'maybe'.

He made a brief visit to Amsterdam a short while before the inquest began. Thames Television interviewed him for a *TV Eye* programme. The finished programme was shown the week before the inquest started. Gill, deciding that the inquest could not wait upon Hayter, ordered the film to be shown together with the footage from which the film had been cut. A video had been installed at the end of Gill's desk.

The footage is shown first. Jacques Texier had arrived and sat in the witness gallery together with his interpreter, watching the film.

Hayter tells the camera, 'Helen was a fun-loving girl. She was very basic, down to earth and a very nice girl. We talked together and enjoyed each other's company . . . on the night she was happy . . . Johannes was drunk . . . I looked on her as a friend, not just somebody to make love to . . . In Jeddah everybody looks to see who they can go to bed with. With Helen and me it was not that way . . . She enjoyed going to bed. She enjoyed making love. That's quite basic. Many girls all over the world enjoy going to bed. She was very honest about it.'

He says she was engaged to a Malaysian man but he 'went away' (he was deported) and she enjoyed the company of other men.

The plan that night was for him to drive Texier back to the Frenchman's boat, moored up in Jeddah Creek, fifty kilometres outside the city. He felt he had had enough to drink and they decided to sleep in the flat. He says that there had been a search for Helen and Johannes but the guests thought they had probably gone to the nurses' quarters or some other residence to make love.

As far as Hayter knows, nobody checked the balcony because the main doors had been closed all night and there were curtains in front of it. Here he contradicts Mrs Arnot. He then contradicts every witness on the alcohol. The guests drank whisky, a bottle of gin, half a bottle of vodka, and, 'Sadikki . . . brewed on a home still, it means my "old friend".' He grins. Sadikki is a very potent drink. Fabled variants of it stretch through the Middle East and up through Europe, to Scandinavia, where it is schnapps.

How much alcohol was drunk, he is asked. Hayter replies it was not really a lot. A question of measurement. Two or three people could drink, without getting really drunk, two bottles. For eight or nine, a case is a fair amount.

'How merry were the people there?'

'Merry? . . . I wouldn't say drunk. Maybe one or two.'

Otten drank through the night. Hayter says Otten was drunk before he reached the party. As for Helen, 'She drank quite an amount, she was very very happy.'

Each witness took pains to emphasise this happiness. She had handed in her notice, the workplace was not a good workplace, she had drunk a considerable quantity. She was described as being quiet at the beginning of the party. Her progression through the night had been from quiet good humour into greater happiness. No shouts, tantrums, screams, anger, tears.

Hayter then comments: 'No drugs, no Arabs. If either came it was the unwritten law, the party finished.' There are obvious reasons. Saudi jails are known to be hell on earth. Drugs and Saudis, Arabs, all may mean compromise, imprisonment, for the white, especially the white drinking. This comment contradicts both Kirwen and Arnot's, 'It was a quiet drinks party much as one would find it in this country.'

We had heard Arnot, 'The curtains were closed so the neighbours could not see in.' Lights were dimmed, candles lit. Hayter's comment states the basic premise – it was an illegal drinks party and should not be known by the outside culture.

A group of people using an illegal drug knowingly. It echoed the 1960s hash dens, both in overtones of paranoia – the closed curtains – and the fear, the party finished if Arabs should arrive. Schlaeffer expressed it eloquently: 'Getting back to port smelling, it is very very dangerous . . . dangerous.'

Hayter then surprises us. He repeats that the balcony doors were closed, the curtains pulled in front, and then mentions that the balcony was L-shaped, and there is a door from the dining area onto the side balcony. This door was never checked by himself, nor any other person.

No one at the party checked Helen's whereabouts. If Otten wanted a lift back, sure he'd get one. If he's not there, that's his problem, Hayter tells us, his voice shrugging.

Texier drank little: 'Starts with one, finishes with one.' Texier and Hayter bedded down by the balcony doors.

INTERVIEWER: Was there any noise of lovemaking from the balcony?
HAYTER: If it was loud enough, sure we'd have heard. We heard nothing.

The music was on through the night, played low. The lights were off. He is asked if there was any noise between 3.00 and 4.00 a.m. He replies, 'During that time, I don't recall anything. I had my mind concentrated on other activities.'

INTERVIEWER: You went back to sleep?
HAYTER: 4.00 a.m.

He awoke at sunrise. Five o'clock, six o'clock. He shrugs again. Probably he had been woken at about twenty minutes to six. They went out onto the balcony and watched the sun rise. They were looking out at the city and Texier said, 'Look.' Hayter cannot remember his exact words, but the scene was 'a very big shock . . . I didn't recognise Helen.' Hayter looks at the camera, 'I could recognise Otten. Helen had a pair of pants on, down a leg. John, he had a shirt on, looking down, it wasn't possible to see his exact position. I didn't stay and stare.'

INTERVIEWER: Did you think of getting rid of the bodies?
HAYTER: It went through my mind but there was no way we could do so . . . whether guilty or not, we were in deep trouble.

Hayter describes the next events, massively contradicting Arnot, who sits watching.

HAYTER: The next thing, I told Penny to wake up Richard. We woke up Richard Arnot. First thing, Jacques got down to the Embassy. He stayed there. For me then it was to get down to the port and get everybody together. Before that I assisted Richard to get rid of whisky, sadikki. We had the booze, it can cause problems . . . after the whisky went down the drain I left. I went down to the car. I could see Otten's left leg impaled, I couldn't see his torso . . . he was inside the rails.

INTERVIEWER: Did anything strike you?

HAYTER: Nothing at all. I didn't stop to study.

INTERVIEWER: Could they have fallen together?

HAYTER: They weren't very far apart . . . very close. I'm not an expert. I didn't study the situation.

INTERVIEWER: Were any efforts made to see if they were still alive?

HAYTER: No. If they fell, no way in the world they could have survived that distance.

Arnot told Hayter he would ring the Embassy. Hayter left at about 6.30. He went to the port. He sent Fleischer out to get their boss, Gutzeit, who had a flat in the city. The police came. 'It was better to have everyone back in agreement.' Hayter's words come off the screen, his contradiction of Arnot on whether anybody went to examine the bodies echoing. Referring again to the removal of the bodies, he says, 'If it had been one o'clock in the morning, for sure, we would have taken the bodies on a tugboat. This is only because we know Saudi law. Nothing to do with escaping the law.'

He gives examples of Saudi law, with people imprisoned for long periods for traffic offences. 'What sort of law is this?' he asks.

INTERVIEWER: How long were you in prison?

HAYTER: Five months, five days, twelve hours. [Two hours longer than Ritter.]

INTERVIEWER: You were kept in a cell with your colleagues and Dr Arnot?

HAYTER: At first, in the police cells with my colleagues, including Richard Arnot, but not including Jacques Texier. He was still on the jump. During this period Penelope Arnot was coming in for very severe interrogation. Very, very severe. I feel she had it worse than anyone else. After one, two days, the police picked up Jacques Texier, pulled him in. He was there for one, two days. Then we were transferred to the main prison ... Texier was separated. I don't know why he was treated separately.

INTERVIEWER: Why do you feel Jacques Texier was treated separately?

HAYTER: I did not say feel, I know he was treated separately. He had very good contacts with an educational officer in the French Embassy. People were also behind us but we didn't get the same treatment.

Was this due to the state of Anglo-Saudi relations? And what was the state of Saudi–German relations? According to Schlaeffer, the work of Harms Salvage was of great strategic importance. Hayter was chief diver in Harms. By the time that Harms could act, and provide possible protection for Hayter, the employees were already inside the police station, embroiled. At 6.30 Hayter could have set the ball rolling. Instead he sent Fleischer to Harry Gutzeit, the manager. Harry went to the port and found everyone, including the police, waiting, without time to get onto the phone to Hamburg, Bonn, or his contacts in the harbour.

Texier was put into a separate section of the prison, and immediately received library facilities.

INTERVIEWER: Were the police investigating accidental death?

HAYTER: They were investigating a murder. There is no doubt about that.

INTERVIEWER: During the interrogations, did they ever make it plain who they thought was responsible?

HAYTER: Never at any time. Interrogated the worst was Penny Arnot ... They gave her a very hard time. According to some, the woman's section is very bad, lesbians, you name it ... she was told to make a statement, you sign it saying you make love you get on the plane ... she signed the statement. I didn't want to sign it but then I thought, you're in the shits already, a little bit more won't make any difference. But making love you lose your head . . . it was a plain con job. They lost interest in murder then.

INTERVIEWER: Were they accusing anyone of murder?

HAYTER: Normal police tactics, one against the other one. You said, he said, etc., etc. They didn't accuse anyone direct. They had ten days' intensive interrogation then got her on that. They did their job. That's what they were doing, their job.

In the jail they discussed the deaths. How it could have happened. The height of the balcony, humidity, the slippery tiles. It looked like an accident to all of them. Hayter mentions the broken sunlounger, says it looks as though they tried to make love on it.

INTERVIEWER: They toppled over?

HAYTER: Sure.

INTERVIEWER: Did you accept it?

HAYTER: No point in not accepting it. You've got to accept it. If I was guilty, inside, something comes up . . . you get overheard, you'd know it.

INTERVIEWER: Has anything made you change your mind that it was not an accident?

HAYTER: No, not until discussions afterwards. There were certain points, then the pathologists' reports, internationally renowned experts – their reasoning I couldn't argue with – on the basis of their reasoning I now have my doubts.

Inside the jail he had not followed the emergence of the evidence outside, the talk. No one heard anything inside.

INTERVIEWER: Did any of you believe that they were out on the balcony?

HAYTER: No. Everyone in the flat, also people who'd left, had believed they'd gone to another place. The

way they were acting, it was a one-way ticket for sex.
No arguments.

He refers to how people perceived both Otten and
Helen. 'Both of them, especially Johannes, is an adult,
not a baby. If he couldn't look after himself, then no one
else could.'

The interviewer refers to a search for the couple.

HAYTER: Search for them? If I'd known earlier those
bodies had been out there, I'd have jumped, for sure,
not to escape the law, but to report it from another
country.

INTERVIEWER: The autopsy reports, have they changed
your views?

HAYTER: Hypothetically.

INTERVIEWER: How do you mean, hypothetically?

HAYTER: Nothing except for reports from the medical
fraternity. There is nothing proven ... but I have
definitely changed my views. On the basis of what I
have read, I suspect foul play.

INTERVIEWER: You go along now with the injuries?

HAYTER: ... I'm not in a position to question the experts. An expert who's spent many years, who's done
so much, I'm not in the position to say this is how it
was. I'm a bum, I can't argue. On reading those reports, I can say, I agree something must have
happened.

INTERVIEWER: If that is right, then how does the accident fit in?

HAYTER: The version that I have accepted up to now, it
wipes it off the slate ... it can't stand.

He then spotlights Texier.

INTERVIEWER: Not everyone was in the prison with
you?

HAYTER: Jacques Texier was in another unit [he pauses,

looks at the camera]. Okay, why Jacques Texier? [he leans back] Previously a good friend of mine . . . [his eyes are steady in their gaze, but blurred in expression – perhaps jetlagged] we've done some good jobs . . . Not until someday somebody comes up, can't say yes or no . . . There is a certain amount of hypothetical evidence pointing that way.

Texier, in the witness bench, leans forwards, hand touching his sock, face expressionless.

The interviewer asks whether anyone else came to the party.

HAYTER: Some came in, came out . . . it all happened before the morning. The hardcore people were in prison . . . Because we got questioned about this so often. You can say what you like, as far as I'm concerned, who did it, did a very good job. Definitely nobody else there except those people previously discussed . . . leave it there.

The footage ends. Texier talks with his interpreter.

The transmitted programme, *TV Eye*, follows. Hayter adds only that they were drinking and Helen was happy. Otten was always drinking. Hayter went to sleep around 2.30 and woke up a short time after, not long after 3.00 a.m. He goes on to say: 'Penny Arnot came out and we started getting intimate and from then on carried on. We made love together for about an hour.'

The question of Ron Smith comes up. 'Now I do not speak for anybody else. I speak for myself. I speak very straight, very hard. But he is the cause for me to do four months extra in prison, in a Saudi prison, which is, I think, one of the worst in the world . . . Under these conditions I came out with a very big chip on my shoulder and I was very close, I quote, but I did not, to putting a contract on his head.'

'What sort of contract?' asks the interviewer.

'To hurt him. I considered maybe he has a problem walking from then on.'

The transmitted film also has a brief interview with Fleming and Lise Aaen. He was the catering manager at the Bakhsh hospital and she was a nurse there. They both obviously believed she was murdered.

It ends with a home movie. A kitchen door opens. Helen is at the kitchen sink playing. She turns to the camera, faces it, smiles. She is about six or seven. Two days later, waiting for the verdict, the image burns.

Just after noon, Jacques Texier takes the stand, held in that changed moment. His interpreter is alongside him but is silent for most of the day. A tall, broad-shouldered man, greying hair cut short, a round, heavy face with thick glasses. He came to Saudi Arabia after twenty years in South East Asia, mainly Vietnam.

He met Tim Hayter in the harbour. Hayter was then a yacht crew member. Texier was putting together an exhibition at the French Institute. Hayter got a contract with Harms and some time later sent jobs Texier's way. Texier was also a diving instructor. They worked on the sea bed laying pipes.

Texier lived on his boat, moored in Jeddah creek, fifty kilometres from the city. Hayter went out to see him two or three days a week.

One day he was driven into Jeddah by Hayter for a shopping trip. 'I saw two heavy-duty batteries I needed for the boat. I ask Tim Hayter, "Will you lend me the money?" . . . no money with me. He lent me money. Two weeks later he said he was going to Singapore. Did I want to attend a party? I say "yes" . . . maybe one, two weeks attend the party, give him his money back.'

GILL: He invited you to come?
TEXIER: Yes.
GILL: What were your arrangements? How would you
    meet him?

TEXIER: At a friend's house – he gave me an apartment at the Cultural Centre. Waiting. Eight to nine. I went to bed because nobody come. About ten somebody knocked on door. Chinese guy Jim . . . Jimmy Yeong. He took me in the car, I said, 'Don't,' I could walk, about five minutes, he said, 'No, drive.'

GILL: Did Mr Yeong drive the car?

TEXIER: It was Hayter's car. He drove it. Drove me to flat, showed me door, I knocked . . . he left. He didn't want to stay.

GILL: You arrived in the flat on your own?

TEXIER: Yes.

GILL: A number of people were there from the Harms company?

TEXIER: Yes.

GILL: Did you walk upstairs?

TEXIER: Yes. Mr Arnot and his wife . . . Hayter . . .

GILL: There were people there you didn't know?

TEXIER: Yes. Know people by sight.

GILL: You had never met the Arnots before?

TEXIER: No.

GILL: Did you see Nurse Helen Smith there?

TEXIER: Yes.

GILL: Had you met her before?

TEXIER: Boat fifty kilometres from Jeddah . . . don't attend too many parties.

GILL: How would you describe the situation?

TEXIER: It was party.

GILL: What sort of party was it?

TEXIER: Illegal drinking.

GILL: Did you see the drinks?

TEXIER: Whisky.

GILL: Was there anything else?

TEXIER: I didn't notice.

GILL: Could you give the jury an idea of how many people were present?

TEXIER: About a dozen.

GILL: What happened during the evening?

TEXIER: Singing, dancing, Germans spoke German. I was bored.

GILL: Did you have much to drink?

TEXIER: Only one or two. I don't smoke.

GILL: Did you dance?

TEXIER (laughing): No.

GILL: Did you talk to any of the guests?

TEXIER: To Mr and Mrs Arnot in English. They say, 'I know about you.'

GILL: You felt you were the odd man out?

TEXIER: Yes.

GILL: How were you intending to get back to your quarters?

TEXIER: First, fifty kilometres ... Hayter drinking ... then I ask to sleep on sofa because Mr Hayter could not drive me back. I could go back to French Cultural Centre – a room in flat there – in the morning.

GILL: During the evening, you had one or two drinks, did you notice Nurse Helen in the evening?

TEXIER: Drinking like everybody, talks, mainly with Otten. Start dancing, do as you do at a party, kiss and so on. Had a liking for him you know.

GILL: They were together for most of the evening?

TEXIER: She was in the room.

GILL: That was to start with?

TEXIER: She start with everybody then at end of evening – after start dancing – I know she only stay with Mr Otten.

GILL: She was drinking with everyone else. Have you an assessment of how much she drank?

TEXIER: Difficult to say ... I see her ... One or two glasses she hold ... but not more.

GILL: Merry, cheerful?

TEXIER: Ouff no ... no I think not drunk. She doesn't fall down on the floor.

GILL: Mr Otten?

TEXIER: For Mr Otten it is different. Mr Otten always drinking a lot. This evening he was drunk you know.

[Texier full of gestures. Shoulders, mouth, smiles.]

GILL: This evening, Mr Otten was drinking a lot?

TEXIER: You don't notice, this one drinking, this one drinking a lot, this one drinks. He always drinks. He was sweating, a very good laugh, but he was drunk.

GILL: He could hold his drink?

TEXIER: I should say so. Because he was a very strong man.

GILL: The Germans left. Can you remember when they left?

TEXIER: About two o'clock. Around two o'clock.

GILL: What happened later on?

TEXIER: I make a sandwich. I came to kitchen to make a sandwich, before the Germans leave. There I see Otten and Miss Smith going to balcony.

GILL: Before the Germans left?

TEXIER: Yes.

GILL: You went to the kitchen?

TEXIER: Yes, near balcony.

GILL: You saw Helen and Otten go onto the balcony?

TEXIER: Yes.

GILL: How long was it before the Germans left?

TEXIER: One hour maybe.

GILL: When they went onto the balcony, which door did they use?

TEXIER: Door near to kitchen, near opening from kitchen and balcony. I think kitchen close to lounge, between – a door. I think more to kitchen, it is why I see them go.

GILL: They didn't go through the kitchen door onto the balcony but you were going to the kitchen when you saw them going to the balcony?

TEXIER: Yes . . .

GILL: They didn't come through the kitchen?

TEXIER: I looked for the talking and the kissing. They were holding each other.

GILL: Did you see them on the balcony later?

TEXIER: No.

GILL: The Germans left an hour or so later?

TEXIER: I was pleased they left. I was sleepy.

GILL: Was this occasion the last time you saw them?

TEXIER: Yes.

GILL: At that point when the Germans left, were there any arguments?

TEXIER: Nothing at all . . . Germans feeling . . . they get up . . . very sleepy . . . more stoned.

GILL: There was no hostility, no arguments?

TEXIER: No.

GILL: When the time came to leave, was any search made for Otten?

TEXIER: No, no, no. He was supposed to leave. You at party, someone come, go, you don't notice . . .

GILL: Did anyone look for him?

TEXIER: I know Otten, know each other working, but maybe someone tried to find where they are . . . I don't know.

GILL: When the Germans left, who did that leave in the flat?

TEXIER: 'Dr Arnot, Hayter, Mrs Arnot, me.

GILL: Dr Arnot?

TEXIER: Dr Arnot told me he had surgery to perform. He was holding technical books, studying – I ask him why read. He say because you have to study surgery before. Then he go to bed early to be in shape for next morning.

GILL: When did he go to bed?

TEXIER: Maybe 1.00 a.m. or midnight, I don't know.

GILL: Before the time you saw Helen and Otten go out to the balcony?

TEXIER: Yes, I think so, I think before.

GILL: So when the Germans left, that left Mrs Arnot, Mr Arnot, Mr Hayter and yourself. What happened then?

TEXIER: I asked Mrs Arnot go to sleep now, she said yes, so I went to sleep on the sofa.

GILL: Which room was this?

TEXIER: In the corner, where the music was – a small lounge where all the people sit down.

GILL: It was very near to the balcony door, was it?

TEXIER: Yes.

GILL: Do you know where Tim Hayter went?

TEXIER: I don't know. I think he told me he was going to sleep in the armchair.

GILL: Can you remember if Tim Hayter slept in the room you were in or not?

TEXIER: He told me he was going to sleep in the armchair. I thought he was sleeping there . . . between kitchen and place I was sleeping. I think he move in armchair and sleep.

GILL: How long were you asleep?

TEXIER: Yes, until . . . just before dawn. Always wakes me up, even now. I heard noise . . . somebody . . [He lifts his shoulders.]

GILL: Yes, what was the noise, Mr Texier?

TEXIER: Somebody making love. Then I did not want to get up because I didn't want to . . .

GILL: You didn't want to embarrass them?

TEXIER: No.

GILL: You pretended to be asleep?

TEXIER: Yes . . . that's the only statement I did not make to the Saudi police.

GILL: I'm afraid I have to ask you who was involved?

TEXIER: Only can be two people involved.

GILL: That may be so, but just so there can be no misunderstanding.

TEXIER: Mrs Arnot and Tim Hayter.

GILL: It is most important, this. A very important piece of evidence. Where was this taking place?

TEXIER: Behind me . . . in the dining room. [He points over his shoulder with a movement of his elbow and hand.]

GILL: In the adjoining room?

TEXIER: Yes.

GILL: How long did this go on for?

TEXIER: Not too long, maybe ten, fifteen minutes maybe . . .

GILL: And then, how did you come to get up?

TEXIER: They went into the kitchen to make coffee.

GILL: You then got up and followed them?

TEXIER: I got up and joined them.

GILL: You all took coffee?

TEXIER: Yes. Mrs Arnot made the coffee.

GILL: What did you do then?

TEXIER: We were talking and went to the balcony.

GILL: You went to the balcony. Which door? The one from the room you were sleeping in?

TEXIER: The one straight to the kitchen from the balcony. The other door.

GILL: It wasn't the door from the room you were sleeping in, it was the door from which you had seen Helen and Johannes going onto the balcony.

TEXIER: Yes, the one close to the kitchen.

GILL: Why did you go out onto the balcony?

TEXIER: We had coffee . . . to see the sun rising. I don't know. Mrs Arnot came too.

GILL: You went merely to take your coffee out and enjoy the scene on sun rising?

TEXIER: Yes . . . always do that. Early.

GILL: And then, Mrs Arnot?

TEXIER: Mrs Arnot say, she looked over, she said, 'Oh my God,' and I looked over . . . without my glasses . . . Mr Hayter by my side . . . then it was panic.

Gill calls for a lunch adjournment. It has been a heavy morning. Texier was enjoyable, smiles coming from all quarters as he spoke. He contradicted Hayter by an hour over the time of the love-making and contradicted what Arnot had said about going straight to sleep.

He was the first witness to state the Germans were speaking German to each other, and the English, English, so that the party was split some way. He described the party as illegal drinking in such a manner that said, 'what else do you think it could be?'

There was also the memory of Fleming Aaen's electrifying appearance in the television programme, when he joked, 'You tell me how a man can make love with a girl without his trousers on, holding his passport in his hand.' Gill had been asked twice for the Aaens to appear as witnesses, but had refused.

Back in the afternoon, Gill shows Texier some photographs.

GILL: You came out onto the balcony from the door into the dining area, in from that door, then where did you go?

TEXIER: Drinking coffee . . . just came out from inside.

GILL: Can you remember the position you were in when you looked over?

TEXIER: Go out. Mrs Arnot say body, booohh, very panicky, everybody, me too.

GILL: Do you recall where it was?

TEXIER: I see Mrs Arnot.

GILL: Was anything on the balcony?

TEXIER: No.

GILL: Was there any furniture at all?

TEXIER: Furniture on other side . . . at the corner . . . opposite kitchen.

GILL: What was the furniture?

TEXIER: A camping bed. It was folded, not opened.

GILL: Folded, not opened?

TEXIER: Yes.

Eyebrows go up. Forty-five minutes later on that morning, Matron Johnstone went out and saw an unfolded camp bed.

GILL: Was it against the building wall or the balcony?

TEXIER: It was very narrow. [He studies the photograph,

hand around his chin.] It was in the middle of the
balcony.

GILL: Not against the wall or the balcony?

TEXIER: Near the middle, I remember I saw bed. I
remember it was folded. No clothes.

GILL: Was it near to the building wall, near to the place
where you looked over or somewhere close to it?

TEXIER: As I went there to look, and I do that, and I see
in corner this bed. I think it was a bed.

Gill asks him to look at photograph number 38.

GILL: Was it there?

TEXIER: No, because it was on other side. At the
corner.

Gill tries him with the position of the photographer.
Texier sticks to the corner.

GILL: You saw the body of Helen?

TEXIER: It was very high. I didn't wear glasses. I didn't
know if it was near or far.

GILL: Look at the photograph. Where was Helen lying?

TEXIER: It was a very quick look. We all panicked, we
went inside. Mr Arnot came and they were first thing
hiding the whisky.

GILL: When you saw bodies, panic?

TEXIER: Yes . . . oooooohhh.

GILL: What exactly happened?

TEXIER: If you see two bodies and you are in Saudi
Arabia . . . [He shakes his head.]

GILL: Was the fact of the two bodies being there cause
of your panic?

TEXIER: See two bodies in Saudi Arabia . . . not
something, even in street, someone run over . . . I
think Mrs Arnot called Mr Arnot. I didn't know
where Mr Arnot was.

GILL: Mrs Arnot left to call her husband?

TEXIER: He came quick. He had a towel around him I think.

GILL: What did he do?

TEXIER: Main concern was the alcohol. So quick.

GILL: He was getting rid of the alcohol?

TEXIER: Mrs Arnot crying what had happened. Even if you have to go to the police you hide alcohol – offence in Saudi Arabia.

GILL: The next thing Mr Arnot did?

TEXIER: I just told him, 'Look, I'm leaving, I must go to Embassy.' At the main entrance I did not even look at the bodies. Told Mr Arnot, 'You know where to find me.' Outside a Lebanese. He said, 'What's happened?'

GILL: You left, what was happening?

TEXIER: They were emptying the bottles – Mr and Mrs Arnot.

GILL: Had anybody been to look at the bodies?

TEXIER: I don't know because I leave before.

GILL: Was it possible Mr Arnot looked before you left?

TEXIER: No, he was still in flat ... impossible ... he was still in flat with alcohol.

Texier saw the Lebanese and another man on the landing. He did not see anyone else around.

GILL: As you were leaving, you didn't look, you didn't see anything on the street at the time?

TEXIER: I didn't even look at the bodies. I went straight to the Centre. I was very frightened.

He had been sponsored in Saudi Arabia by the French Cultural Centre. He raced around to the cultural attaché from the Embassy. He said somebody had fallen off the balcony. The attaché said, 'All right, Jacques, come in.'

In the afternoon he went back to his boat. Next morning someone called him from the shore. It was Tim Hayter with the police. He went with him to the police station and was put inside in a cell with some of the others.

Gill questions him about his statement to the police in which he said he went to the balconies to look for Helen and Johannes.

> GILL: Is that right?
> TEXIER: No.
> GILL: The statement is wrong?
> TEXIER: I don't know.
> GILL: It is signed by you. Do you remember saying that?
> TEXIER: No.
> GILL: You only went on the balcony as a pleasant place to have coffee.
> TEXIER: Yes.

During the first questions from the Saudi police, Texier received the impression that they thought it was an accident. But later, they appeared to be investigating something more serious. They never made any accusations of murder, however.

Gill asks him whether, if there had been a struggle on the balcony, he would have heard it. He doubted it, the air conditioner was so noisy, but he would have heard a scream.

> GILL: If it had been suggested that someone could have assaulted Helen or used violence against her, what would you say?
> TEXIER: I think maybe on the balcony something happened between her and Mr Otten because both fell down from the balcony.
> GILL: Was there music playing?
> TEXIER: The music stop . . . Germans leave. After, go to sleep.
> GILL: The only hindrance is the air conditioner?
> TEXIER: Yes.

GILL: Sufficient to prevent you hearing?

TEXIER: Depends on noise . . . shouting, screaming, just a wall, window, heavy curtain.

GILL: You would expect to hear if there was a scream?

TEXIER: Sure . . . I was on this sofa. I was very close.

GILL: Was Mr Otten a big man? How would you describe him?

TEXIER: Very strong. One metre 85, 90. I think he was a little taller than me.

Robertson rises. Texier describes the balcony. Mrs Arnot going to the balcony looking over, Hayter then leaving the balcony wall against which he had been standing, to look over the balcony rail. Again he states he was the first to leave.

ROBERTSON: Can you recall if the balcony door was opened?

TEXIER: I don't recollect very well about this door, but it would be open because I see Otten and Helen Smith going out. I look outside and see them kissing and holding on the balcony.

ROBERTSON: You saw them from where you were in the kitchen?

TEXIER: Yes . . . all I remember . . . difficult.

ROBERTSON: Which balcony were they on? Did you see them through the kitchen window?

TEXIER: When I came back to the lounge, I saw them like this.

ROBERTSON: Did you go and draw the curtains aside?

TEXIER: Curtains not in room to my knowledge . . . windows closed.

Texier tries to remember. It was on the way back from the kitchen. He saw them dancing, leaving the room. He did not like that kind of party; it was more interesting walking around. He couldn't remember how long it was before the Germans left. He was sleepy.

He does not think there was any search. He cannot recall anyone calling out 'John, John.' If the Germans were inquiring about Johannes, he would not know because they were speaking in German. It was not his concern where Johannes was. If it was anybody's concern, it was the manager's.

He could not recall any conversation after the Germans left. He went to sleep. Robertson reads out Mrs Arnot's statement to the West Yorkshire police in which she states that after the Germans left the three of them – herself, Texier and Hayter – had been in the room together and had realised no one had seen Helen and Johannes go out with the Germans, so she had checked the balcony and the side balcony.

ROBERTSON: Can you recall that conversation?

TEXIER: No . . . no. I was sleepy . . . no talk.

ROBERTSON: Can you recall Mrs Arnot looking outside on the balcony for them?

TEXIER: I can't recall, but it was not possible. I just wanted to go to sleep . . . they were friends . . . What's Helen and Otten's disappearance for me? Otten and Helen, I see them for an hour. I do not see this happening.

ROBERTSON: You do not recall any conversation as to where they might be?

TEXIER: No.

ROBERTSON: Did you say anything to anyone about the time you needed waking up?

TEXIER: No, I don't need anybody to wake me up.

They discuss the manner of his waking.

ROBERTSON: You heard noise coming from the direction of one of the big armchairs?

TEXIER: From somewhere behind.

ROBERTSON: This made you discreet?

TEXIER: I slept this way. [Texier turns inside the box,

puts his head to the right. His left hand jabs behind his shoulder, his right hand goes up against his cheek.]

ROBERTSON: You didn't look. You pretended to be sleeping?

TEXIER: Yes, very embarrassing . . . I don't know Mrs Arnot at this time. I just come in house.

ROBERTSON: You cannot recall how long it went on for?

TEXIER: Ten, fifteen minutes.

ROBERTSON: You went out then, had some coffee. Were you going out to sit?

TEXIER: Nowhere to sit . . . just standing there. Talk about life . . . nothing particular, just this, that. Morning is very fresh. My main pleasure is to take coffee on boat when the sun rises. I don't like to stay in a flat.

Robertson ends by questioning Texier about the sun-lounger. But Texier remembers nothing other than that he saw it. Napley stands. Texier has contradicted Arnot. Napley begins: 'How good are your eyes?' Texier explains that now he needs two pairs of glasses. That morning his glasses had steamed up. They discuss Mrs Arnot's position on the balcony when she saw the bodies. He could not be specific. They discuss the sunlounger – it was there, folded.

Napley takes the statement Texier made to the British police in October 1982. He reads it aloud, facing Texier, holding it in his right hand, left hand in his pocket. 'I looked out of kitchen window and saw them embracing each other, leaning against the balcony rail.'

TEXIER: Yes. Maybe they were leaning on something. The fact was they were standing there.

Napley reads through it again and then,

NAPLEY: Is this accurate: 'I cannot recall which one of

the two had his or her head against the rail but certainly one was leaning against it?'

TEXIER: Yes ... it was dark ... there was some light from the flat.

He had not seen anyone else go out. Napley mentions the love-making and then turns to the coffee trip onto the balcony. In his police statement, Texier had said he looked down, saw something, and drew Mrs Arnot's attention to it. But Texier is now adamant that he did not do this. He only remembers Mrs Arnot saying, 'Oh my God.'

NAPLEY: This was the first time you knew anything was wrong?

TEXIER: Yes.

NAPLEY: Mr Arnot has given evidence, and he has said that after he was awoken, he went to the balcony and ran down the stairs.

TEXIER: No, I left before Mr Arnot went downstairs.

NAPLEY: Mr Arnot said he went out onto the balcony, went back into his room, got himself dressed, then went down to examine the bodies.

Texier shakes his head.

NAPLEY: Mr Arnot gave evidence and he said he went back to the bedroom, put on his clothes, and ran downstairs to look at the bodies. You say that could not have happened?

TEXIER: I went before.

NAPLEY: Mr Arnot said he put his clothes on – that takes a minute or two – and then went downstairs. Are you saying you left in two or three minutes?

TEXIER: As soon as I saw the bodies, came back to the apartment. Mrs Arnot, Hayter, Mr Arnot too ... I said to them, 'I'm going away, I need to make my report to my boss. You can get in contact.'

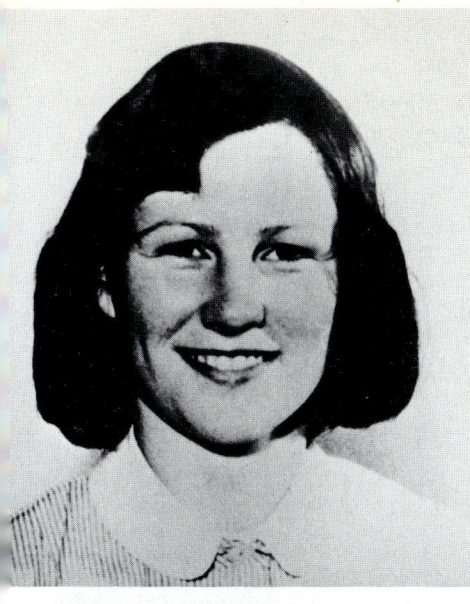

1a. Helen Smith.

1b. Ronald Smith, Helen's father, leaving the Leeds Town Hall on the sixth day of the inquest.

2a. Richard Arnot arriving at the inquest in Leeds in November 1982. It was at his flat in Jeddah that the illegal drinks party was held during which Helen Smith died.

2b. Ron Smith arrives at the inquest with his son Graham and solicitor Ruth Bundey.

3a. Leeds Coroner Philip Gill.

3b. Leeds pathologist Dr Michael Green, who performed a post-mortem examination on Helen Smith's body in June 1980.

4a. Geoffrey Robertson, the barrister representing Ron Smith at the inquest.

4b. Sir David Napley, the solicitor representing Richard Arnot.

5a. (*above left*) Dr Muhammad Kheir, the Saudi Arabian pathologist who conducted the first post-mortem examination on Helen Smith's body in Jeddah in May 1979.

5b. (*above right*) Danish pathologist Professor Jorgen Dalgaard, who examined Helen Smith's body in December 1980 at her father's request.

5c. Professor Alan Usher, the Sheffield pathologist who conducted a joint post-mortem examination with Professor Dalgaard.

6a. German electrician Martin Fleischer, a guest at the Arnots' party who gave evidence at the inquest.

6b. (*above right*) Gordon Kirby, Vice Consul at the British Embassy in Jeddah at the time of Helen Smith's death.

6c. Francis Geere, Second Secretary and Consul at the British Embassy in Jeddah.

7a. Richard and Penelope Arnot.

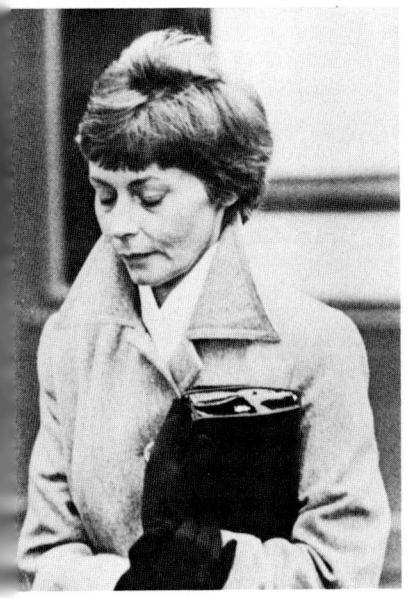

7b. Agnes Johnstone, matron of the Bakhsh Hospital in Jeddah where Helen Smith worked.

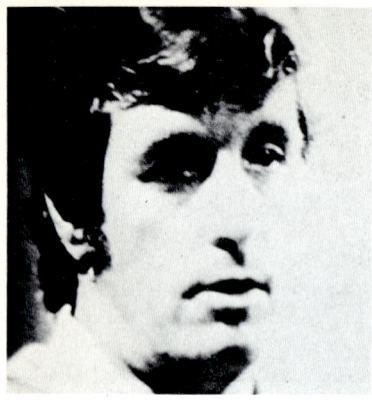

8a. Timothy Hayter, the New Zealand diving
instructor in whose honour the Arnots held the party
at their flat in Jeddah at which Helen Smith died.
Hayter did not attend the inquest.
8b. Jacques Texier, a French marine biologist and
friend of Hayter's, who was also at the party and was
the penultimate witness at the inquest.

NAPLEY: In other words, you left immediately?

TEXIER: Yes.

NAPLEY: When did you first learn that the two people you saw below were dead?

TEXIER: I learnt about it much later on, but I thought it was a fall.

NAPLEY: You were in the apartment, you slept in it. Was there anything there which would make you think that this was not the most dreadful of accidents?

TEXIER: No . . . my opinion . . . they were on the balcony . . . fell. That was my impression.

Napley asks him if he had ever been a mercenary. Texier laughs. No, never. Nor anything like it. He had been a conscript in the French army and then worked in Vietnam as a marine biologist. Texier pulls out French press cuttings where it is reported that he and Arnot were spies and had killed Otten because he knew too much and Helen because she knew too much about Otten. He laughs.

The court adjourns for the day. Texier seemed a good witness. His evidence was full of massive contradictory statements of the other witnesses. He also seemed sometimes to contradict himself, contradicting both murder and accident.

The riddles and the cul-de-sac seemed more open than ever, more closed than ever. Two witnesses were saying at the end of day twelve that Arnot did not go down to the bodies; on the other hand, Helen and Johannes did go out onto the balcony. The closer to the verdict, the more open-ended it became.

Day Thirteen

Tuesday 7 December: Texier is again in the witness box. This time his interpreter speaks mainly for him. He tells Gill he saw no clothes on the balcony.

GILL: You've lived out in Saudi Arabia. Are pairs of jeans sought after and expensive?

TEXIER: They can be bought very easily. They are cheap. I buy them myself.

Sedley takes over.

SEDLEY: When you speak of Helen and Johannes leaning against the balcony, did you actually see that they were leaning against the balustrade?

TEXIER: It was just a glance. It was difficult to say.

SEDLEY: Did you actually see them leaning in that vicinity?

TEXIER: After three years, three hours . . . it was just a glance. I was bored. Then I talked to Arnot.

SEDLEY: Your answer is that they were leaning against the balustrade?

Texier discusses the question with the interpreter. The interpreter nods towards Sedley, whose own command of French seems to be the best in the court, and who has been listening and peering very intently. 'He said yes.'

'Didn't he just begin his answer by saying, "It is difficult to say?"' asked Sedley.

The interpreter and Texier talk again. The interpreter states that Texier had a brief glance for a couple of seconds and it was an impression.

SEDLEY: When the time came for the Germans to leave, Tim Hayter has said that he was positive there was no one on the balcony. Do you agree with that?

The translator and Texier talk.

TRANSLATOR: He says he cannot reply because he was not really interested. This affair is important because something happened, but at the time it was not interesting. He only saw Miss Smith for half an hour.

SEDLEY: Did anyone call out for Otten before they left?

TEXIER: I do not hear. If they called Otten, because he belonged to company, whether he goes or does not go, doesn't matter to me.

According to Texier, apart from Mrs Arnot and Arnot and himself, most of the men were drunk. There is a period of some minutes, perhaps five or ten, before he bedded down. He saw no clothing in the flat in that period, no trousers.

They discuss his waking. He tells the inquest that on the previous day he had been asked if he had heard people making love during the night. In fact, he had heard the noise waking up – 'It was the moment of orgasm, so I heard the noise.'

He did not think that it happened between three o'clock and four, or four and five, but around five, since, as he had stated often, he always woke at that time.

He is asked if he had any knowledge of what Mrs Arnot and Hayter did before they made love. The interpreter replies, 'I have to place this story in context. Before I came to Dr Arnot's flat I didn't know the relationship and the kind of relationship which existed between Tim Hayter and Mrs Arnot. When I went to bed I remember Mr Hayter saying he would sleep in the armchair.'

He slept himself through the hours between three and five. He thought it 95 per cent certain that someone could not have come back into the flat after the guests had departed, but it was a large flat, and he could not be completely certain.

Sedley asks him about the balcony in the morning.

SEDLEY: On the balcony Mrs Arnot said, 'Oh my God.' You immediately looked down. Did you recognise who's the bodies were?

TEXIER: It happened very quickly.

SEDLEY: You looked?

TEXIER: Yes.

SEDLEY: Did you recognise who the bodies were?

TEXIER: I do not know . . . Mrs Arnot did not say. I do
not remember. I know two bodies.

SEDLEY: Did you recognise them?

TEXIER: What do you mean, recognise?

SEDLEY: Did you see that it was Helen and the other
one Otten?

TEXIER: I saw this – two bodies.

SEDLEY: You did not recognise them?

TEXIER: I thought it was them.

SEDLEY: What made you think that?

TEXIER: Because they were at the party.

SEDLEY: Was there any other reason?

TEXIER: Perhaps Mrs Arnot and Tim Hayter mentioned
they recognised them.

SEDLEY: Did you hear Mrs Arnot say, 'What's Helen
doing asleep down there?'

TEXIER: No.

SEDLEY: You didn't hear her say that?

TEXIER: No.

He is asked if Hayter had said anything to indicate who
the bodies were. He remembered Hayter saying something but could not remember what it was.

They discuss the flat; the panic; the dispersal of the
alcohol.

SEDLEY: Did you understand at the time what the logic
was? The connection between two bodies and the
alcohol in the flat?

TEXIER: In Saudi Arabia, two different causes, first accident or murder, then alcohol, because if this accident
or anything, police are going to come and find alcohol,
case finished with two, three months in jail, 45 lashes.

SEDLEY: Was the logic this, the police would come if
the bodies were connected to the flat?

TEXIER: Yes.

SEDLEY: Was it you, Tim Hayter or Mrs Arnot who initiated getting rid of the alcohol?

TEXIER: I think it was Mrs Arnot . . . It was not in my home.

He is asked about Mr Arnot. Again he repeats what he has said. Arnot came into the room, he discussed what had been seen over the balcony, Texier told him he could be contacted at the Embassy. The cultural attaché had been his sponsor and it was most important that he should be told, not for Texier himself but for the Embassy.

SEDLEY: How long elapsed between the moment that you saw the bodies and the moment you left the flat?

TEXIER: Personally I saw the bodies, went into kitchen, saw the excitement, told Mr Arnot going, perhaps ten minutes elapsed.

SEDLEY: When you left the flat, Mr Arnot was still in the flat with the towel around him?

TEXIER: I think he went back to get dressed.

SEDLEY: When you left the flat, Mr Arnot was still in the flat?

TEXIER: Yes. I was the first one to leave and go down the stairs.

They discuss Dr Suktian, who stated he saw two men leaving Arnot's flat. Texier agrees he could fit the description of the elderly man in his mid-fifties. He agrees with Sedley that the description of the younger man Suktian had given fitted Hayter more than it fitted Arnot.

SEDLEY: At the time Mrs Arnot came back from the balcony, she went to raise her husband?

TEXIER: Yes.

SEDLEY: Did you go with her into the bedroom?

TEXIER: No.

He is asked about the conversation at the door between Arnot and another man, possibly a doctor. Texier replies that on leaving there was an Arab on the landing in western clothes. 'I think he said, "What is happening?" I went through and came downstairs.' Texier did not wait to listen.

They discuss the prison. He had been kept separate from the others. During the whole inquiry he was kept isolated from the rest of the partygoers, but after the inquiry had ended he was given permission by the prison director to use the prison library. There he met Arnot, who was helping prisoners and therefore had the same facility. In meetings with Arnot, they had discussed certain aspects of the case.

Sedley refers to Texier's statement made to the English police. He reads out the same quote which had been read out the day before in which Texier said he saw Helen and Johannes on the kitchen balcony, leaning against the rail.

Texier agrees that he had said it to the court but it was very difficult to say how, or which way, since there was a curtain there. He knew he saw them, but whether he saw them through the door or the window he did not know.

He disagrees with Hayter that he knew more about the deaths than Hayter. How could he know, since he did not know the Arnots or Helen Smith, and this was his first visit to the flat.

Napley rises again and asks the question in people's minds.

NAPLEY: You said this morning, it is difficult to say precisely that you saw Helen and Otten leaning against the balustrade?

TEXIER: I know I saw them together but they seemed to be leaning. It happened in two seconds.

NAPLEY: It was the impression you got, you can't say more?

TEXIER: No.

They discuss the panic at finding the alcohol.

NAPLEY: If it was necessary to get rid of it, it could have been done earlier?

TEXIER: Yes.

NAPLEY: Finding the bodies made it necessary to get rid of it?

TEXIER: Yes.

NAPLEY: Mr Arnot first appeared with a towel around him?

TEXIER: Yes.

NAPLEY: Within a short span of time he came back clothed?

TEXIER: Yes.

In that span, Texier thought he himself was in the kitchen. He did not see Arnot getting dressed.

NAPLEY: You will not disagree that Arnot was out of your sight for three or four minutes when he went to get dressed?

TEXIER: No.

NAPLEY: When Mr Arnot went to get dressed, was he away for some time?

TEXIER: I think he just had time to go into bedroom and get dressed. He went to get dressed, since he came back dressed.

NAPLEY: Did several minutes elapse?

TEXIER: The time to go and get dressed and come back.

NAPLEY: Mr Arnot went to the balcony?

TEXIER: No, no, no . . . only know we went to the balcony. Mrs Arnot, they talked, he went back to get dressed.

He is emphatic that Arnot only went to get dressed and came back.

He steps down. Napley has managed to insert a possibility that Arnot could have raced down, but he has only a few minutes to race down six floors, examine the bodies, come back. But then Texier was emphatic.

The last witness, called suddenly over the weekend, is Paul Roberts. He had worked in a Jeddah shipping agency. He shared a flat with a Vittorio Bagnasco who worked for the same shipping company.

He describes how there was a loud banging on the door. He opened it to Peter Schmidt, the German national referred to as a party guest. Schmidt was very flustered and wanted his friend Bagnasco to get him out of the country through Bagnasco's connections in the harbour. Roberts tells the inquest, 'Anyone can get out if you put your mind to it. It's easier through the harbour.'

It was the early hours of the morning. He estimates it was around 5 a.m. but he could not be certain because the blinds were down.

GILL: Could it have been later than 5 a.m.?
ROBERTS: To be honest, it could have been.
GILL: As late as 6.30?
ROBERTS: To be honest, I think it was unlikely to be that late, but there is a possibility.

He showed Schmidt in to his flatmate and returned to bed. He could not remember the exact date but later he heard that there had been a party and people had been killed. Schmidt had not told him why he wanted to leave the country so urgently and Roberts did not ask Bagnasco later, 'It wasn't the thing one should know about.'

Gill begins his summing up. Texier sits through the afternoon on the witness bench. He has raised more questions than he has answered. After the afternoon session, he comes out of the court, onto the precinct, and is surrounded by journalists.

'Mr Texier,' Paul Foot asks, 'last week the Foreign Office said your mother suffered a stroke. How is she?'

Texier snorts. 'How is she? Her heart just went . . . what is it? . . . palpitation, shock.'

We laugh. The Foreign Office had translated '*coup de coeur*' as stroke.

7. *Coroner Gill Sums Up*

Coroner Gill began his summing up just after lunch on Tuesday 7 December 1982. It was to last for almost two days.

'This must be the most difficult, complex, involved case it has been the lot of a coroner's jury to have heard,' he began. He went on to pinpoint seven major problems.

Firstly, there was the great publicity that had surrounded the case since the deaths of Helen and Johannes Otten three and a half years earlier. He reiterated what he had said at the beginning of the inquest: the jury should forget all that it had read, seen or heard and make up its mind purely on the evidence presented to it at the inquest.

Secondly, Helen had met her death abroad and this had presented enormous difficulties to the West Yorkshire police in visiting the scene, drawing up plans etc. Thirdly, it had been very difficult to trace and interview witnesses and often it had had to be done through Interpol, and fourthly there had been the problem of availability of witnesses to attend the inquest. 'All have come on their own volition, at great expense and inconvenience, as a gesture of goodwill,' said Gill. (This was an interesting comment because all witnesses from abroad came at great expense to the West Yorkshire County Council).

Fifthly, there were people abroad who had not been able to attend – especially Penelope Arnot and Timothy Hayter. It was with great regret that Timothy Hayter came as close to Britain as Amsterdam for the *TV Eye* interview, and Gill had not known he was there.

Sixthly, there were the problems facing the pathologists in Britain who were faced with a body getting on for two years old, and one which had had all its internal organs removed.

Finally, there was the problem of the evidence. The jury had to decide how much was speculation and opinion, how much solid, reliable fact. It must weigh up dispassionately, 'without fear or favour'.

Coroner Gill then went on to explain the 'purpose and form' of an inquest. The purpose was laid down in the coroners' rules. The jury had to: 1) decide who the deceased was; 2) decide how, when and where the deceased came by her death; 3) record such matters as are required to register death in the United Kingdom (in this case, the death was not registrable, as it occurred abroad).

Number 2 was the most important of these, and the big question was 'how'. 'You are the sole arbiter, the sole judges. All the evidence before you, you can accept and reject at will,' Gill told the jury. It should simply record the medical cause of death, and if this was unnatural, in what circumstances. Finally there was the 'conclusion of the jury' – often referred to as the verdict. The jury would decide here whether the death was suicide, unlawful killing, accident 'or whatever'.

Turning to the form of an inquest, Gill stated that it was an inquiry: 'The purpose is not to decide differing points of view between conflicting parties. The purpose is to inquire about the circumstances objectively. We are all here with the common role to examine the evidence and decide where the truth lies. At an inquest, nobody is on trial . . .'

Coroner Gill's summing up proper began by telling of the events in broad chronological order. He started with the Harms Salvage employees: how they came to be invited to the party; how they found it a friendly, happy party, if somewhat boring; how Helen became more and more attached to one of their number – Johannes Otten – as the night wore on; how Helen and Johannes were merry but not necessarily drunk.

The divers left around 3.15 a.m. after only a cursory look for Johannes. They saw nothing on the railings as they stepped outside but because of unfamiliarity with driving the jeep at night, they set all the lights flashing before driving off in a hurry, in case they had drawn attention to themselves.

Coroner Gill singled out Martin Fleischer of the Germans. He had left earlier than the others and Helen and Johannes were dancing then. At about 6.30 a.m., he was awoken by Timothy Hayter who told him that Johannes was dead – he had been trying 'to screw Helen'. He was to go and inform their boss, Harry Gutzeit, who lived in the city and not at the port with the others. But Fleischer went back to the Arnot apartment instead and saw the tragic scene. He helped Richard Arnot to compile a list of the party guests for the police.

Coroner Gill dealt briefly next with Alan Kirwen as supplier of the whisky before moving on to Timothy Hayter as he appeared in the *TV Eye* film. He reminded the jury of Hayter's description of Helen as fun-loving and nice, someone who enjoyed making love. She had been happy at the party, but Johannes Otten was drunk, according to Hayter.

Gill went through the sequence of events according to Hayter. After the other guests left, he bedded down in the same room as Jacques Texier. At 5.45 a.m. they woke up, had coffee with Penelope Arnot and went onto the balcony. Texier said, 'Look down there, there's bodies.' They woke up Richard Arnot and tried to get rid of the booze.

After their arrest, Hayter was sure the police were investigating murder. He later admitted in the film that he had made love with Penelope Arnot that night. He also remembered a broken sunlounger on the balcony and had thought Helen and Johannes had tried to make love on it.

Coroner Gill emphasised how Hayter at first thought the deaths were an accident, but, on reading the pathology reports, was now doubtful. For some reason, Coroner Gill also referred to Hayter pointing the finger at Texier.

Jacques Texier, however, had turned up at the inquest and Gill emphasised his good character. When he was awoken to the sound of Penelope Arnot and Timothy Hayter making love, he pretended to be asleep because he did not want to embarrass them. It had not occurred to him that they might be embarrassing him, Gill pointed out. And he reminded the jury that Texier needed two pairs of glasses to be able to see properly.

As for his evidence, he had seen Helen and Johannes go onto the balcony and had seen them embracing there. He generally confirmed Timothy Hayter's account of the discovery of the bodies. The sunlounger became a camp bed, however, and this was folded up in the corner of the balcony. The Saudi police never suggested murder when they questioned him. While he was asleep in the Arnot flat, the noise of the air conditioner would have stopped him from hearing anybody fall off the balcony, but he would have heard a scream.

It was getting on for 4.30 p.m. Gill decided to adjourn.

Wednesday 8 December, 10.30 a.m.: Richard Arnot. Gill repeated his evidence that had been confirmed by the other witnesses. He had gone to bed early at around 2.00 a.m., he was woken by his wife on discovery of the bodies, he went downstairs and checked they were dead. Gill had pointed out earlier the variance with Texier's evidence here. Texier had claimed he was the first to go downstairs.

Gill again drew attention to the sunlounger/camp bed in Richard Arnot's evidence. Arnot described it as a sunlounger and, like Texier, thought it was folded up in the corner. Arnot's description of the balcony as slippery when wet or damp was also emphasised.

Coroner Gill then dealt in some detail with Richard Arnot's description of the bodies. Helen was in the court-yard, lying at an oblique angle, with her head towards the building wall. Her left arm was raised above and around her head, which Gill said could be of some significance. He did not notice where her pants were, but her pubic area was exposed. Otten was impaled in the middle of the railings with his head towards the building. There was congealed blood underneath him and his underpants were around his thighs. He appeared to be in a state of sexual excitement.

The rest of Richard Arnot's evidence was taken up with him trying to get rid of the alcohol, searching in vain for Otten's trousers (but finding Helen's abeya, handbag and shoes), and his dealings with Embassy staff, the police, Dr Bakhsh and other hospital staff.

Coroner Gill also made use of Arnot as a medical expert. He reminded the jury that Arnot had seen an in-dentation in Helen's forehead and thought she may have struck a button. Arnot was also not so surprised at the lack of obvious external injuries to Helen. He had seen this before in sudden deaths, although he was not familiar with falls from a height.

Finally, Gill pointed out, Richard Arnot had disagreed when it was suggested to him that Penelope's admission of adultery with Timothy Hayter was an 'alibi for murder'. He thought she had told the truth then.

Penelope Arnot was the next to come under Gill's scrutiny. Her evidence was based on an interview given to the West Yorkshire police in a London hotel, he reminded the jury.

Like Jacques Texier, she said she saw Helen and Johannes go onto the balcony, and she pulled back the curtain and saw them there later. After the Germans had gone, she went to look again, but they were not there. She assumed they had slipped away.

Coroner Gill pointed out that she also said there had been no violence that night, Johannes and Helen were merry although not intoxicated, and that her husband had gone to bed at 2.00 a.m. All this repeated what had been said in evidence by the party guests and Richard, and she largely confirmed Hayter's and Texier's descriptions of the discovery of the bodies.

Turning to the evidence of Dr Rahman, Dr Suktian, Dr Keith, Matron Agnes Johnstone and Dr Bakhsh, Gill tried to build up a consensus of the position and state of the bodies. It was difficult. Dr Suktian and Matron Johnstone agreed with Richard Arnot when they said that Otten's head was towards the building. Dr Bakhsh and Dr Keith thought it was the other way round. Dr Suktian thought that Otten's underpants were around his thighs, again in accord with Richard Arnot, but Dr Bakhsh thought they were in the normal position. With Helen there was more agreement; or at least less disagreement. Dr Suktian, Dr Keith and Matron Johnstone said her left arm was raised. Dr Bakhsh, Dr Suktian and Matron Johnstone agreed that she had only one leg in her pants, and these three each either commented on the lack of blood around Helen or the fact that she was not 'a ghastly mess'.

Coroner Gill also drew attention to Dr Rahman's comment that Otten's face was bruised and that when he went up to the Arnot flat, there was a short white man with a beard standing behind Richard Arnot as he answered the door.

The loud noise heard by Mrs Keith was then briefly referred to before Gill dealt with Matron Agnes Johnstone's evidence in more detail. She had noted that Helen was wearing a loose dress and her bra was in place, but what interested Gill more were her references to the sun-lounger on the Arnot balcony. When she went out there, it was opened out ready for use and the framework was bent as though somebody had stood on it.

Coroner Gill then spoke of the British Embassy's role in the case – as one of non-interference. Nor did they go to the scene to interrogate, as this was a matter for the Saudi police. Kirby's minute was regarded as confidential because it talked of illegal matters (Alan Kirwen supplying the alcohol) and 'this was quite clearly a matter which they did not wish to bring to the attention of the authorities'.

Ron Smith's evidence was dealt with next, and Gill emphasised the points where he and Richard Arnot seemed to be in complete agreement. Like Richard Arnot, Ron Smith was struck by the lack of obvious injury; like Richard Arnot, Ron Smith noticed an indentation in the forehead; like Richard Arnot, Ron Smith noticed that Helen's left arm was raised. Ron Smith's estimation of the height of the balcony was seventy feet above ground, and that of the railings on which Otten was impaled, 6 feet 8 inches.

Ron Smith, of course, went to see the body twice, and on the second occasion, the Bakhsh hospital pathologist, Joe Deguara, was with him. Coroner Gill stressed that Dr Deguara did not do a detailed examination of Helen, and he was not acting in a professional capacity. But he too was struck by the lack of massive injury. He would have expected crushing of the face and arms. He advised Dr Bakhsh to 'get a proper pathologist to fly in from England', but this was not acted upon. He thought it was murder but he was never interviewed by the Saudi police, and he was not invited to attend a meeting of the other pathologists who later examined Helen's body in Britain.

Coroner Gill broke off here to tell the jury that this was where the doubts about how Helen met her death really came to the surface – she was apparently free of serious injury. It was the lead-in to the pathologists' evidence, which he took in the order that they examined Helen's body.

Dr Kheir actually visited the scene and stepped out onto the balcony, Gill noted, where he saw the sunlounger but no evidence of a struggle. There were no clothes on the balcony.

Taking the jury through Dr Kheir's examination of Helen, Gill noted the vital injuries he found. These included abraded bruising and contusions on the head, fractures to the right rear ribs and to the sternum. There were also abraded and bruised wounds to the back of the left elbow, the left hand and the left foot. On the left half of the forehead there was blood covering the brain. The bones of the face were not broken and there were no bruises on the face suggesting criminal assault.

Coroner Gill then stressed that Dr Kheir (whom Gill now began to refer to often as 'professor') was the only pathologist who examined the whole body. The others had not had the benefit of his information about the internal injuries when they performed their autopsies.

These internal injuries included tearing of the right lung substance, slight haemorrhaging from the lower part of the liver and around the right kidney, and bruising around the spleen.

In conclusion, Dr Kheir felt that there was no technical reason why Helen's injuries could not have resulted from a fall from a height, which he fitted in with his estimation of the distance of the Arnot balcony above ground – forty-five feet. The abraded bruising suggested that Helen landed on a rough surface, and Dr Kheir mentioned building work going on. This had not been borne out by the later evidence, Coroner Gill noted.

During examination, Dr Kheir had agreed that the abraded wounds were all on the left side of Helen's body and there was no skull fracture. He also said, however, that he saw no abrasion or bruising inconsistent with a fall, and no injuries to Helen's genitalia indicative of rape. In his opinion there was no evidence of strangling or beating and he had been satisfied that her death was an accident.

He was, however, curious of one aspect, Coroner Gill reminded the jury. He had had the feeling that Otten must have gone over the balcony with some element of momentum.

Gill now turned to Dr Green's autopsy, and told the jury that he would not go through his report in detail as this 'may blur the issues'. He pointed out the difficulties facing Dr Green in being presented with a body that was over a year old. It was shrunken, dried, embalmed and showed many post-mortem marks. It had been subjected to insect activity and pressure from storage.

Gill went through Dr Green's findings. He had noted bruising, mainly to the right side of the body, but also some to the left. There were multiple fractures to the right side of the body too. There was no spine fracture or skull fracture, but the breast bone was fractured and Dr Green thought that this may have occurred during Dr Kheir's autopsy.

Dr Green did note various injuries to Helen's head and face but, although concerned about these, he concluded that her injuries were consistent with a fall from a height of thirty feet or more and a landing on the right side. She was not dead when she dropped. If she had been, there would not have been the extensive seepage of blood round the right-side fractures.

Dr Green was also concerned about the injuries to Helen's genitalia which he found, and there was bruising on the insides of the thighs. He thought the latter could be due to secondary impact after a fall (i.e. the thighs slapping together), or it could have other causes.

Coroner Gill referred to Green's computer print-out of the statistics of falling bodies and said how it 'was almost impossible' to predict the injuries. The nature of the ground, the age of the person falling, the manner in which the fall occurs – all have to be taken into account.

Gill pointed out that once Dr Green had seen Dr Kheir's report at the inquest, which detailed serious internal injuries, he was more inclined to favour a straight seventy-foot fall. He had also agreed that Coroner Gill's own theory that Helen's fall was cushioned in some way could probably solve some of the difficulties concerning her injuries.

Gill turned to Stephen Sedley's examination and pointed out that Green had agreed that Helen's injuries were consistent with her having been beaten, raped and thrown out or dropped. Sedley had also been concerned about the injuries Helen did not have, such as: no fractures to the skull, thighs, legs or spine. There were no marks on the right side of the skull.

The last autopsy on Helen was performed jointly by Professors Dalgaard and Usher. They, in fact, found more injuries overall than Dr Green had done. In particular, they had discovered a large bruise beneath her left forehead – lesion 13 – which Dr Green had mistakenly thought may have been henna dye. This injury by itself could have led to loss of consciousness.

Professor Dalgaard thought lesion 13 could not have originated in a right-side fall. It was caused either by a blow or by falling against something that was not too rigid and not too flat. He thought that the blow had caused bleeding some way down the spinal column, and this indicated that by itself it could have caused death.

But, Gill pointed out, Professor Usher thought that it could also have been caused by a glancing blow to the head as Helen fell. According to Professor Usher, there could have been more than one blow in that region.

Both pathologists referred to Helen's genital injuries, which indicated at least rough sex. There was no proof of rape, however. These genital injuries, taken with the head injuries, raised the possibility that Helen had been subjected to physical violence, and Professor Dalgaard was more emphatic on this point than Professor Usher.

Both pathologists felt that her injuries only indicated a fall of moderate height – not more than thirty feet.

Coroner Gill finally emphasised Professor Usher's point about the problems involved in dealing with a body that was then nineteen months old and from which all the organs had been removed.

The day was coming to an end. Coroner Gill said that he would require about half an hour in the morning to attempt to relate the pathologist evidence to the witness evidence. Sir David Napley rose and asked Gill to make it clear to the jury that, once he had seen Dr Kheir's evidence, Professor Usher had agreed that a fall from a

greater height than thirty feet was a distinct possibility.
Gill thanked him for pointing it out.

The Smith barristers looked aghast at Sir David's apparent audacity in telling the coroner how he should sum
up. It had been done in front of the jury too. Stephen
Sedley suggested that Gill might like to hear some representations on their behalf of what to include in the
morning, once the court had adjourned. Gill agreed.

Gill began the Thursday by 'tidying up' the pathologists'
evidence – probably as a result of the representations
made to him. He pointed out that neither Dalgaard nor
Usher had ever excluded the possibility of a fall from
seventy feet and that Dalgaard had said that a real assessment was difficult.

The caution of Usher and Dalgaard was mentioned – if
they had not been sure that a certain lesion was sustained
in life, then they had dismissed it. Gill again mentioned
the left forehead bruise and Usher's opinion that a glancing blow as Helen fell could not be excluded. Usher had
also said that her inside thigh bruises could be cross-over
injuries or they could indicate rape.

Gill commented that the head injuries 'may be consistent with a whole range of different circumstances' and it
was difficult to come to conclusions because of the problems presented by a nineteen-month-old body.

He referred to the sternum fracture, merely to say that
it showed all the signs of being post mortem and he ended
by taking up Sir David Napley's point of the previous
day. Having seen Dr Kheir's report, Professor Usher now
felt that a fall in the forty-five to fifty-foot range was by
no means out of the question.

Coroner Gill's long summing up the previous day and
a half could hardly be faulted. So far that morning he had
caused a few eyebrows to be raised in the press gallery
as he seemed to bend just that little bit towards one interpretation of the pathologists' findings – that she
simply fell from a height. But, again, to find fault would

be little more than nit-picking.

He now turned at last to what seemed an intractable problem: to make the pathologists' evidence compatible with that of the witnesses. This is what he said:

> As a jury at an inquest you're not deciding between opposing points of view, you are trying to look objectively at everything that has been said, weighing it up as best you can ... You have to, in your own mind, if you can, try to devise a picture of what has happened in relation to the death of Helen Smith. How did it come about?
>
> This must mean a certain amount of conjecture I accept but what I ask you to do is to rely on the evidence, look at the various pieces of evidence which have emerged and put them together and try to form, if you can, as coherent and as complete a picture as is possible on the basis of the evidence you have heard ...
>
> The first thing inevitably that you have to do is relate what the pathologists have said with the actual evidence that has been given to you and these must be considered together because they all form an integral part of this picture ... And so, if I may start, and I think this is obviously the matter that has been baffling us all, here was a problem of relating what the pathologists said to the events as the witnesses have described them to us. If we're going to try to analyse it let us look at the two sources of evidence and see how they shape up when we try to consider them.
>
> So, turning to the witnesses first of all do you believe what you've heard from the witnesses who came to give evidence? Did you feel that they were honest, genuine, truthful people who were genuinely and sincerely coming here to help you by telling you precisely what had happened and did they convince you of the accuracy of their stories? Members of the jury, there may have been differences on various points in the course of their evidence, perhaps that's hardly surprising after

all the passage of time, but were you able to get a general picture from them as to what had happened and did you feel that they were basically honest and truthful in what they were telling you? This is a matter that you have to decide, having heard the witnesses. And if you are satisfied with their evidence, if you do accept what they said to you, certainly so far as the general situation of the party is concerned and the events leading up to the time when the main German party left the building at about three o'clock as we understand is the case; so far as the events up to that stage are concerned do you accept what you were told and do you feel that the evidence has given you a clear picture both of the situation at the party and the circumstances leading up to their departure?

If so, then you have to look at the period following that departure, to what happened after the Germans had left. Members of the jury, the next stage of which we have further information is after the bodies were found some time after half past five in the morning. And so, we have a period of some two and a half hours between three o'clock and five thirty, or just after, in which presumably it would appear that the death of Helen and Johannes occurred. Members of the jury, you have to look at that period and ask yourselves what exactly happened during those crucial hours.

So far as the death of Helen is concerned it seems to me, on the evidence, that the choice is a simple one. Either it was the result of an unlawful killing or it was an accident and that is what you have to decide. Members of the jury, so far as the question of unlawful killing is concerned, the only evidence which there is to support that suggestion is the evidence of the pathologists and the possibilities and speculation which their observations create. They have told you, as I said, of the pattern of bruising which they found and which indicates slaps or punches or whatever and if that evidence is accepted then the indications are that some sort of physical assault has taken place.

And so, let us see how that evidence in fact fits in with the other. Let us assume for a moment that that evidence does give a very real suspicion of foul play. How does the other evidence help you in deciding whether that is the case or not? Do you accept for example the evidence of Mr Arnot? Do you accept the evidence of Mr Texier. Both of those gentlemen you saw in the witness box. You heard them giving their accounts. Did they convince you that they were truthful, honest witnesses doing their best to tell you what they recall of events of three and a half years ago? How did they come across to you? ...

If you do accept their evidence then any incident involving Helen must have involved either Mrs Arnot and/or Mr Hayter or Mr Otten, because the evidence of Mr Arnot and Mr Texier was that Mr Arnot himself was in bed. He had retired to bed earlier in the evening and in fact was asleep until his wife woke him just after half past five. Members of the jury, not only is that Mr Arnot's evidence it was the evidence given to you initially by the Germans who said he had retired to bed before they left and it was the evidence which was supported by the evidence of Mr Texier who described how Mr Arnot was woken when the bodies were found. And, members of the jury, so far as Mr Texier was concerned, he told you how he came to stay the night there because it was late and the person who was going to take him back to his accommodation then had decided that, because they had had drink, it wasn't wise to drive. So he stayed the night and he gave you an account of how they bedded down on a couch for the night and how he woke the following morning. Members of the jury, did you accept what he said, that that was really what happened? And if so do you accept his account of the events during that period? He said that at three o'clock he went off to sleep very quickly and he slept until somewhere just after five to five thirty. He talked about his almost built-in alarm clock which caused him to wake up almost automatically every morning at about that time and, members of the jury, it was put to him that during those sleeping hours, of course, anything could have happened and he might not have been aware of it and he accepted that that was always possible.

Members of the jury, when he did wake up he told you that he became aware of something going on in the room just behind him. Members of the jury, how did his account of that incident come over to you? Did you feel that as he was trying to relate it to you he was under some embarrassment in describing precisely what it was that was happening? As though he didn't particularly like the idea of having to speak from a witness box and describe such events to a court and to all the people present? Was he embarrassed by it and was he in fact being truthful when he told you of what he heard and saw and found out? Members of the jury, if you accept that evidence, this is extremely important because when we come to look at the evidence of Mrs Arnot and Mr Hayter, it is their account of those two and a half hours which is also of great importance, because they are on the spot, they were in the flat.

Members of the jury, one of the great misfortunes, if I may say so, in this case is that we haven't had the benefit of hearing their evidence in person. You've heard Mr Hayter's evidence on film and I come back to what I said yesterday about the caution with which you accept that which is given in a recorded interview of that sort when the evidence hasn't been tested. But you've heard his explanation given to the interviewer. You heard from various witnesses of the account which Mrs Arnot had given to various people about what had happened. You may have detected a certain inconsistency in her stories, indeed I drew attention to it when I was going through the evidence with you. But taking together their two accounts of what happened in those two and a half hours and bearing in mind what Mr Texier told you, do you find the version that came across to you as acceptable? Do you believe that they were in the room together, that Mr Hayter in fact prepared for the night and that later on he and Mrs Arnot did become involved in sexual activity together? Is this account true? And does Mr Texier's evidence in fact corroborate and confirm it to your satisfaction?

Members of the jury, it has been suggested or the thought was put forward and the question asked, was this just a made-up story or was it simply an alibi? Members of the jury, did Mr Texier confirm it to you to your satisfaction? And if it was an alibi, if they were responsible for some vicious assault on Helen Smith, it's not a very successful alibi is it? It's landed them in an awful lot of trouble and we know that from the evidence that we have, one of the greatest problems that Mrs Arnot subsequently was faced with was the effect of the admission that she and Mr Hayter made about that activity.

And members of the jury, let us look at it a little more carefully. Suppose that that story wasn't true, supposing they had in fact been involved in some assault on Helen and were involved in her death and knew about it and this was just intended as an alibi, would they have left it until just after half past five to be involved in all the panic in getting rid of the alcohol? Would they have left the bodies where they were and done nothing about it? In his television interview, Mr Hayter was very clear about what he would have done at an earlier stage if he had known about the presence of these bodies. He said that if 'I'd have known earlier I'd have tried to get out of the country but, when we found out, it was too late.' Members of the jury, it was only a comment on a film, but did it ring true to you? And, in fact, it's something that you will have to consider — whether or not that was a true account of what happened. And if they were involved in any assault on Helen what on earth was the motive? What precipitated it? What was the reason for any assault of this sort? No suggestion has been made of any hostility at the party either towards Helen or anyone else. Would they really be able to get involved in an assault involving Helen to the complete absence of knowledge on the part of Mr Texier. Had they succeeded in fooling him about what they had done and fooling Mr Arnot? Were *they* [Arnot and Texier] aware of the activity and not telling the truth when they came and gave you evidence?

Now, supposing Mrs Arnot and Mr Hayter were not involved. Well, then we are looking, aren't we, elsewhere? We're looking for either Mr Otten to be involved or we're looking for some other person or persons about whom there has not been the slightest indication of evidence. Not even a hint.

But let's look at the relationship between Helen and Otten first of all. What was the nature of that relationship as it's been described to you by the witnesses? They'd met for the first time at that party and they gradually as the evening developed became more and more attached to each other and more and more close. And we heard that indeed various descriptions of that realtionship were given. I think one of the descriptions given by Mr Hayter was that it was a one-way ticket to sex. They became more intimate and more attached to each other. Was there any indication that Otten was violent? In fact, it was often said that when he was drunk he became quieter, so was there any basis at all to think that there was a risk of his using violence towards Helen? And what in fact happened, if you accept the evidence of Mr Texier, if you accept what Mrs Arnot has reported to have said in interviews and to others, that they were seen at one late stage to go out onto the balcony? Mr Texier mentioned this, if you remember. In his evidence he said that he had been to the kitchen and made a sandwich and saw them going towards the balcony. He said he wasn't really concerned about it, he didn't know them and this was a party. He was only there for the first time and didn't know very much about the place ... So did they in fact go to the balcony? Did a sexual act take place between them and was it consensual or was it, in fact, against Helen's consent and was, in fact, rape?

Now members of the jury, so far as that aspect of the matter is concerned, you have got to consider what we've heard about the distance of the bodies, the position of the clothing and all aspects of their condition when they were found; the fact that Otten was found with his underpants down round the lower part of his thighs, that his trousers were missing, that Helen was found with one leg out of her panties or whatever the garment was that she was wearing, that she in fact did have fitted a contraceptive device ...

What do you make of this? Was this in fact a case where these two people have become attracted to each other, had left the party, had gone onto the balcony to find a secluded and private place and had, in the end, indulged in a consensual act of intercourse? This is a matter that you will have to decide and you will have to think about when you consider all the evidence and try to formulate a picture of what happened. And then, members of the jury, you have got to consider the question of how the bodies came to be where they were found. And here there has been a considerable amount of difference of opinion ...

How did the two bodies come to land where they were? Let's look at them individually. The position of Otten's body, jackknifed over the railings, impaled on the railings, with railings that had penetrated his body, according to Professor Kheir, to a depth of about twenty centimetres. Members of the jury, did that indicate to you that he had got into that position as a result from a fall from a height? What degree of force would be necessary to cause a person's body to be impaled to that extent and in that position? What conclusion do you reach about the circumstances that he came to be where he was?

And then, what about Helen: did she fall from a height or is the suggestion that she fell from a height totally unacceptable?

Members of the jury, as you've gathered, as I've read the evidence over to you of the various pathologists, their attitudes and views in this respect have tended to vary as more information has come to light. Initially Dr Green was sceptical and thought that she had fallen from a height but not as much as seventy feet. Professor Dalgaard is still unconvinced that it is as much as that and puts it at a much lower figure, but has to agree that it is extremely difficult to be certain and accepts that it might be perhaps more than he had originally thought in the light of Professor Kheir's details of the internal injuries. And Professor Usher too now says that in the light of those internal injuries the possibility of a fall from a much greater height becomes more likely. And, members of the jury, the proposition was put to Dr Green, in the course of his evidence to Sir David Napley, that the possibility that Helen might have fallen in conjunction with Otten and her body had been cushioned in some way on his could well have accounted for some reduction in the injuries which she had sustained.

The possibility that they had fallen together, clutching each other possibly, and as a result of his coming into contact with the railings and she had fallen off from that height of the railings about seven feet six inches onto the floor, might account for a lesser degree of injury. Or alternatively, they had parted, she had fallen a second or two after him and struck his body as he was impaled and again glanced off him onto the ground. This might also create a reduction in the amount of injury that she had sustained. Members of the jury, the curious thing is that when that possibility was put to Dr Green, who had had some difficulty in accepting initially that she had fallen from a height of seventy feet, his reaction was rather surprising. He didn't say, 'Yes that could be the answer,' he turned round and he said: 'As a result of what I've now heard of Prof. Kheir's evidence and the nature of the internal injuries I think we are looking at a straightforward fall of seventy feet on to the ground . . .

And so, members of the jury, having regard to the nature of the injuries to Helen, and having regard to all the views which have been expressed by the pathologists, do you feel those injuries are consistent with her having fallen from a height of the order of the height of this balcony and fallen directly onto the ground below? Members of the jury, I dealt with the question of the relationship between Helen and Otten and I have dealt with the matter of Otten and I have dealt with the matter of any sexual activity that took place. It's for you to decide, having heard the evidence about that to decide whether it was consensual or whether it was part of a criminal act, which, of course, rape would be. And so, members of the jury, I come back to the question of the bruises, bruises which really are the basis of the suspicion that there is foul play involved in this.

Members of the jury, I have dealt with the problems which are associated with any view that foul play is the answer. Now let us look at the bruises themselves. Were they really bruises which were sustained at the time of Helen's death? Members of the jury, you've had the benefit of the evidence of Professor Kheir, the Saudi Arabian pathologist who made a post-mortem examination. Indeed, members of the jury, he is the only pathologist who has seen the whole body and he has done so when he made the examination in Saudi Arabia. He has concluded what the cause of death was and issued a death certificate on that basis. Members of the jury, he was concerned to examine that body and to investigate the death on behalf of the authorities, and, as he said in his evidence, one of his concerns would be to see whether there was evidence of foul play. Members of the jury, he made his examination and he expressed himself to be satisfied that death was accidental . . . Much has been said about the experience of Dr Green, Professor Dalgaard, and Professor Usher, I hope, members of the jury, that you won't underestimate the experience and knowledge of Professor Kheir as well. A man of considerable experience, admittedly perhaps not operating quite by Western standards, nevertheless a man who had a responsible position in Saudi Arabia and still has such a position in Egypt now, is it conceivable, in your view, and you saw him in the witness box, you were able to assess his ability and qualities, is it conceivable that if those bruises were there at the time of death, that he's just missed them or that he's failed to see them? Is he as incompetent as that when he's looking for evidence of any criminality and the possibility of any assault?

At the end of his examination he was satisfied that all the injuries he saw were the result of a fall. Members of the jury, may I also draw your attention to the evidence of the other witnesses who saw Helen's body just after this – to Mr Arnot, to Mr Smith, to Dr Deguara, to Matron Agnes Johnstone? When they all looked at the body, the thing that struck them was not that there were marks on the body, that it was bruised as if the poor girl had been assaulted, but it was the complete absence of any marks which was striking to them.

Mr Smith told you how his daughter's body appeared to him as being perfect but he'd expected to find it badly damaged and badly injured if it was a fall from this height. Matron Agnes Johnstone said very much the same thing. She had expected to find her 'a ghastly mess' and was surprised that she wasn't. Mr Arnot too, I think, indicated that he expected to find much more injuries and it was the absence of the obvious injury which alerted Dr Deguara and made him suspicious that there was something more than what was apparent at the time.

Members of the jury, Mr Smith it was who said that when he examined his daughter's body he noticed that there was no sign of external injury and he noticed also that 'the abdomen seemed to be full of blood', indicating no doubt that there was some indication there could well be serious internal injuries.

Members of the jury, the one thing that none of those people could know was just how serious the internal injuries were ... Deaths which occur as a result of a fall can, in a rather surprising minority of cases, produce remarkably little external injury and it may come as some surprise. I think many instances were quoted, in the course of this hearing, that this sort of situation can arise and, members of the jury, I ask you to consider whether in fact what has happened here is that serious internal injuries have been sustained as a result of the fall, and the basic suspicion has arisen because those who came on the scene later and looked at the bodies had expected to find much more external injury than there was. But does that mean that in fact Helen had not fallen from the height which was at first believed to be the situation?

And so, members of the jury, what about these bruises? Were they there as a result of the fall or immediately afterwards? Dr Kheir's examination was some twelve days after she had died. Would they have been obvious at that time? Would they not have appeared to him when he made his examination? Members of the jury, he picked out, if you remember, and they are mentioned in his report, certain lesions which he observed ... If he had spotted those lesions, is it not conceivable that he would have found all the others if they had actually been there?

And so, members of the jury, one comes up against a daunting fact. Can it possibly be that the pathologists have been misled? Can this mirage of lesions perhaps be nothing more than artefacts? Could they perhaps be nothing more than marks which have developed after death due, and I quote Dr Green's evidence about this, 'amongst other things due to rough handling of the body subsequently on death'. This, members of the jury, he indicated was often a cause of marks developing on the body which it is sometimes difficult to identify. And he and the other pathologists told of the difficulties which they had in determining whether marks were a result of the handling of the body post mortem or whether they were bruises which had occurred in life. And, members of the jury, so far as that is concerned, perhaps I might just indicate to you very briefly the comments that they made in that particular respect.

I mentioned the comments of Professor Dalgaard about the nature of the body and the position of the body when he found it and indeed the general condition and the problem of examining a body so many months after death. In his report, and I did mention this to you yesterday, he does say how the skin was discoloured, namely yellow brown, darker than usual with extensive darker discolourations, and then he goes on to say part of the hands and all the fingers and the feet and the toes were nearly black, dried and shrunken like mummification. The skin was rather dry and hard like leather and there was a heavy growth of mould. Members of the jury, that is the condition of the body that Professor Dalgaard found it in.

Dr Green's comment, if I can put it simply from his evidence, was this: he said the body was shrunken and dried, it had been embalmed but there was a heavy growth of mould over many parts of the trunk. Then he goes on to say there were many marks on the body which were due to post-mortem spillage of embalming fluid, the activities of insects and to pressure from the way that the body had been stored in the refrigerator, packed in the coffin and so on. Members of the jury, there I think that Dr Green is indicating the problems which he found in examining the body.

And then, Professor Usher, himself, when he began to give evidence, members of the jury, before he had really dealt with the questions that were going to be put to him, he found it necessary to just say one thing by way of introduction. He talked first of all about the difficulties which he had had, he mentioned the complete lack of information and he said it was often misinformation which they had had. He said they were told originally that they were thinking of a height of seventy feet. He said now, having heard Dr Kheir, it sounds probably as though it's nearer forty-five feet.

And then he went on to talk about the condition of the body itself. He said the problems were the length of time since the incident happened and their seeing the body, and the state of the body when they did see it. And he said that the body had been subjected to being moved from the scene, placed in storage, taken out of storage, post-mortemed, put back into storage, embalmed, brought to Leeds, taken out of the refrigerator, re-post-mortemed, put back into a refrigerator and then he and Professor Dalgaard came on the scene and tried to look at it and examine it and decide on the marks which they found on it. He said there were all sorts of marks and stains upon it due to mould and possible post-mortem falls. He said: 'It's now very difficult to tell which marks are significant, one can interpret the marks in a great variety of ways. Some things I've heard are extremely speculative, it's extraordinarily difficult in my view to come to any conclusions which are absolutely firm. It has been a most difficult case. Injuries to the right side support a fall from a considerable height sustained in life.'

He said: 'The height I believed to be twenty to thirty feet. It's very difficult to quantify-falls from a greater height do produce less injury, I cannot exclude a fall from seventy feet.

And so, members of the jury, this is the problem which the pathologists were faced with. Is this evidence acceptable to you, are you convinced by what they say that the bruises were there and that Professor Kheir has missed them altogether, or could it be, in fact, that they were not there at all? Members of the jury, so far as the circumstances in which these marks may have arisen are concerned, Dr Green, in his comments, refers and indeed Professor Usher does, to the various activities in the mortuary. Members of the jury, we have not, of course, had direct evidence about the actual place in the mortuary but an implication has been made in what Professor Usher said about the various actions which occurred in relation to the body, the storage of it, the taking out of storage, and the general handling of the body.

Members of the jury, you are entitled to think about, and to consider, what would be involved in those questions of storage examination, post-mortem examination and replacing in the refrigerators and so forth. And I ask you to just think carefully and to visualise how a body would be handled in those circumstances. How would a body be taken from a post-mortem slab where it has been examined and put onto a trolley, or into a refrigerator? How would it be picked up, where would it be grasped, where would it be held, where would marks be likely to develop?

This is a matter you will decide. I am not going to make suggestions to you, but I invite you to consider this and decide what might have occurred in those circumstances. Members of the jury, when you're considering what may have occurred in the post-mortem room, consider also what may have occurred in relation to the head. Is there anything in those activities in the handling of the body in the mortuary which has come to your knowledge as a result of you knowing the examination of the head, particularly the examination of the skull and the brain? Is there anything there which in your view could account for a grasping or holding and supporting of the head? Members of the jury, this is the matter you will have to think about to decide whether or not, in your view, having regard to all the evidence, and having regard to your assessment of what may have taken place in the post-mortem room, whether in fact an explanation for those marks can be found in that source.

Is that the answer – that these marks, in fact, have been misleading to the pathologists and have set us all on a wild goose chase trying to find out how they can possibly be explained, and what evidence there is of the circumstances in which they were sustained? Members of the jury, in the television film, Mr Hayter made a little comment. He was asked, if you remember, in the film, whether he had been satisfied if this was an accidental death. And he said he had until he heard the pathologists' reports and then he said: 'But having heard what the experts say,' I think his words were, 'I'm only a bum, who am I to disagree with them.'

Members of the jury I hope you won't feel under the same disability. You are the jury in this case, you are able to accept or reject whatever evidence you wish, whether it comes from experts or otherwise. Experts can be wrong. There is an old saying that some things are too important to leave to experts and, members of the jury, I ask you to look at all the evidence objectively from whatever source it comes and, as I said earlier, accept or reject that which you will, according entirely to your convictions. You're the judges in this matter and you have to decide.

So, members of the jury, if you came to the conclusion that you were not satisfied that these bruises had genuinely existed at the time of Helen's death, members of the jury, then you would have to consider the other alternative, because, if those bruises no longer existed, then the evidence of assault or attack upon her disappears.

The question still remains about the nature of the injuries connected or believed to be associated with a fall. Were they the result of a fall from a height and was this, in fact, an accidental matter? Members of the jury, so far as that possibility is concerned what conclusions can you draw? You can look at all the factors that are known about the circumstances in which these bodies were found – Helen with her clothing disarranged, Otten impaled over the railings, underpants down and his trousers having totally disappeared.

Members of the jury, how in your view could they have reached that situation? Could it be that in fact they had gone out onto the balcony quite simply as a couple wanting to be alone and ultimately engaging in sexual intercourse? Could it be, members of the jury, having regard to the time on Mr Otten's watch that we were told had stopped just after three o'clock, could it be that they were out on the balcony? And, members of the jury, at that time, if you find that the time on the watch is an indication of when the fall has occurred, is that not just the time when the German party was leaving – the German party with whom Mr Otten was supposed to be going back to the port?

Members of the jury, we heard, didn't we, from the Germans about problems they had when they went outside the building. They went across the road, nobody noticed anything on the railings at that time, they didn't really look but they said they didn't see anything. They went across the road to their vehicle which was parked on the other side of the road. They got into a frightful mess with the lights and the lights started flashing because they got the wrong switches on.

Members of the jury, they were worried that the

police might see them and come along, and they'd all been drinking, and there was a danger they would be taken into custody if the police saw it, and they were panicking, but they did have this period of flashing lights. Members of the jury, might those lights have been seen by somebody up on the balcony? Somebody who realised that something was going on in relation to a car across the road, a car in which he was supposed to be departing?

Members of the jury, if at that time he was engaged in sexual activity with Helen, possibly with his trousers down round his ankles, his underpants down and Helen with her clothing disarranged, would it be a natural reaction for him to try and see what was going on and see what these flashing lights were and perhaps even attract the attention of his friends across the road? And, members of the jury, did that happen? It's for you to say: you have to form a picture from the items of evidence which you have.

If that happened, might he not hurry towards the balcony edge? We know that there was a sunlounger bed at the side of the balcony with various descriptions about its position, whether it was opened up or closed up or whatever. The matron said that it was opened up. It was alongside the balustrade and it looked as if somebody had stood on it. Members of the jury, the evidence which we have was that the balcony would be dark. Might it be that in his hurry, he, with Helen clutching him, had in fact came into contact with that sunlounger and pitched forward over the edge of the balcony and she clutching him went with him? Members of the jury, Dr Kheir said that in his view so far as the angle of precipitation was concerned he was of the view that there was some element of momentum behind Mr Otten's fall. Could that be the element of momentum that he was talking about? Members of the jury, if that is how they fell, what would happen as they fell? If they were clutching together there is the possibility, and it is no more than a possibility, that they would remain clutched together and, as he became impaled on the railings, as I said earlier on, she may have fallen from him and on to the ground at the side of him. Or they may have parted as they were falling, she may have struck a glancing blow on his body a second or two later. Or indeed, as Dr Green was quite prepared to accept as a possibility, she may have fallen directly onto the ground below onto the pavement.

Members of the jury, her injuries were such that it was said that death might not have been immediately instantaneous. You have, members of the jury, the position of her left arm referred to by many of the witnesses. Was this in a position which was indicative of an attempt at a fall? It is something which you will have to think about and apply what conclusion you reach about that. Members of the jury if, in fact, Otten's clothing situation was as I suggested, if in fact, this did happen at three o'clock in the morning, could it be that, as he fell, his trousers either fell off or came from his body as he landed and then dropped into the street outside? And in the two and a half hours from three o'clock until five thirty when we are told the bodies were first seen, is it possible that there were people passing along the street in the darkness, going to prayers at shortly after four, who might have found these trousers lying in the roadway? We are told that in his trousers he would have his wallet, his documents and other possessions. His wallet would contain a considerable quantity of money, we know that his identification papers were found in the road later on.

Could it be, members of the jury, that some passer-by had found those trousers, helped himself to the trousers and the wallet, and taken care to get rid of any-thing which would help to identify the source? Members of the jury, this is a matter of conjecture, I appreciate, but we have this problem. These trousers are missing, you have to consider what possible circumstances there were in which that sort of situation might have occurred.

And so, members of the jury, it seems to me that these are the issues which you have to decide. You have to decide whether you're satisfied that the bruises to which the pathologists have referred really were bruises which were in existence at the time of Helen's death. If so, then you have got to ask yourselves how they came to be inflicted by whom in what circumstances, and what relevance they had to the circumstances of her death . . .

If that fall was the result of, or in association with, the commission upon Helen of some criminal act, if she had been knocked unconscious and then dropped over the balcony, then that of course would be a criminal act and your findings would be that her death was due to her being killed unlawfully.

Members of the jury, as I said to you at the beginning of this inquest, it is no part of your function, or mine, to name, or accuse, any particular person of an offence, but it is open to you to say her death was the result of being killed unlawfully if you came to that conclusion. If, on the other hand, as I've indicated, you feel that the evidence about those bruises in all circumstances is not sufficient to satisfy you, and if, on a survey of the whole of the evidence and all that witnesses have told you and what you know from all the surrounding evidence, your conclusion is that you're drawn inevitably to the possibility or likelihood that the fall was from the balcony and purely accidental, if not in the circumstances which I've described, then in something like that sort of context, then, members of the jury, you would record a verdict simply of accidental death.

Those are the two possibilities. Members of the jury, I have to put to you the third one. The third possibility, of course, is that of an open verdict – always an unsatisfactory verdict to record because it means and can mean a variety of things. It can mean that there was insufficient evidence to enable you to come to a reasonable conclusion one way or the other on the other two verdicts and inevitably it means that there remains a suspicion in your minds that in fact accident or foul play is not wholly ruled out and that suspicion remains. Members of the jury, that is the situation which would be unfortunate but, nevertheless, if it exists, it would be perfectly right and proper for you to record.

Coroner Gill turned away from the jury and immediately Stephen Sedley rose. 'I have a duty to point out one or two matters of fact,' he began.

Gill interrupted hastily. The coroners' rules made it clear that he could not raise any matters of fact in the presence of the jury. 'If you feel I have failed in any particular respect, I am sorry that you should feel that way, but I must insist on that rule,' he said.

Sir David Napley had, of course, got away with raising a matter of fact at the end of the previous day and Coroner Gill had thanked him. Sedley now tried to raise a matter of law instead – which he was entitled to do. 'It is an essential part of law that it is not open for this court to reject uncontested evidence at will,' he pointed out.

He was, of course, referring to the pathology reports of Professors Dalgaard and Usher. At no stage during the inquest had anybody contested their evidence about the head bruises. All their evidence was one way – these head bruises had been sustained during life. 'I ask you to give a proper direction not to disregard the uncontested expert evidence merely because one person does not like what that expert evidence says,' Sedley added acidly.

But Coroner Gill would not accept that it was uncontested. He referred to Dr Kheir's evidence again, which was 'just as expert as that of the other pathologists'. Dr Kheir had thought there were no injuries inconsistent with a fall.

Stephen Sedley tried to argue – Dr Kheir had found head bruises too – but Gill interrupted again. We were getting back to the facts.

The jury was sent out. It was 11.15 a.m.

Several of us from the press gallery went for a cup of coffee in the Town Hall canteen. We were shaking our heads in disbelief at those last twenty minutes of Coroner Gill's summing up and felt that the jury would be out little more than quarter of an hour. We did not hang around in the canteen, therefore.

But at one o'clock there was still no verdict and we were told we could go off for lunch. We were safe until 2.00 p.m.

The afternoon wore on and we milled around outside the courtroom doors which were guarded by two police officers. At least the press were able to do this. The public gallery was full, however, and nobody sitting there dared risk losing his or her seat by leaving the court for even a few minutes.

We ran through the case again at least a score of times among ourselves. Different angles were discussed with different small groups of journalists, the same angles were dissected and analysed *ad nauseam*. But what was the jury doing at that moment? That was the big question – and the big speculation.

If there was any consensus, it was that the more time passed, the more the jury was looking at the evidence in detail, and the less notice it was taking of Coroner Gill's last twenty minutes. He had said: 'Some things are too important to be left to the experts.' Were those words now rebounding?

At 3.45 p.m. we rushed back into the court. The jury was returning.

'I gather there is a matter on which you would like some guidance,' Coroner Gill addressed them. Ripples of anti-climax went through the court.

'If as a result of a struggle of an aggressive nature between Helen Smith and Johannes Otten, would this be an accident?' the forewoman of the jury asked.

Gill advised that the jury would have to decide whether the aggressive activity was 'consensual or against the girl's wishes'. If the former, it would be an accident; if the latter it would be unlawful killing. At 3.50 p.m. the jury retired again.

Argument raged among the press. Many felt that if the jury now returned an unlawful killing verdict, then a dead, probably innocent, man would be blamed, and this would be diabolical. Others thought that if such a verdict was returned – and it now seemed a real possibility for the first time since the early days of the inquest when the pathologists gave their evidence – then at least the campaign could go forward. Helen had been killed unlawfully. The next step would be to find out who did it.

We hung around the press gallery for a while thinking that the jury would soon resolve the point and there would be a verdict, but we began to drift outside as we realised we were wrong. 'Never underestimate a jury,' someone said and we agreed that, despite all its faults, the jury system was better than anything else around in the world. Outside the court, Ron Smith went off to take photographs and Richard Arnot lost the smile he had held since the morning.

At 5.55 p.m. the jury returned a second time. Once more it was an anti-climax as we learnt it could not reach a unanimous decision. Gill said he would accept a majority verdict provided that not more than two dissented. He asked the forewoman if that would help. 'Not at present,' she said, and smiled. Gill sent them out, saying he would give them another hour. If they had not reached a verdict by then, he would make arrangements for them to spend the night somewhere.

8–3, 7–4, or completely hung at 6–5: we did not know of course. Some of us speculated that it may be split on sex lines, with the four women saying she was beaten and raped, the seven men saying that she obviously asked for anything that came to her.

Leeds Town Hall possesses a huge central hall which holds around 1,500 people. A continuous corridor encircles the hall and on the outside of this corridor are the courts. The wait outside the old Crown Court No. 1 suddenly took on a surreal aspect as hundreds of schoolchildren in their school uniforms arrived with their teachers for a concert. They were ushered in and out of the toilets which were just by where we were standing.

A Christmas concert as the world's press amassed for the verdict of the inquest of the century – the contrast could not have been greater. Someone commented that if there was a verdict at that moment then some poor child might get crushed in the ensuing press stampede.

At 6.47 p.m., with the children safely at their concert, the jury did return. The forewoman spoke. The deceased was Helen Linda Smith and she died in Jeddah on 20 May 1979 from multiple injuries caused by a fall from a top-floor balcony at the Bakhsh hospital complex flats. The jury wished to record an open verdict because it was 'impossible to decide from the evidence available'. It was a 9–2 majority verdict.

Before closing the case, a not very happy looking Coroner Gill paid his appreciation to Peter Smalley of the West Yorkshire police for his involvement over a long period, to the Foreign Office for being the 'postmen' in this inquest, to his professional colleagues, and to the jury who had performed a 'very important public service'.

Finally he read out a letter from Matron Agnes Johnstone.

She had come to the inquest, she said, hoping to be able to speak of Helen's character but had not been able to do so because of the rules and procedures. Could this letter now be read out?

*

Helen Smith was an excellent nurse, exceedingly obedient and if from time to time she erred it was only in unimportant aspects and then only under the influence of others. She was a kind-hearted person, loyal to her colleagues, caring to her patients and a first-rate member of my staff. Despite all the complications our over-riding sentiment is sadness at her untimely death which was a grievous loss to the nursing profession.

Outside Leeds Town Hall, TV cameramen began to run round in circles, carrying or tripping over their gear in the dark as they heard whispers of the whereabouts of the various participants. In the pub opposite, a press conference room had been booked earlier in the day by Ron Smith's solicitor, but was now occupied by a bridge club. Some of the bar staff stood at the doorway of the pub and laughed at the antics of the cameramen. The sound of children singing came from the Town Hall.

8. The Unanswered Questions

> **Answer the questions**
> **Question the answers**
> **Question the unquestioned**
> **Answer the unanswered**

Was Helen Smith assaulted?

All four pathologists who examined Helen officially found injuries to her head. The three who examined her in Britain also found them to her face and genitalia. These last injuries, taken with bruising on her inner thighs, raised the possibility of rape.

Such injuries provided the main evidence for foul play. Professors Dalgaard and Usher and Dr Green agreed that the distribution of these on the face and head could not be equated with a right-side fall. Also, the major blow to the head, lesion 13, found by Professors Usher and Dalgaard (and which, in the latter's opinion, could have caused death by itself), was more to the left side.

How did Coroner Gill deal with this evidence? Basically he invited the jury to ignore it and concentrate on Dr Kheir, who had reported no facial or genital injuries. Coroner Gill told the jury that he thought it highly improbable that Dr Kheir had simply missed them. He added weight to this by pointing out that what struck such diverse people as Ron Smith, Richard Arnot, Matron Agnes Johnstone and Bakhsh hospital pathologist Joe Deguara was the lack of obvious signs of injury. Actually this was not quite true. Ron Smith noted dark marks on Helen's face, 'as if she needed a wash'.

'I hope you will not disregard the experience of Dr

Kheir,' Gill told the jury during the final twenty minutes of his summing up. He failed to add at this crucial point, however, that Dr Kheir had described twenty-three-year-old Helen as a woman in the fourth decade of her life and that he *had* noted head, if not face, injuries. Also, Dr Kheir had seen bleeding on the lining to the brain, which Professors Dalgaard and Usher later said was natural to equate with the major left-forehead injury that they found.

There was another point regarding Dr Kheir's evidence which was never properly clarified. How carefully had he thought through his findings when he told the inquest that he was satisfied the injuries were due to a fall from the balcony to the ground?

Did he actually look carefully at the injuries and come to the conclusion that if Helen fell, it was on her right side? Did the head injuries fit in with this? His report noted various left-side lesions on Helen's body, so did he consider whether these were consistent with a right-side fall? Or did he merely think that this woman had a lot of injuries consistent with a fall without really considering their distribution?

It would have been impossible for Coroner Gill to concentrate on Dr Kheir in those last twenty minutes without making some reference to the other pathologists and their evidence. This reference came in the form of suggesting they had been 'led on a wild goose chase'. The body had been subjected to various changes during the long period that had elapsed between Dr Kheir's and their examinations. The face and head injuries could be due to handling Helen in the post-mortem room. What they found were nothing more than after-death artefacts.

This theory does not stand up, however. Post-mortem changes do not have blood around them. Professors Dalgaard and Usher only counted a lesion as having been sustained during life if they could detect the presence of blood, and rejected it when in doubt. Their findings cannot be discounted so easily. Nor, as Stephen Sedley

pointed out at the end of the summing up, had these
findings been challenged during the course of the examination of any of the pathologists.

Clearly the jury did not think they could be discounted
either. Why else did it return to ask about 'a struggle of
an aggressive nature'? It was trying to reconcile injuries
that it accepted did exist with the witness evidence that
neither saw nor heard a thing.

What can be agreed is that bruises change their shape
and size in time. For example, the major head lesion 13,
Professor Usher said, could have been caused by more than
one impact. The individual bruises caused by these impacts could have merged together with the passage of time.

So although, provided there is blood present, a lesion
cannot simply be discounted as post-mortem, it is difficult
to say on a nineteen-month-old body how serious an
injury was when first sustained. The left-forehead lesion
13 was obviously serious to Professor Dalgaard because,
in his view, it had caused bleeding down the spinal
column. The face injuries, on the other hand, could have
been no more than slaps in a misguided attempt to revive
Helen.

Similarly, it was impossible to say from the genital
injuries whether or not Helen was raped. A woman can
be penetrated against her will and not be bruised at all, as
Professor Dalgaard pointed out. She could be 'gang-
banged' and suffer serious genital and thigh injuries. Professor Usher said these injuries could be due to kicks between the legs and not necessarily be sexual at all.

If they are sexual, however, they do indicate rough sex
– but the extent is unknown. One possibility is that Helen
and Johannes Otten were indeed getting it together but
that Otten's approach was perhaps rather crude. Certainly
he had drunk a lot, and perhaps, also, sex did not come
his way very often, given the laws of the land. The result
that night might well have been penetration with difficulty and premature ejaculation – unsatisfactory all round
– followed by rough 'play' with the hands by a Johannes

Otten who was rather angry with himself and who sought
to regain control of the situation. It is known that rapists
are often nearly impotent, only penetrating with difficulty
and ejaculating prematurely. The dividing line between
consent and sexual assault in the relationship between
Helen and Otten could at this point have become very
blurred.

Were Helen's injuries consistent with a seventy-foot fall?
Professors Dalgaard and Usher and Dr Green agreed that
if Helen fell anywhere it was onto her right side. The
right-side rib injuries and the outside right thigh bruise
indicated such a fall. Tearing of the right lung substance,
slight haemorrhaging from the lower part of the liver and
around the right kidney, and bruising around the spleen,
as found by Dr Kheir, added weight to this.

The damage to these internal organs also added weight to
the supposition that Helen fell from a considerable height.
The problem, however, was not the injuries she did have,
but those that she did not, as Professor Dalgaard put it.

There was no:

* Fracture of the right leg, thigh, arm or of the rim of the
  pelvis.
* Fracture of the right shoulder indicative of a fall. The
  tiny flake fracture of the right shoulder was more consistent with Helen being restrained, according to Professor Usher.
* Fracture to the skull, neck or spine.

The extensive right-rib fractures did indicate a fall onto
this side, however. But all these ribs remained in position.
A fall from a height should have spread them about like
matchsticks.

It has to be remembered that this was a woman hitting
a solid marble floor at about 45 m.p.h. In this context the
computer print-out that Dr Green produced was statistically meaningless. He examined a variety of people
wearing a variety of clothes and falling onto a variety of
surfaces. His sample was eighteen females and thirty-one

males. To produce a statistically reliable result, Dr Green would have to consider this number where all of them were wearing light clothes and fell onto a hard, unyielding surface on their right side.

There is, of course, Coroner Gill's theory that Helen might have bounced off Otten and this cushioned her fall. Generally the pathologists thought that this was not very likely with two people having different builds and weights. Their trajectories would be different.

On hearing Dr Kheir's description of the internal injuries, Professor Usher was prepared to accept that Helen may have fallen a straight forty-five to fifty feet to the ground. At the time he said this, such a distance was finding favour as the height of the Arnot balcony. It was Dr Kheir's estimate and it was only towards the end of the inquest that all parties agreed on a height of sixty-five feet – close to Ron Smith's and Dr Bakhsh's figure.

Putting on his medical hat, Richard Arnot said he had seen sudden and violent deaths where there was no obvious sign of injury – although never any involving falls from a height. Coroner Gill's final scenario did not make Helen's death so sudden, however. He pictured her trying to crawl, which explained some of Dr Kheir's abraded bruises and the position of Helen's left arm above her head.

The final possibility is that Helen did not fall at all, or that she fell only a short distance. Professor Dalgaard felt that it was possible she only fell ten feet, and Professor Usher agreed with Geoffrey Robertson when he said: 'You are not prepared to exclude the possibility that she did not fall at all.' Professor Usher also told of groin bruising that had nothing to do with the pelvic fractures and was not easily explained, and felt that the genital injuries and three of the four pelvic fractures could have resulted from kicks. Could a kick in the right ribs have produced the injuries found there?

More intriguingly, Professors Dalgaard and Usher commented that there was only a small amount of blood around the fractures that appeared to be associated with a right-side fall. Was it possible that Helen had been dropped or thrown to the ground from only a moderate height – after she had died?

The mysterious sternum fracture

The three pathologists who examined Helen in Britain all thought the fracture of her large breast bone (the sternum) occurred post-mortem. Their reasoning was simple. It showed little sign of any blood around it, so it was unlikely the fracture occurred while she was alive.

Their best explanation was that it fractured during the earlier autopsy in Saudi Arabia. Of course, they did not know Dr Kheir's evidence when they first made these pronouncements, and when he said at the inquest that it was already broken when he examined Helen, their theories had to be rethought.

The problem was not simply one of lack of blood. The concensus of these three pathologists was that if Helen had fallen anywhere, it was on her right side. How could such an impact break this very strong bone to the front of the body? A fall to the front – yes; Dr Green's computer print-out of falls from a height showed that the sternum tended to fracture when the distance was greater than forty feet. But a fall on the side?

Could a punch fracture the sternum? Stephen Sedley had asked Dr Green. He had never known it. Another theory – that Otten had been lying on top of Helen on the balcony sunlounger when this collapsed, causing Otten to land heavily on Helen – was also discounted. Breast bones are very difficult to fracture.

Coroner Gill suggested to Professor Usher that Helen might have fallen chest first onto the railings wall next to where Otten was impaled, broken her sternum and then bounced the remaining 6 feet 8 inches to the ground on her right side. But there was no other evidence on her body that she had done this, and, anyway, there was still the stumbling block of no evidence of bleeding around this fracture.

So the sternum fracture became one of the mysteries of the inquest. In his summing up, Coroner Gill referred to it as having all the appearances of being post mortem, but he did not elaborate.

Yet it deserved far more than such a passing reference. During the pathologists' evidence, Geoffrey Robertson had worked hard to explain it – and with some success. He knew that such a fracture was known to occur when desperate attempts were made to revive dead people by heart massage. Could this be the explanation?

He put it to Dr Green. 'It is a well-known complication of cardiac massage,' Green replied, but then all but dismissed it in this case. He knew it happened with old people, where the bones fracture more easily, but this was a twenty-three-year-old young woman.

Geoffrey Robertson persisted, however, and found Professor Usher far more positive. He too had known the breast bone to fracture with heavy heart massage, although, agreed, generally with older people. It would take a lot of force to break it, but you are in a 'no-lose' situation. If the person is dead, it hardly matters if you break the breast bone trying to bring him or her back to life again.

Such a vigorous massage, Geoffrey Robertson put to Professor Usher, could also explain two left-rib fractures that Helen suffered which were difficult to equate with a right-side fall. The broken right ribs were all still in their correct position, yet the two broken left ribs were out of alignment. The heart is on the left side of the body. Could not a massage account for these fractures too?

'Yes, this is a much more convincing explanation for the sternum fracture,' Professor Usher agreed readily. And for the lack of blood too, if Helen Smith was already dead at the time? 'Yes.'

Many of the party participants (doctors and harbour workers) would have been familiar with heart massage. It

is fairly basic first aid. Richard Arnot was the only one
who was actually asked at the inquest if he performed it
on Helen Smith and he denied doing so. The German
Harms Salvage guests all said they left before the deaths
were discovered, so were not asked the question. Neither
was Jacques Texier, but his appearance in the witness
box suggested that he would not have been capable of
massaging a heart forcefully anyway. Penelope Arnot and
Timothy Hayter could not be asked because they were
not at the inquest.

Was the balcony sunlounger folded or unfolded?
The sunlounger on the Arnot balcony figured promi-
nently in Coroner Gill's summing up. In his scenario,
Johannes Otten was making love with Helen when he
stood up, put his foot on it and leaned forward over the
balcony to see what was happening in the street below.
The departing Germans had managed to set every light
flashing on their company jeep. Helen was clutching him
as he overbalanced and fell, with her following.

This scenario depends on one description of the sunlounger – that given by Matron Agnes Johnstone. She
said that when she visited the balcony it was opened out
ready for use and the frame looked as though somebody
had stood on it. It was positioned directly above where
the bodies lay.

Her view was partially corroborated by Tim Hayter on
the *TV Eye* interview. He talked of a sunlounger on the
balcony that he thought had broken while Helen and
Otten were trying to make love. Obviously, this evidence
could not be questioned at the inquest.

The scenario is a neat one – at least up to the point of
Helen 'clutching' Johannes Otten – but unfortunately it
does not square up with the descriptions of the other witnesses, including that of Richard Arnot. He told the inquest that the sunlounger was unserviceable and had been
for some time. It would only be with great difficulty that
anyone could lie on it. He thought that it was stacked up

in the corner when he first looked over the balcony rail and saw the bodies.

So did Jacques Texier, and pathologist Dr Kheir, who visited the balcony later that morning, did not think it was unfolded. Interestingly, Coroner Gill mentioned Dr Kheir's sighting of the sunlounger during his Wednesday-afternoon summing up but not Dr Kheir's opinion of its position.

So Coroner Gill's scenario also depends on three descriptions of the sunlounger being wrong. Yet it is possible that these witnesses and Agnes Johnstone are all correct and telling the truth:

* At 5.30 a.m., Jacques Texier told the inquest, he went onto the balcony with Penelope Arnot and Timothy Hayter, and they saw the bodies below. The sunlounger was folded in the corner. Richard Arnot was awoken and he said that he rushed to the balcony. 'No, I did not trip over the sunlounger,' he added at one point during the only moment of light relief in his evidence. He thought it was folded in the corner, unserviceable, but did not really notice it.

* Richard Arnot went to the hospital to telephone Dr Bakhsh, the police and the British Embassy. He saw Agnes Johnstone and she went to the scene. After looking at Helen, she made her way up to the flat and onto the balcony. It was now 6.15 a.m., and the sunlounger was unfolded, ready for use and above where the bodies lay.

* Around two and a half hours later, after the police had removed the bodies, Dr Kheir arrived on the scene. He went up to the balcony and, to his recollection, the sunlounger was folded in the corner.

The clue to these conflicting accounts lies in the time difference between the sightings. The sunlounger could have been folded up at 5.30 a.m., opened out at 6.15 a.m. and folded up again by 9.00 a.m.

In other words, did someone open out that sunlounger while Richard Arnot was away from the flat making his telephone calls; and, if so, why? Did Richard Arnot say,

on returning to the flat, words to the effect that this is
ridiculous, the sunlounger is broken anyway, so there is
no point in opening it out to make it look as if Helen
and Johannes were using it? And did he or someone else
fold it up again, but after Agnes Johnstone had seen
it?

Were Otten's shorts up or down?

Otten's 'shorts' were actually his underpants. All bar one
of the witnesses who expressed a view on the subject said
that they were down around his thighs when he was seen
spiked on those railings. The exception was Dr Bakhsh,
and Richard Arnot claimed at the inquest that Bakhsh
may have been playing down the sexual aspects of the
tragedy when he said they were up in place.

Yet one person who did not see the body on the railings
also had a view. This was Dr Kheir. His argument was
simple. Those shorts, when he examined the body in the
mortuary, had holes in them which corresponded to
where Johannes Otten had been impaled – around his
groin. They also had tears in them from where Otten had
been taken off the railings. Dr Kheir's conclusion – those
shorts must have been up in position when Otten fell
onto the railings.

We can, again, apply a 'sunlounger type' analysis to
this apparent contradiction in the evidence. The shorts
may well have been in position when Otten fell onto the
railings. Someone, however, might have seen fit to lower
them shortly afterwards, and created the tears then. The
question now becomes one of motive. Why should anyone
want to expose Otten's pubic parts?

The departure of Harms Salvage

Manfred Schlaeffer said in the witness box that Klaus
Ritter, looking for Johannes at the end of the party, went
to the balcony curtain and called out, 'John, John.'

Klaus Ritter said Schlaeffer was wrong. He remembered he stood in the centre between the dining room

and the lounge and aimed his voice at the curtains in front of the balcony. He called 'John, John,' in a loud voice.

Ritter is a massive man, weighing some sixteen stone. He is tall, broad across his shoulders, broad across his back, walks upright with a large belly. Schlaeffer earns his living as a crane operator. He works now in Bahrain. Ritter is the largest man in the party, the largest man at the inquest. Largest in terms of how much space he occupies in someone's vision. Schlaeffer is the most experienced trained man at the party in using his eyes. It is his daily work.

Ritter must move around furniture to reach the balcony. He has enough alcohol inside him to warrant thirty lashes. Schlaeffer, according to his evidence, is sober. To state that Ritter moved to the balcony, he must see Ritter move. No other witnesses said Ritter went to the balcony. If Ritter is right, then Schlaeffer has made a misjudgement of some metres. If that happened on a building site, Schlaeffer operating the crane, a worker might lose an arm. If Schlaeffer is right, then why does Ritter contradict him?

All Harms witnesses said it was obvious where John and Helen had gone, obvious what they had in mind. So why does Ritter have to call?

No Germans saw Helen and Johannes go onto the balcony. No Germans asked where they had gone. No Germans asked Johannes where he was going before he disappeared with Helen. No Germans, they said, seemed bothered, because it was obvious.

Otten had been with them on the accommodation barge. He had travelled with them to the party. He had drunk with them until Helen arrived. He had taken it in turns to dance with her until they came together around midnight.

Schlaeffer said the arrangement was to take him back. Gutzeit said the group had held a brief discussion at the door, since Johannes needed a lift. Hayter said if John could not take care of himself, no one else could, 'he wasn't a baby'.

Schlaeffer said Otten had not been invited. He had been in the accommodation barge, had taken his shower, when they were ready to go, Otten came along because he was there alone and because the company 'were like that' – with a flush in his cheeks as he said it. Ritter said Otten was his friend.

Security could be tight at the harbour gates. Schlaeffer said it was 'really, really dangerous if your breath is smelling'. Ritter said walking through the gates put attention on where you had been. Both said – every witness said – Otten had drunk a considerable amount.

Geoff Robertson, before Gill stopped him, established that Schlaeffer had earlier given accounts to various media of searches made in the flat for Otten at the time they left. Schlaeffer, at the inquest, said there was no search. Ritter said there was no search, only his calling of John's name from the middle of the room. Chapuis said, in his written statement, that there was no search on the balcony. Texier said there was no search. Hayter said there *was* a search.

All agreed it was Otten's first visit to the flat. All agreed he had drunk a considerable amount. All agreed it was obvious he would be with Helen that night.

When the security was tight, and Otten was without a lift – despite the arrangement made that he should be returning with them – reeking of alcohol, how could they then leave him without a lift, having to pass through the harbour gates on foot, the taxi barred from entering the harbour, unless it was so obvious that Helen and Johannes would finish the night with each other? They had embraced, kissed, in front of them. Why bother calling out John's name at all?

They were 95 per cent certain that Helen and Johannes had disappeared, gone off somewhere together, so if they made a pretence for the last 5 per cent, just to satisfy their minds, then why did they not ask Mrs Arnot, Texier or Hayter where Johannes and Helen had gone?

According to Penelope Arnot's evidence, she knew. According to Texier's evidence, he knew. According to the Germans, no one told them. According to the Germans, no one asked.

Mrs Arnot was in the room. Klaus Ritter waved goodbye to her. Mrs Arnot had not mentioned she had twice seen Helen and Johannes on the balcony within the preceding hour, not even when Klaus stood and called out 'John, John.'

The loud crash in the early hours
When one object hits another, a sound-wave pattern is created which travels. A listener decodes this pattern as a 'bang', 'thud', 'crash'. Otten, travelling at 45 m.p.h. at impact-point, impales on the railings and buckles a lamp. The sound-wave created by this event is not heard by Hayter, Texier, Mrs Arnot or any other guest.

The scientific evidence is unassailable. There had to be a bang. Only Mrs Keith from the flat below heard any bang. Mrs Arnot makes no mention of a bang. Hayter said his attention was concentrated on other matters. Texier said he heard no noise. If Mrs Keith's bang is Otten's impact, then the sound-wave can travel five floors but not six?

Otten's watch stopped at 3.10 a.m. Ritter and Schlaeffer stated they reached the company jeep, parked twenty metres away from the main entrance, at 3.15 a.m. This was the time on the jeep's electric clock. All witnesses stated the lift was not working.

Departing guests had to descend a 'spiralling staircase' from the sixth floor to the ground floor. Ritter, on his evidence, had drunk. Chapuis had drunk and had just awoken, as had Gutzeit. Schlaeffer had barely drunk. Ritter is a big, voluble man and takes his time over most things, judging by his movements outside Leeds Town Hall after he had given evidence.

Texier said the Germans were 'stoned'. In their condition, from Arnot's door to the company jeep will take some minutes. They heard no screams, no bang either inside the building or outside. They saw no body, even though the body landed a few yards away from the main entrance. Chapuis stated that if the body had been there, they must have seen it, since the street was well-lit.

If the Germans are right, if Mrs Arnot is right, if the watch at 3.10 signifies the moment of Otten's death, then the Germans are in the building or coming out, and Mrs Arnot with Texier and Hayter are just noticing that Helen and Johannes are not there and discussing their whereabouts. Hayter, Texier, Mrs Arnot hear nothing.

If we accept Texier's evidence, then Mrs Arnot is wrong. There is no conversation, he has just bedded down. He heard no bang, no scream. He thought it was likely he would have heard if he had been awake – he was next to the balcony windows.

The inquest evidence is one-way. No one at the party heard anything. No screams, no bang. Arnot did not hear the air conditioner when he fell asleep. Jeddah is a noisy city; immersion in a foreign city attacks the senses.

No one, and it is baffling evidence, remembers which music played. Arnot could not even remember the music, and it is his family's tape-deck, his family's music. No one remembers an angry voice. No one remembers a raised voice. Eight bottles drunk: no shouts. A tape-deck plays seven hours: no memory of a tune.

This raises the first question:

* Has the memory of the music been subconsciously obliterated, since music records events as they are stored in memory, and if a tune is remembered, the event around the tune will also be remembered?

A bang on impact had to happen. Mrs Keith heard a bang. She estimated it at 3.40 a.m. Questions which follow are then:

1. If 3.40, then why has Otten's watch stopped at 3.10?
2. If 3.40, who is about in the flat above, the Arnots' flat?
3. If 3.40, why do they not hear anything?

Mrs Keith was nursing her son James, restless with a tonsillitis attack. Mrs Keith was dozing. She may estimate the time wrongly. On the other hand, she is a doctor's wife, part of the hospital *milieu*, a *milieu* which functions on time accuracy. If her estimation is wrong then:

1. If before 3.40, why did those above not hear it?
2. If closer to 3.10 than 3.40, why did those above and the Germans not hear it?
3. If between 3.40 and 5.30, when the bodies were discovered, why did Mrs Arnot not hear it, as she is awake, drinking coffee and using her ears listening to music?

These questions are based on that assumption that the bang is the impact of Otten. If it is not, what is it?

The discovery of the bodies
Michael Weston of the British Embassy told the inquest that Mrs Arnot, either at the meeting in the Saudi lawyer's office in November 1979 or at a later time, said she had been sleeping with Hayter when a guest awoke her and informed her that two bodies were lying below, and that this was the first she had heard of it.

Richard Arnot, giving evidence at the inquest, said his wife had discovered the bodies. He said that at some point Mrs Arnot had said to him that Helen had looked 'as if she was asleep'. Texier confirmed that Mrs Arnot had first seen the bodies.

Tim Hayter, to the television cameras, said they had gone out onto the balcony – himself, Mrs Arnot and Texier – and Texier had discovered the bodies.

Jacques Texier said they had taken their coffees out onto the balcony. Mrs Arnot had suddenly said, 'Oh my God,' and indicated the bodies below. He denied Hayter's suggestion that he had seen the bodies first. Hayter, said Texier, had been leaning against the building wall and came forward to the balustrade when he heard Mrs Arnot's cry.

Texier said all three after the discovery went back into

the flat. Mrs Arnot went into the bedroom to wake her husband. (Hayter said he told Mrs Arnot to fetch her husband.) Richard Arnot appeared in the room with a towel around him. He talked to Mrs Arnot, returned to the bedroom, came out again dressed. The immediate activity, according to Texier, was removal of the alcohol. Texier departed.

Richard Arnot told the inquest that he was asleep. He was awoken by Mrs Arnot. Behind her were Texier and Hayter. She told him she thought Helen had fallen off the balcony. He leapt out of bed, grabbed a towel or 'some garment', ran through to the balcony, saw the bodies, ran back. He dressed hurriedly, 'a day without socks', ran down the stairs, examined first Helen, recorded the time, examined Otten, did not look at Otten's watch, returned to the flat. He told the two men and his wife the bodies were of Helen and Johannes and both were dead.

Texier denied going into the bedroom. He remained in the kitchen and living-room area. He denied that Richard Arnot went out onto the balcony. He was emphatic that he was the first man out of the flat. The most he would concede was that Arnot had a few minutes out of his sight. Texier stood firm that these few minutes were only that time taken for Arnot to dress. Texier was emphatic he was the first man out. Hayter also said Texier was first out of the flat.

Hayter confirmed Texier to a large degree. He said no one went down. He indicated it was pointless. 'No way in the world could they have survived [the fall],' he said of Helen and Johannes.

Both Arnot and Texier were in agreement that neither could comment on the activities of Mrs Arnot and Hayter when both men slept. Texier could infer that they had been making love before he heard the sound of their orgasm. Texier had no knowledge of what they had been doing before they started making love. Arnot had slept from 2 a.m. until 5.30 a.m.

Both Texier and Arnot agree on the towel. Arnot came

into the room wearing a towel, according to Texier. Arnot, according to his own evidence, went out onto the balcony with a towel around him.

The only areas of agreement between Texier, Arnot and Hayter, cover those events before the bodies were discovered and those events after the bodies were discovered.

Texier and Arnot agree on Arnot going to bed and getting up. Texier and Hayter agree on the adultery and Texier being first out of the flat. Hayter and Arnot only agree on getting rid of the alcohol.

If it was an accident, why such contradictory evidence? Why does Texier deny going into the bedroom; Hayter not mention it; Arnot state it? Why do both Hayter and Texier state that no one left the flat before Texier; Arnot state he went down?

If an accident, why did Hayter not run straight down to the bodies? Helen was his friend; Mrs Arnot had said, 'She looked as if she was asleep.' Why is the assumption automatic that death had happened; that they had fallen from the balcony; that immediate action is alcohol removal, an action based on no certainty of death? Why is Arnot pinpointed as the man to examine the bodies when Hayter could have run down?

If it was an accident, why does Mrs Arnot walk over to the balcony balustrade? She is with Hayter. Hayter is leaning against the building wall. She has just made love with him. All the evidence states they were on the balcony to look at the morning. She can look at the morning without peering over a balustrade which only reaches up to her thighs, which is surrounded by slippery tiles. She cannot lean on the balcony. She cannot place her elbows on it and sip her coffee.

Gill asked Arnot if Arnot had to stretch over the balcony to see the bodies. Arnot replied he did not have to stretch over, he looked down, 'Placed both hands on the balcony.' How does Mrs Arnot place both hands on the balcony holding a coffee cup?

If an accident, where does Arnot grab his towel from – bedroom or bathroom? If he acts spontaneously, why does he not spring out naked? Why does he not reach out for underpants, trousers?

If it was an accident, why is there no one babbling alongside him? Why is he not accompanied? Why is no one compelled to explain what they had seen, seek mutual reassurance? Why is he alone when he runs down?

If an accident, why does he not look at the face of Otten's watch? Because of the position of Otten's body, his arms hanging down draping his head, Arnot cannot see the ants in that puddle of blood beneath the Dutchman's head without noticing Otten's arms hanging and the stainless-steel strap of Otten's wristwatch. One minute earlier he had looked at his own watch to establish his recording of Helen's death – 'Standard medical practice,' he said. Next minute, on his own evidence, he notices Otten has a watch. He does not look at the time?

This raises a suspicion. Could Arnot tell the jury what time Otten's watch showed if there was any possibility that Texier would come along and deny he went down to the bodies? The jury, on the contradictions between the evidence of Texier and Arnot, would wonder how he knew the time on the watch. Because Texier *did* come after Arnot had given his evidence – and contradicted him – there is no way he can remove that suspicion.

Certain points can be raised:

1. Who can prove Richard Arnot was asleep at 5.30 a.m.? Both Mrs Arnot and Hayter can support Texier in that he was asleep. Under serious interrogation, if these two deny Texier's claim that he was sleeping, he in turn can claim he believed Hayter went to sleep in the armchair, and, further, claim he awoke to their orgasm. Harms Salvage employees can claim they saw Hayter and Mrs Arnot together on the two preceding days. All witnesses can state Arnot went to bed at 2 a.m. Neither Mrs Arnot nor

Hayter can refute Texier's orgasm evidence without stating what they were doing between 3 and 5 a.m.
2. In the Saudi jail, who is that person who can give the best account for the other three? Arnot retired at 2 a.m. He cannot give an account for Texier, Hayter or Mrs Arnot.

Mrs Arnot and Hayter can state Arnot went to bed at 2 a.m. and be supported by Texier. They can state, and be supported by Texier, that Texier bedded down on the sofa.

Mrs Arnot cannot be supported by either Arnot or Texier that she was awake or asleep. Nor can Hayter.

Texier can state Arnot went to bed, Arnot woke up. He can state Hayter bedded down; he cannot state if he slept. He can state Mrs Arnot went to bed; he cannot state if she slept. If pressed, he can state he awoke to the sound of their orgasm, which puts the onus back onto Hayter and Mrs Arnot and incriminates himself.
3. Arnot can state the other three came into his bedroom at 5.30 a.m. This raises an immediate series of questions – what were they doing before then? Mrs Arnot and Hayter can incriminate themselves again. Texier can flatly deny Arnot. If Hayter and Mrs Arnot attempt to support Arnot and contradict Texier, they open themselves to further questions.
4. If both Texier and Arnot are seriously interrogated, Arnot has two fallback positions. Should Texier flatly deny he went into Arnot's bedroom, Arnot can claim his memory slipped. Should Texier deny that Arnot went down to examine the bodies, Arnot can admit that he hid, saying he did so originally to protect his reputation. At each level of interrogation, whenever Texier is asked as a medical man how he knew Arnot was asleep, Texier can reply, 'Arnot came into the room with a towel around him.' Arnot had just been awoken.

Why was Johannes Otten's passport in the road?
Otten was found on the railings with no trousers. Arnot said he found Otten's passport fifteen yards away and

placed it beneath Otten's legs. Kirby arrived later and found a pile of documents $1\frac{1}{2}$ inches thick beneath Otten's legs.

Arnot mentioned only a passport. From 6 a.m. until Kirby's arrival at 6.45 a.m. there had been any number of people who could have accumulated the other documents – doctors, nurses, porters, onlookers, passers-by, policemen.

Ritter said Otten carried his wallet in his back pocket. Each witness stated Otten carried no bag. Each witness stated he wore a white shirt, blue jeans, sandals. Witnesses stated they kept their own papers in their wallets. Otten was fully clothed when last seen alive; he had merely taken off his sandals to dance.

Because Otten carried his wallet in his trousers, and because both trousers and wallet had disappeared, Arnot offered the hypothesis that a thief had been responsible. The theory struck a response in Gill.

Arnot's theory was that the thief removed the trousers, removed the wallet for the money and dropped the documents. Arnot said Otten carried a lot of money. No other witnesses advanced this. Otten, witnesses said, was a hard drinker. How much Otten was carrying that night, how much drink he was expecting to pay for, is not known. Nor was it known when the company left the harbour, who was expected to pay for the drinks.

Otten could not make money without documents. Saudi law required him to carry a passport, residence permit, work permit, harbour pass. Without a passport – no residence. Without residence – no work permit.

Each witness, each person who attended that party, carried papers. Each needed papers to make an income. Each lived in Saudi Arabia to make an income. Each knew these conditions were exactly the same for each other.

Arnot employed an Ethiopian maid. She was an illegal immigrant. She had no documents. Dr Keith told the inquest the hospital employed illegal immigrants to guard the living quarters. He described their cardboard shanty-

Disappearance before death requires the event of the party to be seen as an event existing before death, with no conjecture of death, and then it requires the evidence to substantiate it. The evidence stated that Helen and Johannes were together, embracing, kissing, dancing. The question then is – how do the others react?

Switch the emphasis from after-death knowledge to pre-death possibility; switch the emphasis from Helen and Johannes to how the others interacted with Helen and Johannes; switch the emphasis from Otten's death to Otten's appearance alive next morning. Every European port knows the practical joke played on the seaman who ends up without his trousers, his papers, his wallet, his money, his ship.

Did Otten's behaviour that night warrant that jape?

The evidence stated he was not a company man. The company took him along, he happened to be around. He received free meals, free showers, free newspapers on the company accommodation barge.

The evidence stated it was a farewell party. Stated it was dull, boring. The evidence stated two women were present. Each man lived without his family, lived with other men, worked together. It stated alcohol was consumed. It stated two women danced with everyone at first. It stated one woman then danced with only one man. It stated this man had been in the company accommodation, was taken along by the company, had no invitation to the party, just happened to be there. It stated he danced, kissed, embraced. It stated there was only one other woman there.

It stated the company men sat together. It stated Helen and Johannes danced alone. It stated they danced in a 'close way'. She did not dance with anyone else after Otten. It stated it was dull, boring. It stated Germans spoke German, English spoke English. It stated Hayter would be flying off next day. It stated each man would go to work next morning.

It stated a one-way ticket to sex. It stated that each man would go back to his bed alone.

It stated Otten knew how to look after himself. Stated he was not a baby. Stated he was a big man. Stated he was a sea captain. Stated it was a dull party. Stated people became merry.

Was a jape played on Johannes Otten that night?

Tim Hayter, 6.30 a.m. to 8.30 a.m., 20 May 1979
According to the inquest evidence of both Tim Hayter and Richard Arnot, Hayter left the Arnot apartment at 6.30 a.m. with the intent of telling the others, getting them together.

Fleischer said Hayter woke him at 6.30 a.m. and sent him off immediately to fetch Harms Salvage manager Harry Gutzeit. Fleischer was not given time to wash or go to the lavatory. He was told there had been an accident.

Klaus Ritter told the inquest he had just woken. Hayter barged in, told him there had been an accident, told him to tell the others. Ritter said it was around 6.30 a.m.

Manfred Schlaeffer told the inquest a message was rung across to him either by Hayter or Fleischer at 6.30 a.m. He was sleeping on the floating crane. He thought the message of an accident was a bad joke until Hayter rang him at 7.30 a.m.

Harry Gutzeit, who was sleeping in his flat in the city, told the inquest that Hayter did not contact him.

According to Fleischer, he misunderstood Hayter and returned to the Arnots' building, then went back to the harbour with the police two hours later. According to Schlaeffer, Fleischer wanted to see the bodies.

According to Harry Gutzeit, he arrived at the harbour to find the company, the police, waiting for him. He arrived there knowing nothing of what had happened.

According to Hayter, Texier was kept separate from the others inside the prison, and received different treatment. The reason, Hayter implied, was that Texier had people pulling strings for him. He was a good friend of the French cultural attaché. As Hayter said, 'We had people behind us as well.'

From this, questions follow:

1. Why did Hayter send Fleischer to Harry when Harry lived in the city, the Arnots' flat was in the city, Hayter was in the city, and Hayter could have driven around to him before he went to the harbour?

2. According to Fleischer, Hayter was angry that the German came back with the police, though he did not express it in words. If Hayter expected Fleischer to return with Harry Gutzeit, and he expected that there would only elapse the time necessary for Fleischer to drive to Harry's and return with Harry, then why did he not fetch Harry himself?

3. Why did not Hayter consider it urgent to see Harry first, explain what had happened, discuss a strategy, get Harry, as the Jeddah manager, to exert influence on the Saudi port authorities and contact the parent company in Hamburg, thereby pulling in the West German government, since, as Hayter stated, 'we were in deep trouble'? Why, as a consequence of not taking this action, did he allow the Germans to be unprepared in terms of Hamburg and Bonn taking both an immediate interest and immediate action?

4. Harry Gutzeit was the manager. Hayter was the head diver. Why did Hayter choose Fleischer to fetch Harry Gutzeit? Fleischer had been in Jeddah only three weeks. He was a student doing a year out. He was not versed in company affairs, work practices. He was young. Harry did not know him as well as he knew Ritter, Chapuis and Schlaeffer.

5. Was Hayter's choice of Fleischer unconnected with Fleischer leaving the party half an hour before the main group? That group who departed together comprised Ritter, Chapuis, Schlaeffer and Gutzeit. Ritter and Chapuis slept in the accommodation barge. Schlaeffer slept on the floating crane. Gutzeit slept in his city flat.

6. Why, if Hayter had to inform the men, did he not get someone to get Schlaeffer from the floating crane and bring him back to the accommodation barge?

7. Why, when the stated intent was to inform the others and get them together, did Hayter send Fleischer away to get Harry Gutzeit, did not summon from the floating crane the sleeping Schlaeffer, and got Ritter to tell the others?

8. When they are in 'deep trouble', and he had the means to get them all together, then why did Hayter choose a series of actions which apparently gave him some minutes alone on the accommodation barge?

9. What did he do in the accommodation barge from 6.30 a.m., when he saw Ritter, until 8.30, when the police arrived? There is no evidence at the inquest to indicate his activities in those two hours.

10. Unless there is something at the harbour which attracts him, then his choice to go there appears irrational. His course of action, once he gets there, appears completely rational if the intent is to give some minutes alone. What does he do then – look for trousers? Think of ways and means of leaving the country?

The differing accounts given by Penelope Arnot
Penelope Arnot told her husband she had seen Helen and Johannes go through the balcony doors onto the balcony. He told this to the police. She told Kirby of the British Embassy that Helen and Johannes had been on their way for sex and had gone out onto the balcony. She repeated this in her statement to the West Yorkshire police on 27 August 1980.

* She did not tell anyone at the party, either before the guests left or while they were leaving – Ritter, according to his evidence, calling out, 'John, John' – that she had seen the pair go out.
* No other person in the party rooms, apart from Texier, had seen Helen and Johannes go out.

The questions are:

Why did no one else see the pair go out?
Why did she tell no one they had gone out?

In the statement to the West Yorkshire police she said, 'I pulled open the curtains and looked quickly out. I saw them silhouetted against the glow of the night lights of Jeddah. They were standing together and not moving.'

Why did she allow them to stay out there when she knew the balcony was dangerous?

Why does she not go out and tell them to be less visible because the flat is filled with people in various stages of sobriety and bottles of alcohol are present?

In her statement to the West Yorkshire police she said that after the Germans had departed, she realised she had not seen Helen and Johannes go with them. She discussed this with the remaining guests, Texier and Hayter, checked the balconies for Johannes and Helen, could not find them, and the three decided that they had slipped through the balcony's side door and quietly gone over to Helen's flat.

1. Texier denied this conversation had taken place. He said he and Hayter bedded down after the Germans left.
2. Hayter made no mention of this conversation.
3. Arnot, giving inquest evidence, made no mention of this conversation taking place as a repeated conversation between himself, Hayter and Mrs Arnot immediately after the bodies were found.

Did this conversation take place?
If it had happened, and the accident had happened, would it not have come up in discussion immediately in the aftermath of the discovery of the bodies?

The brief encounter of Tim Hayter and Penelope Arnot
Penelope Arnot and Tim Hayter gave the following accounts of their encounter in the Arnot flat between the

departure of the Germans at 3 a.m. and the discovery of the bodies at 5.30 a.m.

She told Gordon Kirby, Vice-Consul at the British Embassy, at 7 a.m. that morning of 20 May, that she had spent the period between three and five drinking coffee, listening to music and cleaning up the debris from the party.

Ten days later, after intensive interrogation, she confessed to the Saudi authorities that she had sex with Timothy Hayter in another room in the flat.

In November 1979, almost six months later, at a meeting arranged to ascertain whether the Saudi government would punish their adultery with the full rigour of the law, capital punishment, she told those present – Geere and Weston from the Embassy, Richard Arnot, Hayter and the Saudi lawyer – that she and Hayter had left the room with the intention of commiting adultery in another room and that as far as she was aware, Helen was still alive. Hayter, according to Weston, 'did not deny this'.

In February 1980, three months later, before a Saudi court, she and Hayter retracted their confession of adultery.

In August 1980, Penelope Arnot repeated her denial of the adultery to both the West Yorkshire police in an interview which was not released before the inquest, and in a series of newspaper articles.

In 1980, Hayter went to the British Embassy requiring a new passport, intending to leave Saudi Arabia (New Zealand nationals in Saudi Arabia are looked after by the British Embassy). He had a 'lighthearted' conversation with Kirby. Kirby repeated the conversation to the inquest. Hayter had said that he and another man had stripped down to their underpants and bedded down on sofas. Mrs Arnot, who was interested in sex, woke him, and they had sex together in the same room as the other man. Kirby recorded this but the record could not be produced at the inquest. It was still in the Embassy at Jeddah.

During the inquest, this version was confirmed by

Richard Arnot, Hayter and Texier. Arnot said that his wife had denied the adultery to the British police and public both because she was ashamed of it and because it had become the focal point of the whole case.

He said to the inquest that the adultery was not an alibi for murder.

The word alibi in this instance is very much a misnomer. An alibi presents a suspect in another location. It is quite the reverse in this case. In any normal police inquiry these two were the principal witnesses present in the flat when two people disappeared, who each gave different accounts at different times to different people of their movements at the time in question.

Arnot said at the inquest that he believed the brief encounter did take place and said that the pair were naive and did not expect to be treated with the full rigour of the law.

This begs the question, though. If they were so naive that they did not know Saudi law, and when they had a choice between the 'other room' story and the 'same room' story – the latter confirmed by both Hayter and Texier, though not by Mrs Arnot herself – then why say they were in another room, since in terms of possible punishment for the illegal act, the location has no importance?

If they did know the law, and they chose the 'other room' story for their confession instead of the 'same room' story, then why make the confession of adultery, punishable by death, and *still* keep hidden the exact location?

1. Did the brief encounter take place?
2. Was it the necessary means used to divert attention away from questions regarding the disappearance of Helen and Johannes?
3. If it was, then why was it necessary to divert attention away?
4. Was it the device used to divert British public attention away from the deaths?

The bootleg whisky

Dr Alan Kirwen told the inquest that Arnot phoned him on Saturday 19 May and said he had 'some people coming around', and could Kirwen supply a case of Johnny Walker?

'When did you take it around?' Coroner Gill asked Kirwen.

'Lunchtime,' Kirwen replied.

Arnot remembered it differently. He said he entered the flat at 9.45 p.m. with Helen and a bucket of ice. 'Yes, I'm pretty sure Alan came in next with the booze,' he said. 'I had the ice.'

Arnot remembered he had only a half bottle of whisky and two bottles of wine before Kirwen arrived. Ritter and Schlaeffer said drinks were available when they arrived at 8 p.m. Fleischer said drinks were available when he arrived at 8.45 p.m. Hayter said a case was a fair amount for eight or nine people. Hayter also said there was sadikki, gin and vodka present. Other witnesses denied this.

Kirwen was asked if he was ever paid. 'I don't think I was,' he replied. Twelve bottles at £25 each – £300 in all. Kirwen did not add anything to his answer.

Arnot referred to Kirwen coming in with the drink, Hayter pulling out a roll of money to pay, and Mrs Arnot interjecting, saying, 'Don't worry, we'll pay.' Arnot then repeated twice within the next half hour this exchange betweeen Mrs Arnot and Hayter.

Kirwen said, 'Only Arnot knew I supplied the alcohol.' Fleischer is asked, 'Do you know Alan Kirwen?' He replied, 'No.' He wrote the guest list out together with Arnot and gave it to the police.

Kirwen gave evidence after Fleischer. Schlaeffer and Ritter sat in the witness box when Kirwen gave evidence. Both, when asked who had attended the party, referred to the 'gentleman' they had seen in the witness box. Neither knew his name but both remembered he had been at the party.

Dieter Chapuis in his written statement said that Mrs Arnot maintained the drinks supply. One or two bottles were always on the table. Ritter, Schlaeffer, Fleischer and Arnot all said the same. Kirwen stated he supplied a case of twelve bottles. The only inference possible is that the case was kept elsewhere, and that when bottles were empty, Mrs Arnot replaced them with full bottles from Kirwen's supply.

Kirwen lived 'a fifteen-minute drive away'. Jeddah roads were, according to witnesses, 'pot-holed'. The penalties for supply were 'two years in prison and two hundred lashes'. Gill asked Kirwen, 'What steps did you take to protect your position?' Kirwen received his supply from O'Brien, 'a larger supplier'. Arnot said that generally the police did not raid private houses. Alcohol is tolerated if consumption is discreet. Arnot 'drew the curtains'.

Kirwen 'had a flat in a private villa owned by Lockheeds'. On Arnot's evidence, Kirwen drives fifteen minutes over pot-holed roads, parks the car, crosses the pavement, walks up six flights of a spiralling staircase. He is not spotted by anyone. He enters a flat at 10 p.m., not knowing who will be there, and either leaves his bag in the hall or carries it into the main room, asking Mrs Arnot where he should deposit the whisky.

A conversation then takes place, Kirwen present or nearby, in which Hayter offers to pay, pulls out a roll, Mrs Arnot interjects, Arnot witnesses. The other guests, some of whom have spent almost two hours drinking half a bottle of whisky, do not connect Kirwen's arrival with the sudden presence of full bottles on the table. Kirwen was asked, 'Did the Saudi police inquire after you?' He replied, 'No.'

Kirwen agreed that he knew Hayter. Agreed that neither Arnot nor Hayter named him as the supplier when they were detained in jail. Penelope Arnot was detained in the women's prison. Hayter said of her, 'For her I feel sorry. She had it the worst.' Arnot said the police hammered her continuously, 'We know you're hiding something. What is it?'

She was, Arnot said, 'physically in a very bad shape'. Her 'anti-depressant medicine had been denied her'. According to Kirby's minute, she told him one hour after the bodies were found that Kirwen had attended the party, Kirwen supplied the booze. There is no evidence she told this to the police.

Kirwen heard of the deaths '48 hours later'. The Embassy contacted him two days after this, four days in all after the deaths. Kirwen stated he always kept a supply of drink in case people wanted a bottle or two. He is asked, 'You had American contacts?' and replies, 'Yes, it was difficult for the British community to obtain alcohol.' He played squash and went to parties at the Embassy.

After ten days of 'intensive interrogation', according to Hayter, Mrs Arnot made a confession of adultery. Hayter said the police did their job. They could not get her on murder; they got her on adultery.

The Embassy told the inquest that they could not interfere with the Saudi police investigation. Arnot said he omitted Kirwen's name from the list of party guests for 'obvious reasons'.

Kirwen is asked, 'Did you go round to O'Brien's house at 3 a.m. and tell him all hell had broken loose at the Arnots' flat?' Kirwen denies this.

O'Brien is the larger supplier. O'Brien and Kirwen were both employees of Lockheeds, suppliers of Saudi defence requirements. Arnot makes no mention of ringing Kirwen the morning of the deaths. He rang Dr Bakhsh, the police, perhaps the Embassy.

Penny Arnot gave the Embassy the name of Kirwen. Arnot did not give the police the name of Kirwen. He received an assurance from Bakhsh that prosecutions would not follow and decided 'to be frank with the police'. He told the authorities the bottles for the party were supplied 'by a grateful patient'.

Certain explicit questions can be asked. These questions concern the party and concern the consequences of two deaths and alcohol in a society where alcohol is an illegal drug:

1. That contradiction between Arnot and Kirwen as to when the alcohol arrived is vital. If it arrived at lunch time, guests could drink from 8 p.m. Helen arrived at 9.45 p.m., almost certainly sober. Evidence stated she was in Otten's arms at 12.30.

If Kirwen is correct in the time, what is the sobriety of the guests when Helen arrived? Their sobriety at midnight? How did she perceive them? How did they perceive her? How did she interact with them? What is the position of Otten, a Dutchman, in a party where Germans speak German, English speak English? Otten was also not a Harms Salvage employee? Was Helen driven into Otten's arms? Did he offer protection?

2. If Arnot is correct, can Kirwen arrive at 10 p.m., carrying the bottles, and not be identified as the supplier? If a 10 p.m. arrival is correct, what sort of party was it between 8 p.m. and 10 p.m.? How was Helen's arrival, almost coinciding with the whisky arrival, perceived? What did the party become?

3. Arnot said eight bottles were drunk. These must be drunk between 10 p.m. and 3 a.m. Three guests – Schlaeffer, who said he was sober, Mrs Arnot and Texier, apparently drank small quantities. Arnot said two guests, Kirwen and Peter Schmidt, 'the German national', had left by 12.30. Arnot arrived at 9.45 p.m., was absent from 11.30 to 12.30 at the hospital, returned and remained at the party from 12.30 until 2 a.m. He drank, he stated, no more than five glasses. By 1 a.m. both Gutzeit and Chapuis were asleep.

This leaves Ritter, Hayter and Fleischer as the only guests who drank, stayed awake, did not disappear and were present from 10 p.m. until 2.30 a.m.

Fleischer left at 2.30. He was sober enough to drive home. Ritter, who eventually received a repealed sentence of thirty lashes for alcohol, drove the company car back to the harbour, the sober Schlaeffer alongside in the passenger seat.

Hayter said sadikki, gin and vodka were present. Could he, on his last night in Jeddah, have a farewell party without sadikki, 'my old friend', present?

On the evidence, Helen and Johannes must have consumed large quantities. How was this done? On the evidence, far more explicitly on a 10 p.m. scenario, the pair dance and kiss continuously, are always embracing, dance slowly with their arms around each other, drink considerable quantities. Do they dance holding bottles and glasses in their hands, behind each other's back, break away, take a long swallow? Do they sit on the sofa, embrace, kiss, break off, drink a long glass, kiss, embrace again?

4. What is demanded from Hayter on all the evidence? He must drink so much that Ritter and Fleischer can stand up and drive home. He must drink so much that Helen and Johannes can walk onto the balcony and not collapse inside the flat. Simultaneously, he must be so sober, coherent, attractive, pleasant smelling, that shortly afterwards he can kiss and embrace Mrs Arnot and make love to her.

5. What does all the inquest evidence demand from Mrs Arnot? She is required to be so sober that she can ensure full bottles are kept on the table and she can tidy up, but so bemused she fails to see the belongings of Helen and Johannes when tidying. She can see the same man on Thursday, Friday, Saturday, and offer, without her husband's pre-arranged consent, £300 from the family kitty for his party and then be filled with such sudden desire for this man that she wakes him, kisses him, initiates a brief encounter and months later is thoroughly ashamed of it.

6. When Arnot can remember such detail as 'ants in a puddle of blood' and springs on a 'sunlounger periphery', can he forget when the alcohol arrived? Likewise, Alan

Kirwen can be so worried that he abruptly leaves the
country, but can he forget when he delivered the alcohol,
that act which was responsible for his departure?

7. Immediately the bodies were discovered, Arnot had to
remember when the alcohol was delivered to ensure he
knew what he *should not* say to the police. Kirwen, as
soon as he heard of the deaths, had to remember his
movements to remember, if he was picked up, what he
should or should not say to the police. How can one of
the two forget three and a half years later?

8. Hayter said, 'We were in deep trouble.' At 6 a.m., the
bodies discovered, the alcohol being removed, how could
Arnot and Hayter be certain another guest would not
identify Kirwen as the supplier? On the evidence presented by Kirwen, Arnot and Hayter, neither Arnot nor
Hayter warned Kirwen.

9. Kirwen faced two years in prison and two hundred
lashes as supplier of the alcohol. Kirwen, according to
Arnot, could perhaps remember Arnot's telephone call,
perhaps remember Mrs Arnot's offer to pay, perhaps
remember, unless he did not talk to anyone, that it was
Hayter's farewell party, perhaps remember that Hayter
pulled out a roll of money. All damaging memories if the
police discover that the grateful patient as the supplier is
a lie and pull in Kirwen, and Kirwen talks. Arnot and
Hayter in the flat; two dead bodies outside. Despite this,
neither contacts him. How can Arnot and Hayter be certain that Kirwen will not talk if identified and arrested?

10. Can they remove the alcohol and not discuss the supplier? Can Hayter, especially, be certain that the police
will swallow the 'grateful patient' lie? Can they be certain
the police will not separate the prisoners, apply pressure,
get someone talking, get Arnot and Hayter identified as
remaining in the flat, get Hayter identified as the man
who flashed money, who had a farewell party?

11. Both men are at the centre of alcohol and two deaths.
Arnot can claim sleep. He cannot, if pressure is applied,
state what Hayter did while he himself slept. Texier can

claim sleep. He cannot state what Hayter did while he himself slept. If pressure is applied on Hayter, he can only offer two stories – he slept, or some account of what happened. Mrs Arnot, in another jail, can only offer sleep or some account of what happened.

Both Texier and Arnot can claim sleep. The police can dispute this on the evidence of the Germans in the case of Texier. Texier can support Arnot in that Arnot went to bed at 2 a.m. The Germans can support this. Texier can be implicated in the deaths. He can only be implicated on the question of alcohol if the Arnots, Hayter and the arrested Kirwen lie. Can Hayter accept this forseeable situation with such equanimity that he does not warn Kirwen?

12. Ritter, Schlaeffer Gutzeit and Chapuis can support each other that they departed together, that Arnot was in bed, that Texier, Mrs Arnot and Hayter were awake and in the flat when they departed. Any guest might implicate Hayter and the Arnots on the question of alcohol. How can Hayter make certain the guests accept Arnot's lie without indicating to them the truth? How can he make certain no guest remembers Kirwen without identifying, to a degree, Kirwen?

13. Kirwen supplied the British community with alcohol. British expatriates worked in the hospital. The community is small. Expatriates mix with each other. Some expatriates may be at risk if Kirwen is arrested and talks. How can that community grapevine break down to such an extent that Kirwen is not told of the deaths until 48 hours later?

14. The Embassy knew Kirwen as an Embassy party guest and squash player. One hour after the deaths, they knew he supplied the alcohol. Evidence stated that Saudi jails are hell on hearth. Evidence stated that the Embassy agreed with Kirwen's suggestion that he should leave the country immediately. Why does it take them four days to contact him?

15. Kirwen brings forward his leave, departs. This coin-

cides, in time, with inquest evidence that police questioning toughened. Ron Smith was in Jeddah asking questions, becoming suspicious, talking to the police. Hayter, as a consequence, considered having Ron knee-capped. Was Kirwen's departure at this point coincidental?

16. Inquest evidence stated that Mrs Arnot was kept in a separate jail. Arnot described her bad physical shape, the denial of anti-depressant medicine. He stated that the police hammered her – 'We know you're hiding something.'

On the inquest evidence, Mrs Arnot always had two pieces of criminal information – events of the night and Alan Kirwen. The inference from Arnot's evidence is that her bad physical shape is in some way connected with denial of her medicine. Kirwen's gratefully accepted name and identification as supplier of the drink might have ensured medicine, create a diversion from what happened that night in relation to adultery or death, give her a breathing space. How does she keep herself so together that she can admit adultery and not mention Kirwen?

17. Witnesses state they are first placed in the police-station yard. Mrs Arnot is present in the yard until 4 a.m. the next morning. From inquest evidence there are four possibilities for Mrs Arnot not naming Kirwen.

He is a friend, and she does not wish to implicate him. She was in such a bad state she forgot his existence. The police only demanded a confession of adultery. Her husband had told the authorities the supplier was a grateful patient. On this final reason, if she delivers his name, it contradicts Arnot, and who, and what, is then caught on this contradiction?

18. Is it another coincidence that she confesses to adultery after Kirwen had departed? How does she know Kirwen had left Jeddah? According to the inquest evidence, only Arnot and the Embassy visited her.

19. Alcohol and two deaths together present one conclusion. Keep alcohol separate from the deaths, and there are no conclusions. The conclusion, when the two are viewed together, is a conclusion of who has the power in an extremely nasty situation. To reach this conclusion we need not imagine that Hayter did ultimately pay, nor do we require the 'grateful patient' ploy to be exposed.

Who can always be supported, despite the 'grateful patient' exposure, by Kirwen if Hayter's offer to pay is stated, if Kirwen states he was never paid, and states why?

Who, without considerations of either the grateful patient or Kirwen's presence and absence in Jeddah, can always be supported by others in that he was in bed by 2 a.m. and was awoken at 5.30 a.m.?

Who can always state, 'My wife offered to pay, Hayter pulled out a roll?'

Who always has a let-out clause? Which two are always without the let-out clause? Who must always be beholden? Who always has the power? Who can always, supported by others, distance himself from whatever happened that night? What does the adultery confession look like from this angle? What do the differences in the adultery statements look like from this angle? What inferences can be drawn from the contradictions of the inquest evidence from this angle?

9. *The Politics of Pathology*

There is nothing about this girl's injuries inconsistent with an accidental death, enquires Sir David Napley of Professor Usher. No, there was not, he agrees, even though the injuries were consistent with other causes too.

The jury listens attentively. Coroner Gill makes a note; so does the press. The expert hath spoken, risen above the mud-slinging: an objective opinion, based on irrefutable, scientific data.

This is the experts' function, and their knowledge gives them power. Everybody listens, everybody treats them with respect. And if that opinion happens to substantiate how you think a certain event occurred, then you use it to legitimise your view. Hence Sir David's question.

The Smith barristers do the same: get the experts to agree with their line. Dr Green, Professors Dalgaard and Usher are all asked to agree that Helen has injuries consistent with her having been beaten and raped. The Smith barristers want a ten-foot fall to be a possibility, Sir David wants it to be seventy feet. They both are, the pathologists say. This, however, presents a problem for the jury. One expert can be handled with relative ease. He will err towards one extreme or the other 'on a balance of probabilities'. But four pathologists erring towards opposite extremes means that they neutralise each other.

'If Otten fell backwards, might he have somersaulted on the way down?' asks Sir David Napley, this time of Dr Kheir. 'God knows!' What an admission – Dr Kheir is not God. We were beginning to get the impression that Sir David is expecting him to be.

It should have been so simple. Dr Kheir was told by the police that Helen Smith had fallen from the fourth or sixth floor. Find injuries consistent with a fall from this height. Easily done – plenty of injuries on her body from which to choose.

Back in England, Coroner Coverdale to Dr Green: please find out whether the injuries are consistent with a fall from a height. Dr Green does his work. Yes, they are; she fell on her right side. Coverdale accepts this finding and puts out a press release to this effect. The accidental fall theory has been legitimised by the science of the pathologist. There need be no inquest, although we will not rule it out entirely. If there is one, we can rely on Dr Green's report in the witness box.

But Dr Green has found other injuries – to the head – 'not entirely consistent with' a fall. Minor are they? enquires Coverdale. Agreed, approves Green. Well then, they have not contributed towards death. We can accept them as being present with this proviso.

Wait; Dr Green also has evidence of genital injuries – again more consistent with things other than a fall. All right, she may have these, but have they contributed to her death? No. I don't accept them then. Leave them out entirely; we do not wish to cause Mr Smith unnecessary upset.

Dr Green and Dr Kheir could have attended an inquest, read their reports in black and white, and, apart from a few uncomfortable moments over Dr Green's head injuries, their evidence would have been accepted totally. It reinforced the existing position. Helen fell by accident. It legitimised the views of all those who said so.

But wait! Enter recalcitrant father. He has spent a chunk of his life trying to prove that his daughter was murdered, and is not going to give up on the basis of this. It certainly does not reinforce his position.

He commissions another expert independently, and at his own expense. The man he commissions is world-renowned, a man of integrity and a professor to boot.

Professor Dalgaard, together with Professor Usher,

takes apart Helen Smith's body. They also take apart Dr Green's report, now supplemented with details of the genital injuries. He has made mistakes. There is no significant right-shoulder fracture to suggest she fell on it. There is evidence of a definite head injury which Dr Green thought might be henna dye. So there *is* evidence of violence to Helen's body before she died.

The pathologists appear to be in conflict, but their position is awkward. If one denigrates the other, then the whole profession becomes denigrated, smeared, tarred with the same brush. Can you ever trust a pathologist not to have made mistakes when he speaks in a court of law again? What if the death penalty comes back and someone is sent to the gallows on his word?

Except, if you are accused of murder you can, if you are rich enough, commission your own examination of the dead person. *Your* pathologist is bound to find areas of disagreement with *theirs*. You might then get off because the two experts neutralise each other.

But, in general, the public criticisms pathologists make of each other are muted. They reduce themselves to phrases like, 'It is very difficult to say with certainty . . .', 'I would not disagree with my colleague . . .'. They are searching for common ground, which they can only find on top of an academic fence where they form neither one view nor the other. Conflict among experts makes sure the issue is no longer clear-cut. In itself, this is an invitation to an open verdict.

One way of resolving conflict is to discredit a pathologist, make him appear fallible. Although discrediting is not strictly allowed by the inquest rules, this is the new game played out in the witness box. It is played by both the Smith barristers and Sir David Napley.

With Dr Green it is straightforward. He has admitted mistakes, he has admitted missing out the genital injuries from his report. Of the right-shoulder fracture that wasn't, he has to say: 'It was a mistake which I should not have made.' Of the missing genital injuries, he has to say: 'I accepted the express request of Coroner Coverdale.'

It is also easy to ignore the opinion of a fifth pathologist, Dr Joe Deguara. He was the pathologist at the Bakhsh hospital and he looked at the body with Ron Smith within days of Helen's death. It was not a proper examination, but Dr Deguara could be expected to recognise a body that had fallen seventy feet on to a hard marble floor. He doubted that Helen had, and advised Dr Bakhsh himself to fly in a forensic pathologist from London. Nothing came of it. A year and a half later he gave a statement to the West Yorkshire police to the effect that here was a case of suspected murder. Nothing came of it. He told the inquest all this. Nothing was made of it. His examination was unofficial and carries far less weight than Dr Green's computer print-out on the statistics of falling bodies – a print-out that was effectively criticised by the Smith barristers.

But it is much more difficult to discredit Professor Dalgaard. Did you not talk about the Helen Smith case to a convention of pathologists? asks Sir David Napley. Did not some have grave doubts about what you said? 'Two out of 150,' says Professor Dalgaard. Wasn't it many more? 'They did not tell me.' The accusation has been made, however. It is repeated later by a member of the press arguing for accident. Looking through back copies of Denmark's biggest selling daily – *Ekstrabladet*, read by ¾ million people out of a population of 6 million – reveals no mention of any disagreement at this convention. But the damage is done.

At one point during the examination of Professor Usher, Stephen Sedley stands up to complain that Sir David Napley has a fundamental misunderstanding of the nature of the inquest. 'It is not Smith *v.* Arnot. We are here to get at the truth,' he says as Sir David is working himself up to his aggressive best. Dr Kheir is comparatively lucky. He is buffered by an interpreter and is treated lightly.

Could Johannes Otten have somersaulted on the way down? What a question. These people are pathologists, examiners of dead bodies, not experts in their aerodynamics. Ron Smith or the Harms workers or Penelope Arnot can give an equally educated answer. Yet it is the experts who are asked these questions and it is as experts that they give their answers. There may be no merit in what they say, but this is unimportant. They are the experts, and therefore they can give the credibility to the theories.

A variation on discrediting the pathologists is to have a go at the science of pathology itself. Sir David Napley to Professor Dalgaard: 'Pathology is not an exact science . . . You often have to indulge in speculation and guesswork.' Sir David to Professor Usher: 'Even at best, it is very rare that you do not have to engage in speculation.' According to Dr Kheir, *God knows* what a falling body may do aerodynamically, so let us stir up this inexact science and muddy the waters a little.

Especially muddy them when everything is so clear, and you do not like what you see. The four pathologists do have genuine common ground. All agree that Helen Smith had head injuries, and the probability is, agree three of them, that these were not caused by a fall. Three of them also find genital injuries and thigh bruises that indicate rape. This produces a simple picture: Helen Smith was beaten up and raped. Whether she was then tipped over the sixth-floor balcony or carried down the stairs and dumped outside is now of secondary importance. The fact that violence has been done to her body suggests that her death was no accident.

But for each of these injuries a different cause can be found and, like rabbits out of a hat, the other scenarios are pulled. Helen Smith's thigh injuries could be due to her legs slapping together on impact with the ground; her genital injuries could have occurred at some other time in the week before her death. She could have sustained her severe head injury by striking a glancing blow against the

wall on her way down from the Arnot flat. She fell
clutching her beloved Johannes and he broke her fall. She
separated from Otten, but bounced off him into the
courtyard as he stuck on the railings. She smashed against
the wall lamp to the side of where Otten was impaled.
We are now into the realm of dual impacts (one with
Otten, the lamp or the building wall, the other on landing). All these are possible. All complicate the fall and
therefore the nature of the injuries sustained. It matters
not that these scenarios are challenged as improbable,
simply raising them as possibilities undermines the clear-
cut picture of beating and rape.

Coroner Gill said in his summing up: 'Some things are
too important to be left to the experts.' This may be true,
but Coroner Gill was inviting the jury at the time simply
to throw out the findings of three of the four pathologists
who examined Helen. These related to Helen's head and
genital injuries principally and they did not reinforce the
position Gill was about to take. Nor did he make more
than a passing reference to the sternum fracture so neatly
explained in the dialogue between Geoffrey Robertson
and Professor Usher. *Some things are too important to be
left to the experts*. It's a safe cliché, but every cliché has
its anti-cliché. 'Don't throw the baby out with the bath
water' would seem to be appropriate here. The pathologists *had* found injuries to the head and genital regions.
Professors Dalgaard and Usher had been most painstak-
ing in their work, examining sections microscopically and
only confirming injuries once they discovered the presence of blood. Yet now it was being suggested that these
were after-death artefacts and the pathologists had been
led on a 'wild goose chase'.

Dr Kheir's evidence did reinforce the position that
Coroner Gill took at the end of his summing up. 'The
bruises really are the basis of the suspicion that there is
foul play,' he told the jury. 'Were they really bruises at
the time of Helen's death? You have had the benefit of
the evidence of Professor [*sic*] Kheir. One of his concerns

would be to investigate the body, to see if there was evidence of foul play. He expressed himself to be satisfied that the death was accidental. Is it conceivable that Professor Kheir was wrong? I hope you will not underestimate the experience of Professor Kheir. Is it conceivable, in your view, that if those bruises were there at the time of death he has just missed them?' Dr Kheir happened to get Helen's age wrong by about ten years, and when asked directly, both Professor Dalgaard and Usher said they had to disagree with him over the bruises – Professor Usher almost apologetically so.

This creates a problem for Coroner Gill. On this point the pathologists have stopped searching for common ground – they simply disagree. If Coroner Gill was writing for the newspapers or for television, the concept of balance would come in here. This means that if you are given one view of an event, no matter how plausible, you have also to get 'the other side', no matter how implausible.

The newspaper or television can leave it at that – give the two views – or it can try to average the views out with its own balanced view somewhere in between the two. But how does this help Coroner Gill if one pathologist (Professor Dalgaard) believes Helen Smith was murdered while another (Dr Kheir) believes her death was an accident? Where is the point of balance between these two views? There does not seem to be one. A choice has to be made. Someone's view has to be rejected.

Choices, of course, have to be made when coming to any decision, and they often appear as if they were rational, objective, scientific assessment. But such decisions that pretend they are scientific pull the wool over the eyes. They are invariably political. For example, the local Council wants to demolish a terrace of grand Victorian houses to make way for a hypermarket which will create jobs and bring shoppers into the town – they hope. The planners prepare plans, the environmental health officers survey the houses and find evidence of neglect and decay. They declare them slums. The harsh, political choice between residents and developer becomes reduced to a scientific, rational assessment. Why employ your experts on the Council if you are not going to take their advice?

But what if the residents object and engage their own experts? They force a public inquiry. The hypermarket is not going to increase jobs substantially, their experts argue. Far from increasing the number of people using the town's facilities, it is going to decrease the amount of trade other shops receive as everyone drives into the hypermarket car park, does their shopping, and drives away again. Environmentally, the hypermarket will disrupt life for miles around, and the houses it will replace have nothing wrong with them that a bit of money and security for the residents will not put right.

The experts conflict, they neutralise each other with their facts and figures. Their interpretations are seen to be based on value judgements, as with any other mortal. Whose view is the public inquiry inspector going to take? What expert evidence does he accept? Back to a political decision.

And back to the deaths of an Englishwoman and a Dutchman in Jeddah, Saudi Arabia. The story is put about that they fell accidentally while making love on a sixth-floor balcony. The woman's father disagrees. He thinks the wool is being pulled over *his* eyes. He states publicly that he thinks she was murdered. Consternation ensues. British–Saudi relations tend to be volatile. The deaths are bad enough, but the illegal drinks, the sex, the British nationals in a Saudi jail about to be flogged, and now a stroppy father are all rocking the diplomatic boat. The woman's father is even told at the Foreign Office in London that he is jeopardising those relations.

How political has Helen Smith become? The use and abuse of pathologists at her inquest must be set in that context.

10. *The Politics of the Accident Theory*

'... Some were prostitutes, but perhaps the saddest part of this case is that some were not. The last six attacks were on totally respectable women.'
Sir Michael Havers, Attorney General,
Yorkshire Ripper trial.

1ST DANISH MAN: I walked out last night and went underneath her window. She looked down on me. Her face was like a face in a Cathedral.

2ND DANISH MAN: What did you do?

1ST DANISH MAN: I went up the stairs. She stood at the door. She wanted ten pounds.

2ND DANISH MAN: What happened then?

1ST DANISH MAN: I paid her.

2ND DANISH MAN: And what did you do then?

1ST DANISH MAN: I knelt, I prayed and I thanked my God.

2ND DANISH MAN: I never pay.

1ST DANISH MAN: Well, I can't be paying for all of them.

A Copenhagen joke.

'... the reason was, of course, Helen was a scrubber.'
A journalist, Queens Hotel, Leeds, 23 November 1982.

The cover-up is that process of evasions, lies and statements mislaid set in motion automatically when Ron Smith banged on doors and *Private Eye* wanted answers.

The cover-up is infinitely elastic, stretching from the top to the bottom, bottom to the top. The accident had to be written on Helen's gravestone in the public mind.

Because Helen Smith became a public case, because the public mind consists of individuals, because the deaths were suspicious, the accident must allay all questions. Those participating in the cover-up could still be asked – how did she die? Accident was the answer.

From the first moment, the accident theory required props. The first prop was the height of the balcony. The second was the height of the flats above the ground. The third was the assumptions each of us carry.

Would we, as perceivers of the event, regard the event as an accident? How would we filter and examine the evidence? What conclusions would we draw? How would we get Helen from the flat inside to the balcony at the front?

Through the hard-headed diligence of Ron Smith, his unceasing effort, much of the cover-up was exposed. Professor Dalgaard publicly hammered the foundations of accident by his autopsy. Findings, which indicated that Helen had been beaten.

In retrospect we can see that Coroner Gill, in the final twenty minutes of his summing up, effectively murdered the accident theory he had given life to by combining previously disparate parts of the story.

Arnot prepared the ground for the summing up. He delivered an image of perfect symmetry. He said that Otten's dead body had an erection. It was, said he, 'a most grotesque sight', The questions it answered, dazzling in the image's light. How did Otten get an erection? Otten was making love with Helen. So how did Otten get impaled with an erection? They were making love and fell over the side of the balcony. How would the public remember it? As a coda for the whole Helen Smith case. For what the public knew, it could confirm. It gave to their deaths flesh and blood and the key of the coda, that

'grotesque sight', never said murder. It only said accident.

What a pity Arnot had not mentioned it before, had
not offered it to the pathologists to discuss, for it might
have helped them to form an opinion as to how Helen
died. A pity he waited until there was only Gill's final
summing up – with perhaps Texier – before the jury
reached its verdict.

Compare it with Dalgaard, a Dane of middle age. Dalgaard, who shattered his natural reserve, his voice full of
contemptuous fury, to say, 'She died like a motor accident
victim. If she'd been taken to hospital, like we do, she
could have lived. There was a hospital just there nearby.'

The inquest was a battle for the public mind. It was,
and is, the public who determine the quality of truth. To
support the accident theory, and deliver it into the maw
of posterity, certain assumptions had then to come into
operation. These assumptions needed to filter very con-
crete evidence – evidence concerning Helen's actions on
the night, her movement from the enclosed interior of
the flat out onto the balcony.

Witnesses had to show they had not raped her. Witnesses had to show she had drunk sufficient to fall on the
treacherous, slippery tiles. Witnesses had to show a reason
for her wanting to be on the slippery tiles. She had to be
in a state of drunkenness such that she did not keel over
in the flat, yet was sufficiently drunk to go out onto a
balcony she knew was dangerous. If this was not shown,
then the pathological evidence pointed one way – assault,
rape, blows around her head possibly causing her death.

Helen had to be presented. From the first second of
her death, for the first man there, for the second man
there, for the doctors, the nurses, the Embassy, the
public, the press, the jury, Helen had to be presented,
and the presentation could not exist without the perceiver
of it. The perceiver could not perceive without the
assumptions filtering what is perceived and what is not
perceived.

Every observer had to make a choice. Was she raped, murdered? How did she get onto the balcony? The answer rests on only one assumption – the observer's evaluation of women.

What sort of women get onto a balcony with a man, drunk late at night, and why are they there? She wanted sex with Otten. What sort of women get raped? What sort of women get murdered?

But Helen did not walk into that flat alone. Others were present. Since others did attend the party, and since the inquest was held to determine how she died, and since the circumstances were suspicious, certain questions had to be asked to fit the details already presented as evidence. And certain questions would automatically be excluded to fit the details already presented as evidence.

No single witness was asked how he personally felt about Helen going onto the balcony with Otten. Not a single witness was asked if he had looked at Helen – at her thighs, buttocks, breasts, legs – while she was dancing.

They were asked: did you see her, what was she doing? Was she merry? How much was she drinking? They were never asked, did it make you think of your wife when she and Otten sat kissing? Did it make you think of your love, your loneliness, when they embraced?

The line of questions put to the witnesses was exactly that line of questions put in a rape case. Helen had to prove her case, and she was dead. We all know of the woman, raped, who is asked, what clothes were you wearing? In the inquest, Helen's clothing was her glass, her alcohol consumption. As in rape, the propulsion of the act, the last steps over the slippery tiles – her own desire. Compare this inquest with the Yorkshire Ripper trial. Sutcliffe was never asked about his penis. Helen's pubis was kicked around the court like a football in the name of accident.

The inquest did not discuss a dead body with thigh bruises indicating rape. It discussed how men saw and thought of themselves as men. Sir David Napley questioned Professor Usher on those thigh bruises. Could they indicate rape? Could they indicate how much force was used? How much force does a man normally use to caress a woman's pubis, he asked one pathologist?

After discussing Helen's bruising with Usher, Napley then asked Usher if he knew that Helen's lovers were wanted by the Saudi police? Usher is a pathologist. He examines bodies. He has examined raped women. What has the police wanting her lovers got to do with the evidence of rape on Helen Smith's thighs? Only one thing – the establishment of the thought that she deserves everything she gets.

Compare this with how the party guests were questioned. Fleischer grins when he is asked how he experienced living in a country where sexual relationships outside marriage are illegal, where relationships are difficult to make. He answers, 'I take it as it comes.'

He is not asked, and no man was asked – do you masturbate; do you have relationships with each other; do you get lonely at night; how do you feel at three in the morning; how do you feel waking up on your own; what do you do when you think of your wife, your girlfriend, your lover; do you lie there and think what she is doing, do you clench your fists and put your head in your pillow; do you miss your children; does homesickness sear your mind; does the memory of their faces cut your soul?

Compare Napley's questioning of Usher with the questioning of Arnot. Long, sepulchral silences between each question as he told the inquest of Hayter and his wife. He tells us Hayter had told him in the jail of the brief encounter. He is not asked, what did it do to you? How much, with everything else, did it cost you? He tells us he felt angry and let down. He is not then asked, did you want revenge?

Male sexuality, male feelings, did not exist. It was all Helen. Helen was stroppy. Helen trod on toes. Helen was promiscuous. Helen was difficult to get along with. Helen had a Dutch cap. Helen had a coil. In the end she could not even claim her death for herself.

Helen was a scrubber and every man could use her. She died for the same reasons the Ripper victims died. She left Leeds threatened, as every woman was, by the Yorkshire Ripper, Peter Sutcliffe, then still free. She got off the plane in Jeddah, she had a new life waiting. She died five months later on marble. To support the accident theory, men had to believe that women are not raped and murdered daily. To support the accident in Helen Smith's death, men had to be so blind to her life that they could not imagine what her feelings were when she got off that plane.

11. *The Politics of Cover-up*

'All cover-ups begin at the bottom,' said Ron Smith once in an interview with the *Leeds Other Paper*. 'A couple of coppers do something wrong and the sergeant – unless he is a very honest man – will cover up for them. Then it goes higher and higher, with each superior officer covering up for his immediate junior. Before you know where you are, you are at the Chief Constable's desk. If he now admits that those two coppers did something wrong, then not only they, but all the senior officers are implicated too. The whole police force will become drawn in – so he goes along with it too.'

Ron Smith was drawing on his experience as a policeman in the 1950s, but let us now take up the theme in early-morning Jeddah on 20 May 1979 and the Arnots' flat. Richard, Penelope and two guests who stayed the night – Tim Hayter and Jacques Texier – have two bodies on their hands. It matters not for the sake of this argument how they came to be in that state. The Arnots and their guests also have rather a large quantity of alcohol, which is illegal in Saudi Arabia, to explain. The cover-up begins.

Tim Hayter said on the *TV Eye* interview that he might have shipped the bodies of Helen and Johannes out of the country if he could. Presumably he would have dumped their bodies at sea. 'It went through my mind, but there was no way we could do so. We would have taken the bodies on the tugboat, purely because we know Saudi law,' he said. He did not even want anybody to know that two people had been killed.

Richard Arnot told the inquest that his thoughts were on the drink: 'One thought was uppermost in all our minds. The police would be in the flat and we had a considerable amount of alcohol there, and that we would be wise to get rid of it. My wife at this stage was pouring the remaining bottles of whisky down the kitchen sink. Hayter, Texier and I picked up containers of partly fermented wine in the lavatory and carried them into the bathroom and emptied them into the bath.' But it is a hopeless task. A lot of whisky at £25 a bottle goes down the drains of that block of flats. Those drains will smell for days afterwards.

There is no international conspiracy apparent at that moment – just some frantic people trying in vain to pour away a few bottles of whisky and some home-made wine, and at least one of them fantasising over getting rid of the bodies. It is doomed to failure. Many people must know that Helen Smith was at the Arnots' that night. They cannot simply make her vanish. And as for Johannes Otten – he is well and truly stuck on the railings. Hayter did not say in the TV interview whether he communicated his thoughts to the others. But his plan was nonsense. The deaths have to be revealed. The alcohol? Perhaps at this stage they can still get away with it.

Penelope Arnot goes over to the hospital with her two young children. Diplomats Gordon Kirby and Michael Balmer find her there. They have been sent to the scene by Michael Weston, the Counsellor at the Embassy. 'On the 'phone, Mr Weston was very angry,' Gordon Kirby told the inquest. He has good reason to be. What English fools in this expatriate community have upset the apple cart and drawn attention to themselves? Storm clouds gather on the diplomatic front.

Penelope Arnot tells the two diplomats that another Englishmen, Alan Kirwen, supplied the black-market booze. Kirby makes a note, which he later writes up as a 'minute'. This minute also notes that he finds Penelope Arnot's story as to what happened that night unsatisfactory in some respects. Was she really clearing up the party debris, drinking coffee and listening to music until dawn when she had probably been awake since 6.30 a.m. the previous day? Was Helen Smith really the only other female at the party?

Back at the scene of the tragedy, the temperature is rising. The alcohol has been discovered, and one of Helen's legs is out of her knickers, indicating sex. Alcohol and extra-marital sex – both are very much against Saudi law, law that has been flagrantly flouted by a bunch of disrespectful Europeans. On top of that, two people – one a British national – are dead. Pray that it was an accident or there *will* be trouble.

Kirby's 'minute' of the conversation with Penelope Arnot is a problem. Relations between Saudi Arabia and Britain could be embarrassed by the whole episode. The minute casts doubts on the truthfulness of Penelope Arnot's account and it names the Englishman who supplied the booze. Should they show it to the investigating Saudi police? It is, after all, Penelope Arnot's first account of the events that night – taken completely without pressure.

'I would have held that view,' said Counsellor Michael Weston when asked at the inquest if he thought the minute should not be shown to the Jeddah police.

Alan Kirwen would have faced two years in jail and 200 strokes of the cane for supplying the alcohol, expanded Gordon Kirby. He agreed with Coroner Gill that Kirwen would be in deep trouble, and this was a matter the Embassy would not wish to precipitate.

Kirby also believes that the Arnots will pass on Kirwen's name to the Jeddah police anyway, but he is lucky. Richard Arnot told the inquest that because he left the party early, he did not regard him as being part of it. 'I remember when making the list [of party guests for the police], I thought the less said of him the better,' he explained to a knowing, understanding court.

The Embassy contacts Kirwen, however, about four days after the deaths. He talks to Francis Geere, who tells him what has happened. Kirwen is not concerned that the Embassy knows he supplied the whisky for, and was at, the party, but would be if the Saudi authorities got to know. He is due to return to England on leave and decides to bring it forward by a couple of days. Francis Geere feels it would be wise. The Embassy view, as expressed by Gordon Kirby at the inquest, is: 'It would be improper to advise him to leave Saudi Arabia, but it would be proper to advise him his name had come up.' In other words, if the Embassy told Kirwen directly to get out of the country quickly, and the Saudi authorities found out, then certain diplomats would be *persona non grata*. Back in England, however, the Foreign Office is more straightforward. 'The Foreign Office thought it would be inadvisable to return,' Kirwen told the inquest. So he does not and it is unlikely he ever will. His two-year contract as medical officer for Lockheed International comes to an end – fourteen months early. He will become a medical officer for the Cunard Steamship Company instead.

Back in Jeddah, problems mount over the deaths. Rumours are rife in the Bakhsh hospital that the two were murdered. Gordon Kirby's minute does not actually form any view of this. It simply queries Penelope Arnot's movements in the early hours and speculates on the possibility of more women having been there. Is it a document to be shown to the Saudi police? No. Michael Weston has already formed the view that the deaths were an accident – 'on the basis of what Mr Arnot and Mr Kirby told me.' The telegram to the Foreign Office in London, asking that the next of kin be told, states there has been an accident in which a British subject has been killed.

So there is no need to show Kirby's minute to anyone if it was an accident.

Enter Ron Smith. He looks at Helen's body and believes there is no way that she fell any distance onto that solid, marble floor. He smells murder. Consul Francis Geere is accompanying him but keeps a 'respectful distance' away as Ron Smith examines Helen. A few days later, Francis Geere accompanies Ron Smith a second time to the mortuary. This time he has some staff from the Bakhsh hospital with him, including Joe Deguara, who is Dr Bakhsh's own consultant pathologist. Francis Geere does not hear comments about the injuries to Helen being slight.

And Francis Geere 'has no knowledge' of any murder investigation by the Saudi police. He hears little but the police telling him a few weeks later that they are satisfied it was an accident.

What a pity that later, Penelope Arnot admits to adultery on the night of the party with Timothy Hayter. Does she not know that the penalty is stoning to death? Another potentially embarrassing situation – Her Majesty's Government would not take kindly to one of her subjects suffering that fate. The admission also contradicts what she told Gordon Kirby, but it does answer more satisfactorily one of his queries. She did not simply spend those early hours clearing up, drinking coffee and listening to music.

Michael Weston himself hears Mrs Arnot repeat her adultery admission in a Saudi lawyer's office in October or November 1979. Some time later – in 1980 – Tim Hayter repeats it to Gordon Kirby in what Gordon Kirby described to the inquest as a 'light-hearted' conversation. Tim Hayter is at the Embassy at the time sorting out a new passport so he can leave the country (the British Embassy looks after the interests of New Zealand nationals). Kirby makes a record of the conversation.

There is, however, one important difference between Penelope Arnot's admission and Tim Hayter's. She said the adultery took place in another room, Tim Hayter says the same room as Jacques Texier and therefore not far from the balcony.

With three varying accounts of Penelope Arnot's and Tim Hayter's movements that night – Penelope's original conversation with Kirby, her admission of adultery in front of Michael Weston (and Francis Geere was there although he said he did not listen), and Hayter's conversation with Kirby – the British Embassy are sitting on a hot potato: three different accounts by the two principle witnesses in two suspicious deaths. Will it cool down?

There was a British Embassy cover-up over the death of Helen Smith and at least some of its extent was revealed at the inquest. An Englishman was protected because he had supplied whisky to the party. Perhaps this had less to do with concern over what might happen to Alan Kirwen, and more to do with keeping the situation cool. Catching an alcohol trafficker would certainly have escalated matters.

So, certainly, would double murder. The talk of it around the Bakhsh hospital was dismissed as rumour, and diplomats generally seemed deaf to the word 'murder' whenever it was mooted. At the inquest, Michael Weston could not recall 'clearly at all' a report to the Foreign Office that there were suspicious matters as a result of interviews with hospital staff. Francis Geere, however, remembered a Telemessage to the Foreign Office. Coroner Gill asked if this was 'merely a recital of speculation'. 'Yes,' Geere agreed. When Kirby's minute expressed doubts about Penelope Arnot's story, Geere's attitude was that it was 'a question for the Saudi police'.

Any cover-up would certainly have been confined to the Embassy but for Ron Smith getting wind of the contents of Kirby's minute. He wanted to see it. It was a 'potential conflict situation', as Ruth Bundey aptly put it. The Embassy was protecting one British subject at the expense of another. The latter happened to be a bereaved father; the former faced jail and a beating.

Ron Smith could not win. If he saw the minute and blurted out its contents to the Saudi authorities, the result could be very embarrassing – to use diplomatic jargon. It named an alcohol trafficker who had hastily left the country or was at that moment packing his bags to leave. It contained an account by Penelope Arnot – now in Saudi custody – of the party which was queried. It is possible that the Saudi authorities even objected to the very presence of the minute. The police had stopped Gordon Kirby talking to Richard Arnot at the scene. 'The Saudis were very keen to have uninfluenced statements,' was how Francis Geere put it.

As Ron Smith's demands for access to the minute became more frenetic, the Embassy telegrammed the Foreign Office. Back came the reply – the F.O. had not seen the contents of the minute, but it would be wrong in principle to let it be shown. The Foreign Office stuck to that view for three and a half years – long after Alan Kirwen had left Saudi Arabia for good. Then, with no prior warning, it was read out at the inquest. Nobody knew until the inquest, however, that long before the end of 1980, the Embassy possessed three differing accounts of Penelope Arnot's movements that night.

The day after the inquest finished, Foreign Office Minister of State, Douglas Hurd, said there had been no cover-up over this girl's death.

It is never wise to embarrass relations between countries. It was the murder of the heir to the Austrian throne and his wife in a foreign country that sparked off the First World War.

It is particularly never wise to embarrass relations in sensitive parts of the world like the Middle Eastern countries. They are of the utmost strategic importance to the West both politically and economically. Their oil sees to that. And that is the position of Saudi Arabia, which has the added importance of forming much of the eastern bank of the Red Sea.

Britain also has strong trading links with Saudi Arabia apart from oil, and the English-speaking expatriate community in the main port, Jeddah, is large – up to 6,000. It could be said that Richard Arnot was a British export to Saudi Arabia – the highly respected skills of the British medical profession being brought to a private hospital there.

Until 1974, British trade with Saudi Arabia was relatively marginal. Then, with the OPEC oil price rises, the 'petrodollar' kingdom was born and with it a number-one export market. In 1970 the country's first five-year plan was put into operation and the expenditure on development was budgeted at US $9 billion. By 1974, when Saudi projected expenditure for the second five-year plan was announced, it had jumped to US $140 billion. Western firms were more than happy with this plan – rapid growth, particularly in the construction industry, meant millions of pounds' worth of contracts coming their way. By 1981, Saudi Arabia was Britain's twelfth largest export market, and this and the Saudi oil flowing the other way have caused the UK to hold relations between the two countries in the highest esteem.

It is the role of the diplomat in these circumstances to do as much as possible to promote the relations between the two countries and definitely to avoid anything which may embarrass them. But the presence of a sizeable expatriate British community in Jeddah and other parts of Saudi Arabia can make this task difficult – especially as the community members tend to reproduce their lifestyles from back home. Throwing parties, drinking alcohol, having boyfriends or girlfriends are all especially worrying for the diplomats.

The death of Helen Smith in May 1979, therefore, did not exactly please the diplomats in Jeddah. The sex and alcohol aspects were obvious, and at one point Penelope Arnot laid herself open to being stoned to death by admitting adultery. The diplomats had to tread very carefully, and they said so at the inquest. It seemed a case of the less said the better. The Arnots were sentenced in March 1980, Richard to one year in jail and thirty lashes, Penelope to eighty lashes in public.

Then, while the diplomats were trying to get the Arnots spared their flogging, an incident occurred that had nothing to do with the expatriate community. The documentary film, *Death of a Princess*, was shown on

British television in April 1980. It dealt with the execution of a Saudi princess because she had taken a lover. Behind the story lay an attack on the whole Saudi moral code and the hypocrisy of the Saudi Royal family.

The Saudis threatened to break off diplomatic relations, suspend oil exports and huge contracts between the two countries. The day was only saved by the then Foreign Secretary, Lord Carrington, publicly damning the film.

All the good relations were restored by June and somewhere in the restoration the Arnots were spared their flogging. They returned to England in August 1980.

It had been touch and go, however. The Embassy told the inquest that when the Arnots were first thrown in jail it was a matter for the Saudi police. It was not going to volunteer Gordon Kirby's minute or any other information. It would merely make informal efforts to get the Arnots out of the country. But saying no more than you have to is fine, except when someone comes along with a legitimate interest in hearing the lot. Ron Smith did that.

Dr Michael Alan Green made a bad mistake when he said Helen suffered a right-shoulder fracture. He made another when he mistook a serious head lesion for henna dye. Yet perhaps his biggest error was to omit from his original autopsy report details of the genital bruising he had found on Helen's body. He did so at the express request of Deputy Coroner Coverdale (who was at that time in charge of the body), he told the inquest. Deputy coroner and pathologist rationalised this omission by agreeing that the genital injuries did not contribute to death.

It is not an expert's job to leave out anything, however. The genital injuries might not have been pertinent to Dr Green's brief, which was to discover whether Helen Smith's injuries were consistent with a fall from a height. They are, however, pertinent to other things that may have happened to Helen and which may have led, albeit indirectly, to her death – namely rape.

And Dr Green did see fit to put these injuries into a

supplementary report four months later, which was handed to the West Yorkshire police. But by that time, an independent autopsy was only two months off. The supplementary report was not revealed publicly until the inquest, over two years after it was written.

According to Dr Green at the inquest, Deputy Coroner Coverdale asked him to leave out the genital injuries from his original report so as not to cause further distress to Mr Smith. Yet Mr Smith was already by then suspecting that his daughter was raped. So why leave out the details? Or did Coverdale mean by distress that Ron Smith might start running around even more than previously shouting rape, murder and cover-up?

In conclusion, if Coverdale told Green that he did not wish to cause Mr Smith further distress, was that his real or only reason for his express request? We shall probably never know. Deputy Coroner Coverdale is dead and cannot be asked.

Between the unreported genital injuries and the British Embassy in Jeddah, is there a link? Ron Smith has long maintained that there is, but the inquest did not tell us. If there is, part of it is missing, gone forever, dead in the form of ex-Deputy Coroner Coverdale.

Power in Saudi Arabia is hereditary. It has been since the kingdom was established in 1901 after a long struggle against Turkish domination. For centuries, Turkey had dominated the country both economically and religiously via the Ottoman empire.

The main mover in the struggle was a young sheikh from the Saud tribe. He managed to win the support of most of the interior tribes and eventually the whole of Saudi Arabia came under his rule. He became the first King Saud.

What proved crucial to the struggle, particularly in forging a commonwealth of all the tribes in the region, was a fundamentalist Islamic religious sect – the Wahabis – who had been in alliance with the Saud tribe since 1744 and had long advocated the restoration of an Islamic Arabic kingdom.

When the new kingdom was established, the Wahabis' leader – simply referred to as Al-Sheikh – became a firm friend of the Saud family and the ideological custodian of the new Islamic resurgence in the country. It fell upon him and his descendants to devise the laws and rules that govern Saudi Arabia. In doing so, all matters relating to law, both civil and criminal, were derived from the Koran (the Islamic bible). The Saudi kingdom alone in the Islamic world then reinstated the ancient and strict penal code which had operated during the early days of Islam almost thirteen centuries earlier.

The Wahabis or Al-Sheikh family to this day supply all the senior judges and religious leaders whose task it is to interpret the text of the Koran and deliver judgement on all matters spiritual. Together with the Royal Saud family, the Wahabis are the power in Saudi Arabia.

The basis of Saudi law today – the 'moral code' – therefore shows no distinction between criminal and civil law. It includes not only 'normal' crimes such as murder, assault and theft, but also adultery, extra-marital sex and drinking alcohol.

Its enforcement relies very much on the family and self-policing. The police only become involved when crimes are reported to them. It works a little like industrial relations in Britain. If you work on the shop floor and have a grievance, your first step is to try to sort it out informally with the foreman. Only if this does not work do you go higher.

Saudi law enforcement is pretty informal too. The police have no right of entry into houses and they simply do not go in unless asked, other than in exceptional circumstances.

Two years in jail and 200 strokes is the penalty for trafficking alcohol; a woman who commits adultery is stoned to death; off comes your hand after three convictions for theft. The penalties for breaking the Saudi moral code are severe, but the saving grace is that the police play a passive role. They are not on the streets looking for these infringements. Probably the very fact that an offence ends up in the court at all adds to its gravity. The offence is now outside the family – it is public. The offender has so obviously betrayed the trust bestowed upon him or her to observe the code.

The Royal family and religious elite are few in number, but below them is another increasingly powerful group – the meritocracy. Since the mid-1960s, oil wealth has propelled Saudi Arabia into the modern world. The huge strides taken towards developing a modern machinery of government and a strong economic infrastructure have opened up opportunities for ordinary Saudis to take top jobs in administration, industry or even Government – something that had hitherto been the birthright of the Royal family. These people are now in the forefront of the commercial and financial life of the country, they are chiefs of police, and they own private hospitals – like Dr Bakhsh.

This, then, is the meritocracy. It is self-consciously making itself felt in Saudi life, wary of the privileges extended to it by the ruling elite and heavily burdened by the often contradictory demands of modern industrial life. And these contradictions are at their most acute when European staff are employed (partly for prestige, partly for specific skills) with values very different from those on which the country's laws are based.

The Bakhsh hospital in Jeddah is a prestigious place which, in May 1979, had only been open a few months. Richard Arnot was its head doctor. Private hospitals were almost booming in Saudi Arabia at the time. In Jeddah, Medina and Mecca – the three major cities that form a triangle in the west of the country – there are no fewer than twelve, and more than one was owned by Dr Bakhsh. His competitors were similarly members of the meritocracy.

Yet Dr Bakhsh is not only the owner of a hospital.

The entire staff there comes under his patronage, and in this sense he is a head of a family. So when, in May 1979, the death of one of his staff was reported, it was to him that the police would turn at some point. He had a friend who was a chief of police, anyway, he said in his statement read out at the inquest, whom he telephoned on hearing of the deaths of Helen and Johannes Otten. This is not surprising – there are not many in the meritocracy.

The ethics of the moral code therefore dictated that Dr Bakhsh took more than a passing interest in the case. He made sure the railings were replaced by brickwork within hours of the deaths. Dr Bakhsh would give his view to the police, and there was no doubt he was displeased. Vice-Consul Gordon Kirby told the inquest that he was saying at the scene that it was terrible – the alcohol and the sex aspect. In his statement, Dr Bakhsh admitted that he may well have said such things.

And Dr Bakhsh also came down hard on his staff. The strict rules were made even stricter. Curfew rules were considerably tightened. No member of staff was allowed to babysit. And nobody was to talk about the incident to anyone.

His own pathologist, Joe Deguara, looked at Helen – although with Ron Smith and not in a professional capacity. Dr Bakhsh asked him afterwards what his opinion was and Joe Deguara advised that he should arrange for a top forensic pathologist to fly in from London to examine the body. The advice was not acted upon.

Over a year later, Dr Bakhsh paid for the repatriation of Helen's body to England. Yes, he did remember asking Ron Smith not to mention his name, but that was not a condition of paying for the repatriation, his statement indicated.

But back at the tragedy itself, the police, having been called, did begin to do their job. It was, however, unfortunate that the bodies were removed to the mortuary before the police pathologist, Dr Kheir, arrived. Seeing them *in situ* would have helped him considerably.

A few days later, Richard Arnot accompanied some police officers back to his flat for a short time. He told the inquest that the place was covered in fingerprint powder yet strangely neither he nor, as far as he was aware, the other party guests had their prints taken. Tim Hayter told *TV Eye* that the police were pretty heavy while he was in custody and there was no doubt in his mind at the time that they were conducting a murder investigation. Yet the word 'murder' does not seem to have been used by the Saudi police during their interrogation. Jacques Texier made it clear to the inquest that the police never suggested Helen had been assaulted or murdered. A few weeks later, a police official told British Consul Francis Geere that he was satisfied the deaths were an accident.

The Saudi emphasis on informal self-policing has much to commend it. It does, however, lead to a conflict of interests. What head of a family wants the shame of a murder on his hands and shouted across Jeddah? The moral code puts him in an impossible position.

We have alluded to a British Embassy cover-up, a pathology cover-up and a Saudi cover-up. That far we can grasp by teasing apart the evidence presented to the inquest. There is, however, another type of cover-up which operates at a completely different level. There is nothing crude or sinister about it; it probably operates in all walks of life all of the time and nobody thinks of it in terms of cover-up. But it is probably there that the link can be found between the British Embassy and Deputy Coroner Coverdale.

At the inquest, most of the major participants were soon at ease. The lawyers, the Embassy witnesses, Dr Kirwen, Mr Arnot, soon struck a chord with Coroner Gill. These witnesses had come along to assist him and, although sometimes lounging with arms outstretched in the witness box, sometimes looking rather superior, they were polite and courteous. The inquest would have been so cosy and relaxed but for one man – Ron Smith. He stuck out like a sore thumb. He may have been a successful businessman once, but he had worked for that success and his roots were obviously different – working-class, Yorkshire and proud of being both.

How could Michael Weston, Gordon Kirby, Francis Geere, Alan Kirwen, Richard Arnot *et al* cope with this man who took such a pride in being blunt with them – a real 'cut out the bullshit' type? Coroner Gill understood their problem. Their looks said as much as their words as they gave evidence.

It was not Coroner Gill's fault as an individual, nor that of Michael Weston, Gordon Kirby, Francis Geere, Alan Kirwen and Richard Arnot. But institutionally, this fish out of water was literally in a different class to them and it was their justice and truth that was being meted out.

It was probably the same in Saudi Arabia. Ron Smith was almost certainly uncomfortable in the presence of the Embassy diplomats, and they no doubt in his: he wanting to home in directly on his daughter's death, they aware of the wider connotations. Small-talk would be almost out of the question.

How much easier the diplomats would feel in the company of Dr Kirwen, who knew several of them through playing squash, and Richard Arnot – even if they did have to speak to him in a prison yard. The former was medical adviser for a big American multinational company, the latter the senior surgeon at a private hospital.

Kith and kin – another of Ron Smith's phrases, but an apt one. And if you are a diplomat and want to help your kith and kin, then you do not necessarily even think about it. It comes naturally. Smith *v.* Kirwen – the outcome could have been no other and the term 'cover-up' need not enter the consciousness. It is not part of the vocabulary.

Poor Smithy, when he went to see Arnot in Saudi custody and called a spade a spade, could he not see the difference between 'sun rise' and 'sunrise', the latter meaning the dawn? Could he not see the difference in intonation when you speak them?

And back at the inquest, Ron Smith highlighted the difference when he stood in the witness box and mimicked Richard Arnot's upper-class accent and phraseology, encapsulated by Arnot's use of the word 'super' (pronounced 'soo-per' by Ron Smith); when he used the phrase 'no way' as he was saying that his daughter could not have fallen seventy feet; even when he broke down momentarily and said, 'It's all right. Don't bother.' The others in the witness box, however, used almost a different language. They would have 'no prior knowledge', would remember things to 'the best of my recollection' or they 'could not recall'. At times, the Embassy staff at the inquest were like a parody of a solicitor's questionnaire when house conveyancing. 'Is this house connected to mains drainage?' 'As far as we are aware but please check.' 'Were Helen Smith and Johannes Otten murdered?' 'Not as far as we are aware but please check.'

It was probably inevitable that the evidence of Michael Weston, Gordon Kirby, Francis Geere, Alan Kirwen, Richard Arnot *et al* could never be properly questioned at the inquest. 'Miss Bundey, I am not getting the co-operation I am looking for,' Coroner Gill said almost wearily as he interrupted Ron Smith's solicitor's examination of Embassy staff for the nth time. It was not simply the limitations imposed by an inquest that could only ask how, when and where Helen Smith died that caused these interruptions. The invisible bonds between these witnesses and Coroner Gill created an area of admissible questions, questions that could be understood and which gave rise to answers that could be understood. The kith and kin were not even aware of what they were doing. They thought they were helping to get to the truth. They had covered themselves up a long time ago – before Helen Smith's time.

12. The Summing Up That Adds Up

You are the jury,
We leave you our theory

First, ladies and gentlemen of the jury, we must ask ourselves what is the nature of the expatriate community in Saudi Arabia. We must consider this objectively before we devise a picture of what happened that night. The guests at the party were denied two things commonplace in their European homelands. The first is alcohol and the second is a relaxed attitude to sexual relations. Both of these, as we all know, are illegal in Saudi Arabia. And so, members of the jury, we must consider what that means. There are no night clubs, night places, dance halls. There are no public houses, no bars, everything you and I might consider are the normal artefacts of life as we know it.

As a result, the expatriates could find themselves with no place to go at night to meet their friends and talk. Hardly surprising then, is it, members of the jury, that they visited each other's homes? As Mr Arnot said, we were thrown back into our homes. And in their mutual quarters, members of the jury, they could become European. Consequently, as Mr Arnot again told us, acquaintances become friends very rapidly.

We have then to consider a life of constant high temperature, long hours of work, nowhere to go at night. Boredom sets in, does it not? All work and no play makes Jack a dull boy, and many of these people were intelligent, highly skilled, and needed moments of relaxation. Hardly surprising, then, that breaking the law provided a spice of excitement. Mr Hayter said so in the television interview. You must consider, members of the jury, that most of us partake of alcoholic refreshment, most of us enjoy sexual relations. We do not consider that abnormal or illegal.

But again, there are differences. Over here, in our homeland, we can go to a public house with a friend. We can have a social evening where we sit and talk. We have not gone to the public house especially for the drink. This is not the case in Jeddah. As Mr Texier said, it was a drinks party, and a drinks party is illegal.

Consider what might have happened if an Arab arrived, or a neighbour spotted a chink in the curtains and saw some men and women dancing. The police could have arrived. Everyone at the party could then, as they did, receive two to three months in prison. They could receive forty-five lashes. Consider Dr Kirwen. Supplying the alcohol could have cost him two years' imprisonment and two hundred lashes.

And so that makes it easier for us to understand why the curtains were closed. Why, as Mr Arnot told us, candles were on the table and the lights were dimmed. Why the music was low. As Mr Hayter said, the unwritten law was that if an Arab arrived, or drugs arrived, the party was finished.

They were all whites at the party. While we may disagree with it, we cannot argue that the society outside the quarters of the party had made alcohol illegal, had made men and women dancing together illegal. If you remember, Martin Fleischer was charged with joining that party.

The Arnots had lived in this society for five months, as had nurse Helen. They were, we could say, newcomers. It takes all of us time to acclimatise to a new situation, where everything is different, and not as we know it. Mr Hayter said that Otten was drunk on arrival at the party. The other members from Harms said that he drank considerably and was used to drinking. In other words, we received the impression that he was something of a hard drinker. In a society where alcohol is illegal, then obviously, Mr Otten understood how to get by. It was Mr Hayter who said, 'John was not a baby. If he couldn't look after himself, we couldn't.'

Helen had just finished her duty at the hospital. The hospital was marred by a great deal of resentment and unhappiness, Mr Arnot told us. Helen's fiancé had suddenly been deported back to Malaysia and she had handed in her notice. Mr Hayter, for whom the party was being held, was due to fly off to Singapore the following day.

Mr Hayter and all the Harms people knew Johannes Otten, but he especially befriended Klaus Ritter, the company cook. He was around their accommodation barge, took his meals there, used the showers. He came every two or three days and read the newspapers. Ritter said Otten came along to the party. He was Otten's friend. Mr Schlaeffer, the company crane operator, told us Otten had been in the barge that day and so they invited him along, such was their nature.

According to Mr Texier, who is a Frenchman, the Germans spoke German. As Mr Texier said, he felt an outsider. The English spoke English, Mr Texier saying he spoke English with Mr Arnot, asking him, if you remember, why he was going to bed with technical books. In other words, the guests at the party provided a map of Europe, each generally speaking his or her own language.

Mr Texier again, when asked what sort of party it was, immediately replied it was a drinks party. We must consider that briefly before we get the overall picture together. We know a bottle of whisky in Saudi Arabia would cost about five times as much as it does here. This is because it is an illicit drug. It is not an illicit drug here, but it is there, and so the £25 or so must cover the cost of transportation and other sundries. When we pay that much for drink, we tend to value it more highly. We all know the rush at closing time. In that case, time restricts, so we must get the drinks in. At the party, members of the jury, the very act of drinking is illegal.

We know, members of the jury, that the more we pay for something, the more our attention focuses on it. We can all remember the smile on Mr Hayter's face. He was talking of sadikki, the home-stilled liquor, and he said, 'Sadikki, my old friend', which is the English translation of it.

My old friend, for that is what drink in Saudi Arabia is. It is something from the homeland. Something from a past that is not there any more. Something to remind them of happier and, perhaps, better days. Old friends, colleagues, interesting places they have been to.

Each of us can understand that. Sitting with others in a foreign country, the curtains tightly closed in case the neighbours could see in, drinks in our hands, remembering old times, wishing we were back, telling each other about incidents. In these conditions the alcohol is not, is it, members of the jury, a drink in convivial surroundings? They are hardly the surroundings in which any of us would choose to drink.

But consider the alternatives. What if they didn't drink? How could they pass the time? How could they go through the long hours of boredom, the unhappiness of homesickness?

But to go out for a drink is illegal. The parties must be carefully arranged. As Mr Arnot said, it is accepted that they are held, but one is discreet. One is not advertising the fact. As Mr Schlaeffer said, going past the harbour gate can be dangerous if your breath is smelling of alcohol. And so in these conditions, with all that alcohol is, we must see it in what it represents for the guests. We must try and fit it into the picture.

What does it give to them? It gives them an identity, does it not? They feel themselves to be living in a way they know they have lived before. It gives a break from the monotony of daily work. It gives the moments where the past can be brought alive and remembered. It gives each person something to hold onto and remember next day at work. It gives them a feeling that they may mean something, that even if Saudi culture outside denies alcohol, it is not shameful. They know its value. It belongs to their life and if they deny this, members of the jury, do they not then deny themselves?

And, as Mr Hayter reminded us, it can be exciting, as all pursuits can be where we must use wit and cunning to outwit those who place us in constraints we do not consider unlawful. But nurse Helen took something else into this gathering. She was a woman. Mr Hayter reminded us graphically of what that meant. He called her relationship with Otten a one-way ticket to sex. Everyone in Jeddah was looking for someone to have sex with, he further told us.

Does that not tell us much about expatriate life? Sex is legal in our country. It is illegal in Saudi Arabia, and the penalty is severe. Speaking of that shared confession of adultery with Mrs Arnot, Mr Hayter said, 'We could lose our heads.' We, of course, in this country, know of instances where adultery on the part of one of the partners leads to divorce. It leads to heartbreak in some cases, emotional turmoil. In Jeddah, an affair, members of the jury, can lead to the death penalty.

We must consider then, how does that fit into the picture? What in this country might be regarded as a moment of betrayal, the sort of thing that can always happen in emotional relationships, in Jeddah can lead to much more. So it is always in the background.

And so, of course, sex becomes illicit. It becomes exactly like alcohol; it becomes a way of knowing who you are. It becomes a moment to think about while you are working. And so, the enjoyment of sex, the enjoyment of whisky, these are enjoyed with a taste of their illegality. We all know, members of the jury, that forbidden fruits are tempting.

But then we must consider, to pull the picture together, the white colony living in the Jeddah community. We know from our own experience how that colony lives. It is a ghetto. It is a well-paid ghetto, but it has no roots in Saudi society. It only exists because of work and Saudi demand for skills. If that did not exist then the colony

would not be there. We all know what happens to people
living in a ghetto. They close their doors, they have their
shared habits, and because they are living inside a bigger
society which allows them in on sufferance, they must
stick together. The divers cannot go out and meet a
Moslem friend after that party; they must go back to the
harbour. We must consider this when we consider the
nature of illicit sex and alcohol – they are a way of holding
the community together.

Sex and alcohol help the members of the community to
overcome the irritants of the law within which they must
live. They help them to keep their knowledge of their
homelands together; to surmount the homesickness and
stresses of living away from family and friends.

Gossip is not so much then the prurient interests of the
nasty minded. It is the legend of the outlaw. A way of
telling each member of the community, this is us, and
this is what we are like. It holds the community together.
And so, members of the jury, we can see how these illicit
acts of sex and alcohol fuse the past and present together
for each member of the expatriate community. How they
provide knowing smiles between each and every one of
them. How they revive memories better than any
photograph album. How they remind the expatriates
they have a right to play as well as work. The acts help
to surmount boredom. They add a spice of excitement
to daily life. They give a sense of overcoming re-
strictive dangers.

When we consider this picture, then we must consider
the events of the party. We must see that the relationship
between Helen and Johannes could never be the relationship between Helen and Johannes in this country.
Both had committed, together with the rest of the party,
one illegal act, and with their ticket to sex, they were
moving towards the second. And obviously, since it is a
closed community, both inside the flat and around them
in their colony, their actions together could be recognised
by each member of the community present. As Mr Arnot

said, the full physical details of Mrs Arnot's encounter with Mr Hayter were known throughout the community within two days, even to the woman who looked after the children while they were in prison. Gossip, in this sense, was not the province of the nasty-minded – it was a way of reminding the whole community of what it is.

Now we must turn our minds to that night in question, the night of 19 to 20 May. At the party were bottles of whisky and, according to Mr Hayter only, sadikki, vodka and gin. Two women were present. There were eleven men. With the exception of Mr Arnot, they were living there without wives or girlfriends. Martin Fleischer told us he took the problem as it came. Mr Arnot thought Hayter had asked him to extend a general invitation to the nurses. He had mentioned it to Helen, also to another nurse. We do not know why there were so few women present. We can only conjecture. Perhaps Mr Arnot felt embarrassed asking the nurses. Perhaps as a relative newcomer to Saudi life, he felt he did not know the scene well enough to invite more. Perhaps he felt he hardly knew enough of those likely to be coming to invite more. We do know that at 12.30 he called on Matron Agnes Johnstone to invite her along and, receiving no reply, returned to the party. There, Helen and Johannes were dancing together.

At 2.00 a.m., Mr Arnot retired to bed. At 2.30, Martin Fleischer left. Shortly after – the Germans said around 3.00 a.m. – the rest of Harms Salvage left. There remained in the flat Mrs Arnot, Tim Hayter, Jacques Texier, Mr Arnot, the Arnots' children, and possibly, on the balcony, if not elsewhere, Johannes Otten and Helen Smith. At 5.45 that morning they were reported dead.

It is now time, members of the jury, to study in detail what the witnesses said. Do you accept the evidence of Mr Texier, Mr Arnot and the German guests as being honest and truthful? If you do accept it, then any incident involving Helen involves Mrs Arnot, Mr Hayter or Mr Otten. Do you accept that during the sleeping hours anything might have happened?

Tim Hayter and Mrs Arnot were on the spot. Mrs Arnot said originally that after Mr Hayter and Mr Texier had gone to sleep she cleared up the mess, drank coffee and listened to the music. She later modified this story by admitting in the Saudi jail that she committed adultery with Mr Hayter. Mr Hayter corroborated her story. Is this account true, or is it an alibi?

It is true that as an alibi it was not, on the face of it, a very good one. A woman is stoned to death for adultery. But Mr Weston of the British Embassy said he was under the impression that Mrs Arnot was not aware of the penalty when she made the confession. And it did give a more creditable account of her movements during those early hours. It did apparently stop the police questions about the deaths, and Mrs Arnot did in the end get away with it by retracting her confession.

Supposing Mr Hayter and Mrs Arnot were not involved. Mr Texier was asleep, so that leaves Mr Otten. There are no indications that Mr Otten became violent when he was drunk; in fact, witnesses said he became quiet. So what happens if we accept Mr Texier's story and Mrs Arnot's story – that they both saw Helen and Otten go onto the balcony? Did they go there? Was it consensual?

Here we have another choice. We must consider: was it consensual between themselves, was it consensual with the other party guests? Otten had arrived with people from Harms Salvage. Helen had arrived with Mr Arnot from the hospital. We could ask, were either free agents?

Helen belonged to the hospital; Otten belonged to the harbour. In the society of the party, they could be seen as free agents, but, is it not the case, that in the relationship between the society of the party and the society outside, both existed under constraint? Their presence in the greater society outside existed on sufferance, and if they carried their documents to prove that this sufferance had been extended to them, they were legal and they could live there. Is it not the case that each party member lived under the same constraints? We have the Germans' evidence that Helen's and Johannes's disappearance was not noted by them. We have Mr Texier's evidence. Mr Texier was bored. He went into the kitchen to make a sandwich. He spoke to Mr Arnot. Mr Arnot had technical books with him; he had his thoughts on the following morning's surgery. And so, at first glance, nobody was concerned about their one-way ticket to sex, as Mr Hayter put it. But can two people, who have already committed one illegal act, go out onto the balcony with the intent of committing a second illegal act without disturbing the others? This must be considered.

Then you have to consider the question as to how the bodies came to be where they were. Otten was jack-knifed over the railings. Had he got into that position as a result of a fall from a height? Helen was in the courtyard – did she fall from a height, or is this unacceptable?

Professor Dalgaard said that it was not so much the injuries she did have that made him doubt it, but more those she did not have – no fracture of the skull, arms, legs, no serious pelvic fracture, no neck or spine fractures. Professor Usher was not prepared to exclude the possibility that she did not fall from anywhere. Much of Dr Green's original findings depended on Helen having a right-shoulder fracture which she sustained when she fell on it, and which was protecting her skull. We now know that Dr Green made a mistake over this shoulder fracture. 'It was a mistake I should not have made,' he said.

Having regard to the nature of Helen's injuries, members of the jury, do you think they are consistent with falling on the ground below? Remember it was a hard, marble surface. Helen would be travelling at about 45 m.p.h. when she hit it. And she was only wearing light clothing.

The bruises to Helen's face and head seem the basis of the suspicion of foul play. We have had the benefit of the evidence of Dr Kheir. He told Sir David Napley that there were no abrasions inconsistent with a fall.

Here though we must consider briefly those very same questions which have plagued us throughout. The tragedy did not happen in Britain. Dr Kheir stated that he deals with more cases of male rape than female. He speaks and investigates in Arabic. How many of us understand and know Arabic? How many of us know and understand the differences in perception and understanding of the world that language precipitates? Dr Kheir is also a Moslem. How many of us understand the Moslem religion and its way of looking at the world?

We will not know the Saudis simply by reading about Lawrence of Arabia, members of the jury, but at the same time, there is equally much of us that Dr Kheir does not know. Can we honestly expect him to understand the points which we make, in our minds, when we ask him questions in the court, and can we expect him, an expert giving evidence in another country he does not live in, to understand and appreciate the way that we receive his words? Can we expect him to appreciate and understand the way we expect an answer? An English Sunday dinner is difficult to explain to anyone who is not English and has not grown up here. So is it fair to ask anyone who comes from another country, with another set of values and with an entirely different way of seeing the world, to give us answers which depend wholly on the process of scientific analysis.

I put it to you that Dr Kheir was placed in a very difficult position when asked to interpret the injuries, both in Saudi Arabia and at the inquest. He never saw the bodies *in situ* and he was called upon to examine the body of a white girl who was visually and externally in the very least different from those he was accustomed to examining daily. Hardly surprising that he thought she was in the fourth decade of her life, when in fact she was only twenty-three.

I think, members of the jury, that it is necessary to look at Dr Kheir's evidence from the point of view of the injuries he *did* find on Helen, and then it is up to you to interpret these for yourselves.

He found damage to some of the internal organs which were consistent with a fall. He agreed with the other pathologists that she fell on her right side. Yet he also found injuries to her left side and to her head. He said there was blood on the lining of the brain on the left side. Are these injuries consistent with a fall from a height, on the right side, especially this last one?

Professors Dalgaard and Usher said it was natural to equate Dr Kheir's discovery of blood on the lining of the brain with the major head injury, lesion 13, that they found. Professor Dalgaard thought the injury could not have been caused by a fall yet could, by itself, have caused death within minutes. Professors Dalgaard and Usher both said they had to disagree with Dr Kheir when he stated there were no injuries inconsistent with a fall. They said there were, and Lesion 13, which Professor Dalgaard thought had caused bleeding to some distance down the spinal column, was one of them.

The later pathologists were, of course, working under extreme difficulty. There was Dr Green's comment that the skin was shrunken and dried. Many marks were due to pressure, due to the way the bodies had been packed. And Professor Usher told graphically how the bodies had been moved from one place to another.

But the joint examination of Professors Dalgaard and Usher was also one of the most throrough ever to be carried out. They erred on the side of caution and only counted a suspected lesion as having been sustained in life if they found blood there. Professor Dalgaard is one of the most experienced pathologists in the world, and has dealt with embalmed bodies many times, instructing students in how to deal with them. Professor Usher has examined 15,000 bodies in his career. Is it conceivable that these two pathologists were mistaken when they said there were injuries inconsistent with a fall, yet consistent with assault?

We all know that experts can be wrong. But what forms the way we examine evidence, members of the jury? Is the evidence there in a pristine state, as if it had just been created, with the expert arriving on the scene equally as pristine? Or is always a certain degree of experience in existence, which is then used to interpret what is found?

The expert does, of course, use his or her experience. But what about you, members of the jury? You may not be pathologists, but don't you also accumulate experience? Don't you think that you too have a shrewd idea of what is reasonable and what is not in this case, using that experience? You must all bring to bear what is inside you.

Sir David Napley pointed out that pathology is an inexact science. The body is never experienced in a pristine state; it is experienced by the person who is there. In that situation, people bring their own experience to bear, and the sum of this experience can be vastly different, person to person. Bruises on the face, bruises not on the face – it will be the experiences of Dr Kheir that determine how he approaches the examination, and this is, of course, equally true for Professors Dalgaard and Usher. Professor Dalgaard is a vastly experienced man and has his own refined techniques of measuring a body. Dr Kheir, in Jeddah, in a culture with a different set of values, a long history of medical practice vastly different from our own, with a very different medical technology, will use an entirely different framework to measure that same body. Both experts will be right within the measure of their own experiences.

And so, members of the jury, we must ask you now to stand back and bring your own experiences to bear on this case. You may know nothing of pathology but each of you is an expert in your own life. Is it a wild goose chase to examine the components of that night, to draw out all of it, and then, using the measure of your own experience, reach the verdict on what you consider reasonable?

If you come to the conclusion that the head bruises did exist at the time of Helen's death and they were not due to a fall, then the evidence of assault is very strong. What conclusions can you then draw? It is here that the evidence of Mr Texier becomes vital.

How did his account – given under some embarrassment – come across? Was he being truthful? He said that

Mr Arnot went to bed early, that he saw Helen and Johannes go onto the balcony, and then the Germans left.

Otten, of course, came to the party with the Germans in their company jeep. They said they made a cursory search for him when they left. Manfred Schlaeffer said that Klaus Ritter went to the balcony curtain and called out: 'John, where are you?' But they did not really think he was there. They thought that Johannes had far more important things on his mind than them.

But if this is true, and Mrs Arnot and Mr Texier knew he was on the balcony, why did they not tell the departing Germans? Could it be that they were talking and joking about Otten in German, but were not really concerned to call him at all. With the exception of Manfred Schlaeffer, we know that they each had drink inside of them. One of their acquaintances had obviously become attached to a woman. Consider their position, members of the jury, in Jeddah. Would this not be a rare occurrence, worthy of conversation, perhaps in their merry state also worthy of a joke or two?

Mr Texier said that a short while after the Germans left, he and Mr Hayter bedded down for the night, leaving Mrs Arnot awake. When he awoke, it was to the sound of Mrs Arnot and Mr Hayter having sexual intercourse. He said that he turned over and pretended to be asleep, and then he got up at around 5.00 a.m. Is it possible, members of the jury, that Mr Texier was mistaken about the time? Did he actually wake up to the sound of love-making, turn over and doze off again? The next thing he knew, of course, was that it was 5.00 a.m. and time to get up. Is it your experience, members of the jury, that you can doze off and wake up some time later as if it was only the next minute?

If Mrs Arnot and Mr Hayter were love-making at around 5.00 a.m., it would be leaving it a bit late, wouldn't it? Mr Arnot might wake up in the bedroom and wonder why his wife has not come to bed yet, and come to investigate. Mr Hayter and Mrs Arnot had known each other some time. He had taken her to the company's floating crane the previous day, and he obviously knew her well enough for her to offer to pay for the whisky for the party. So, is it conceivable that Mr Hayter fell asleep with her awake in the room, only to be woken up later by her? You, again, have to draw on your experience, members of the jury.

Suppose that Mr Hayter and Mrs Arnot were indulging in sexual intercourse much earlier, however. What might Helen and Otten be doing on the balcony at that time? They could have been disturbed by the Germans leaving. Remember the flashing lights of the jeep. Was that really unfamiliarity with the controls or was it part of a joke, a joke directed at what they thought might be going on on the balcony?

If it was part of a joke, where did it originate? Was it back in the flat before they left? Do I need to remind you, members of the jury, of the old seafaring joke: the shipwrecked sailor with no money, no ship and no trousers? Did one of the departing Germans go onto the balcony, see the couple there indulging in love-making, and then sneak away, taking with him Johannes Otten's trousers, but being careful to leave behind his passport – his most valuable possession? Is this not a much more convincing explanation for the mystery of the trousers than the only other alternative? (That an Arab passing his body impaled on the railings stole them)? We have heard, members of the jury, that Otten often carried his money with him. But nobody saw it on his person that night. Would you go a party with all your money in your jeans' pocket, or would you consider it safer locked up at home? If Otten had no money on him, and there is no positive evidence that he was carrying any, then the motive for stealing disappears. His jeans are virtually worthless, yet his passport, which is a valuable document because of the large number of illegal immigrants in Saudi Arabia, is left behind. And that is before we even begin to consider the macabre aspects of such a theft.

But why might the departing Germans want to play

such a practical joke? Otten had, of course, come to the party with them in their company jeep. They had accepted him into their company. Did they not now feel some resentment that he had deserted them for something they could not share – a woman? And in doing this had he also not changed the nature of the party? At first Mrs Arnot and Helen danced and talked with everyone. Later, only Helen and Johannes were dancing – closely together. They had changed a drinks party into a sex party. Was there a little 'getting your own back' involved in the stealing of the trousers?

So suppose, therefore, his trousers have gone back to the port with the Germans. Suppose Otten decides he wants to leave after perhaps not an entirely successful encounter with Helen, because firstly he is drunk and secondly he has probably had no sex for some time. Perhaps he has indulged in forceful sexual activity with his hands. However, now he cannot find his trousers. He goes to the room and there the only people awake have their minds on other things. He starts to moan about his missing trousers. Someone reluctantly goes to the balcony to investigate or even joke about their disappearance, and, because of the drink inside them and the general situation, a scuffle develops. Helen becomes drawn in, perhaps becomes hysterical, and receives a kick or two in the ribs and a knock on the head. Professor Usher said some of her injuries were consistent with kicks. In the course of the scuffle, Otten goes over the balcony. Remember what Dr Kheir said about Otten having fallen with some momentum.

Mr Texier has not awoken. The air conditioning has subdued the noise of the scuffle and he has slept through the crash of Otten hitting the railings below. Helen was silenced as soon as she began to scream.

But Otten has fallen. What can be done? Helen too is unconscious. They try to revive Helen by a few slaps to the face, but she will not come round. A few minutes later she is dead. A last desperate attempt is made to revive her by heart massage, but this only succeeds in breaking her breast bone. What can be done now?

Timothy Hayter said during the *TV Eye* interview that he thought of trying to get the bodies out of the country. Is this, in fact, what someone tried to do next? Did someone carry Helen down the stairs with the intention of taking her and Otten in a car to the port? But then came a big problem. Otten could not be removed from the railings. Remember, members of the jury, how they had to get a saw from the hospital to cut him free. So was Helen's body then simply thrown to the ground? Remember, some of her right-side fractures could have occurred post mortem, as there was little blood around them. Is this not a much more convincing explanation for all of Helen's injuries, members of the jury?

What would happen then? The most natural thing to do would be to awaken Mr Arnot, and surely his immediate response would be to go and check that Helen was in fact dead. Mr Arnot, of course, told us he did this, but might his timing have been wrong? He said he did it just after 5.30 a.m. but could it not have been earlier, while Mr Texier was still asleep? Mr Hayter said that at 5.30 a.m. nobody went to check that the bodies were dead – there was no point, he said. There was only no point, members of the jury, if they were absolutely certain in their minds that Helen had fallen from the balcony or if they were otherwise certain she was dead. Mr Texier insisted that he was the first to leave the flat after 5.30 a.m., and Mr Arnot vanished only long enough to get dressed.

If the bodies cannot be taken away, then the next best thing is for the deaths to be an accident. It is essential too that Mr Texier believes this when he awakes. Mr Arnot goes back to bed because he must not be seen to be up and about. It would be a good idea, in fact, if Mr Texier discovers the bodies.

Mr Texier awakes at 5.00 a.m. He, Mrs Arnot and Mr Hayter make coffee and step onto the balcony. Mr Hayter said on the *TV Eye* film that Mr Texier looked over the balcony and said something like: 'Look, there are bodies down there.' Mr Texier, who suffers from poor eyesight and misting-up glasses in the humidity of that Jeddah morning, told us, however, that it was not he who made the discovery. Could it be, members of the jury, that it was *intended* that Mr Texier discover the bodies, but it soon became apparent that this would be impossible? There then followed the panic over the alcohol.

And did someone in the course of this throw Otten's passport into the street to make it look as if his trousers had been with him when he fell, but had since vanished mysteriously? Is this why Mr Hayter drove back to the port and awoke Martin Fleischer? Remember, members of the jury, Mr Fleischer left the party earlier than the other German guests, alone and while Helen and Johannes were still in the apartment. He would therefore not know about the trousers. Did Mr Hayter ask him to go to their boss, Harry Gutzeit, who lived in the city, because he wanted him out of the way while he spoke to the others? It was established that it would have been much easier and faster for Mr Hayter to have gone to Harry Gutzeit himself.

These are the issues you have to decide, members of the jury. You have to combine the pathologists' evidence with that of the witnesses and with your own experience of what is reasonable. If you accept the scenario we have presented here, or something similar, as being reasonable then you have to decide who started the scuffle. Did Otten go over the balcony as a result of someone defending him or herself? Did Helen become knocked unconscious as a result of someone defending him or herself? Or were they both killed as a result of aggressive acts by others? Remember, however, it is no part of your function to accuse anyone.

13. *The Politics of Inquests*

Everybody dies. Every death has a reason. Old age, illness, heart attack, accident, foul play. We must know why people die, unless we do not care. And if we do not care, human life itself becomes cheapened. Why bother about it? Let the bodies lie in the streets of Bahrein, or at the bottom of a block of flats. It has nothing to do with us.

But maybe some people do care. That is why we have inquests – solemn occasions where the object is to get at the truth of the circumstances of a death, especially where there is a doubt.

Helen Smith is dead. She was twenty-three. She died not of old age, nor of illness, nor of a heart attack. Full of life, she went to see a bit of the world. Six months later she was dead at the bottom of a block of flats and apparently nobody saw or heard what happened. Nearby was the body of a man.

It was either an accident or else it was foul play. The choices are simple and there are only two. But in the heat of Saudi Arabia – the temperature, the diplomatic heat, the heat of the police questioning – something became blurred. Those two people, spiked on railings and lying on a marble courtyard, stiff rith *rigor mortis*, isolated from everyone else, could no longer communicate. In the split second before either lost consciousness we could have been told. Now we cannot. The living world is left to interpret, to reconstruct.

Jeddah, late-May 1979. Three groups of people are interested.

1. The party guests, Mr and Mrs Arnot. Definitely – the

dead people were at the same party as them. Definitely, too, every reason to hope it was an accident. Big trouble for each of them if it was not.

2. The British diplomats in Jeddah. They have things to consider other than a dead woman. There are the wider implications of Britain's interest in Saudi Arabia, the West's interest in the Middle East. They too must hope for accident.

3. Ron Smith, father of Helen, has no real interest in anything other than the fact his daughter is dead when he arrives in Jeddah. Then he sees her, becomes convinced that this is no accident, becomes convinced that the State is putting its other interests before that of the truth about his daughter. A contradiction looms. Is not the primary function of the State to protect its citizens? 'Her Britannic Majesty's Principal Secretary of State for Foreign and Commonwealth Affairs Requests and requires in the Name of Her Majesty all those whom it may concern to allow the bearer to pass freely without let or hindrance, and to afford the bearer such assistance and protection as may be necessary.' So speaks the British passport.

Britain trades with Saudi Arabia – a country rich through oil – to create jobs, provide food, shelter for her citizens back home. In those circumstances is it permissible to sacrifice the truth about one of those citizens in the name of perpetuating good relations with the country it has offended. Truth and lies are mere words. Trade, jobs, the existence of the British State are more than words. Helen Smith was dead anyway, and no amount of investigation would bring her back to life.

Accident or foul play: diplomats, police, hospital owner apparently easily satisfied it was an accident. Father believes foul play. The body is brought back to England and is deposited with the Leeds deputy coroner. Pathologists do their work and their findings fuel the doubts.

It is here that we join the same well-worn track that all dubious deaths in this country follow: police called; not sure what happened; inform coroner.

The coroner, who is either a lawyer or a medical person, acts as the first filter as he examines the police evidence, the pathologist's findings and perhaps even takes his own statements. The coroner sifts through all this. All deaths of a dubious nature lead to the coroner – the absorber who makes sense out of the evidence, the purifier of muddied waters, the resolver of contradictions.

The coroner forms a 'view' of the cause of death. He can do this without speaking a word in public. 'The work of a coroner starts from the moment a person dies,' Philip Gill himself was quoted as saying in the *Wakefield Express* a few weeks after the Helen Smith inquest.

Having formed a 'view', the coroner then takes the decision on whether to hold an inquest or not. He takes into account two factors. Firstly, has he satisfied himself as to the cause of death and removed all reasonable doubts; and secondly, is there a great deal of public concern over this death? He can there and then make his judgement.

June 1980: the death of Helen Smith is a matter of great public concern, and there she is, on Deputy Coroner Coverdale's lap. He decides there is not enough evidence to warrant an inquest, although he says he will leave the matter open. Helen remains with Coverdale for one year, and is then transferred to Philip Gill – a more senior coroner than Coverdale. He takes just one month to decide no inquest, despite the public concern. It is how he interprets the Coroners' Act of 1887 – he claims he has no jurisdiction if the death occurs outside the United Kingdom. Gill has, in fact, opened two inquests in recent years on people who have died abroad.

Truth demands an inquest, honesty demands an inquest and justice demands an inquest to find out how Helen Smith died. Truth, honesty and justice are surely words that rise above an interpretation of the meaning of the Coroners' Act. Is the law an ass? Or is the coroner's interpretation wrong? Ron Smith takes Gill to the High Court and loses. He takes him to the Appeal Court and wins. There has to be an inquest. The route has been unconventional, to say the least – from Jeddah to Leeds mortuary, where Helen's body lies, is a long way. From the coroner's judgement that there should be no inquest to the successful challenge in the courts is a hitherto uncharted way.

But we are now back on the well-worn track. The coroner conducts further inquiries, takes statements, appeals for witnesses. Everyone offers advice; Ron Smith is especially to the fore. He sends Gill a list of sixty-three people he thinks should be witnesses, but Gill states that he never receives it.

Further filtering by the coroner takes place. Which witnesses will be called? Which statements will be presented as evidence? It is all in his hands and his hands alone. If he forms the view that it was an accident and he wishes to fulfil that view, then he need only call those witnesses and present those statements that substantiate it. This is not to say that Gill actually did this – pathologists were called who suspected foul play – but the power is there for him to do so and is it right that any one person should possess such power when the truth is at stake?

At the inquest itself, there are two potential flies in the ointment as far as a coroner and his 'view' are concerned. The first is the jury – laypeople – often a problem, although less so in a coroner's court where the coroner has some discretion in its choosing.

One method is for the coroner's officer to stand outside the court on the day of an inquest and simply ask passers-by. This is deemed satisfactory if the inquest is only going to last for an hour or so. Another method is for the coroner to have an arrangement with the local town hall to ask there for secretaries and the like to be released when an inquest comes up. Thirdly, the coroner might use the Crown Court list of jurors.

Only this last gives anything approaching a random selection procedure. The first depends on the coroner's officer (usually a policeman), the second means that only a certain type of person is chosen. The coroner's officer could, of course, go along an unemployment queue, but this has never been known. It is not known how the jury for the Helen Smith inquest was chosen. Coroners do also have the discretion over whether or not there should be a jury. The guiding rule is that there is a jury when there is public interest in the case. Justice must not only be done, it must also be seen to be done. But the jury enters that court, by and large, ignorant. If it is not ignorant, it will be because of what it has read about the case in the newspapers, and then the coroner tells the members straight: they must put out of their mind what they have read, seen or heard. Meanwhile, the coroner, who is not ignorant and who, indeed, has formed a 'view' already, asks questions of the witnesses. It is a certain line of questioning – inevitably in accordance with his 'view'. He thinks it was an accident and asks his questions accordingly. Did Helen fall accidentally from the Arnot balcony, crash into Johannes Otten, who a fraction of a second before became impaled on the railings, and bounce off him? Does that explain her injuries? What was this interesting sunlounger on the balcony? And so on. Some of the questions may stray, but the initial theme remains.

The other potential fly is the witness evidence. We have to exclude here the pathologists, who are predictable even if they do disagree with each other. But the others – what might they say under the piercing questions of a barrister? The simple answer is that piercing questions are not allowed. This is not a normal court. These witnesses have been invited by the coroner to assist him. It is assumed that they are telling the truth. Nobody can cross-examine them or get under their skins. Welcome to the coroner's guests. And they can all sit in the court and hear what each other has to say.

Theory: an inquest is a solemn and dignified occasion to discover the circumstances of a human being's death. Everyone present is there to assist the coroner because they believe human life to be important. The assumption is, however, that everyone there has a common interest – to get to the truth. The inquest works on concensus to 'provide for the public an honest, dispassionate assessment of what had happened as far as one could establish it from the evidence' (Gill's words quoted in the *Wakefield Express* interview).

It probably works like that too in many cases. But what if the death is controversial, involves politics, involves disputes between interested parties, each with separate interests? Arnot – accident. Smith – foul play. Pretend there is a concensus there. It does not work.

It then behoves the coroner to rise above all this. Gill again in the *Wakefield Express*: 'An inquest is conducted on behalf of the Crown. I am not there conducting it for any particular person, but to establish what the truth is and what happened, irrespective of what the interests of other persons might be.' Come fair wind or foul, the coroner must sustain the concensus proceedings even when there are none.

Coroners are employed by metropolitan councils, paid for out of the rates, yet are accountable to the Crown. Gill has said it; politicians on West Yorkshire County Council soon found out how little control they had when they expressed unhappiness at his handling of the Helen Smith case some months before he was finally forced to conduct an inquest. Coroners can only be sacked by the Queen's representative – the Lord Chancellor.

Gill's comments are themselves based on an assumption – the assumption of the Crown (read State) as neutral observer. Only then does the coroner's position become tenable. But what if the State's interests are also at stake at an inquest? What if the State has been accused of covering up murder? Does that not put the coroner – conducting an inquest on behalf of the Crown – in a rather awkward position? Objective judgements have at their very base the independence of the judge.

* Helen Smith (died 1979): father accused British Embassy in Jeddah and Foreign Office in London of covering up the circumstances of her death. Inquest verdict: Open.

* Blair Peach (died 1979): police accused of causing his death at an anti-National Front demonstration in Lewisham. Inquest verdict: Misadventure.

* James Kelly (died 1980): died in police custody in Liverpool. Inquest verdict: Misadventure.

* New Cross (13 black people died 1980): a party was still in full swing when the house went up in flames. Inquest verdict: Open.

These are the inquests which have made the news in recent years. In each of them the State had an interest. In the first three it was obvious; the last occurred when the last thing the Government wanted to do was to fan the flames of racial tension. The Government was, at the time, trying to convince the black community that it enjoys the full protection of British law.

All four inquests were controversial. The arguments still rage, the word 'whitewash' will never dry on some lips. They are testimony to the inadequacy of the procedures.

Gill obviously believes that it is right that coroners become involved the moment a person dies. Others have argued in the wake of the Helen Smith inquest that it is a positive disadvantage in controversial cases. The coroner should come on the case fresh, and with no view – like a judge.

Judges are responsible to the Crown too, of course. But at least they are used to hearing cases from scratch. And their procedures are completely different. There are no holds barred in cross-examination. The only rules are that the legal representatives do not ask leading questions and restrict themselves to material evidence – not hearsay. Interestingly, at the Helen Smith inquest, much hearsay evidence was admitted.

Geoffrey Robertson's examination of Richard Arnot was made extremely difficult and its effectiveness was lessened under the constant barrage of interruptions from Gill making sure the rules of the inquest were applied. This was even unfair to Arnot. He had come saying he had nothing to hide. Why protect him? He is an intelligent man who can hold his own in the company of Robertson and Sedley. Surely he did not wish to leave the old Leeds Crown Court with people under the impression that Gill had been protecting him.

Helen Smith's body bears the marks (or lack of them) that suggest foul play. To prove it, someone, somewhere, must lend human support to that suggestion by saying, 'I did it' or 'I saw it happen'. Nobody has so far volunteered that information, and the procedures of examination at the Leeds inquest made sure that nobody was going to be forced to volunteer it. Yet whatever procedure should have been adopted or may yet be adopted in the future, there remains the problem of getting people from abroad to come to Britain. They cannot be forced. Many did come for the inquest, probably often on the understanding that they had nothing to fear from the proceedings. Inquests do not accuse anyone, even when the verdict is unlawful killing, as Gill constantly reminded the Leeds jury (although if it was, a report would go to the Director of Public Prosecutions).

The verdict was open. Neither can we in this book prove foul play. It would be rather contradictory in a book based on the inquest to be able to do so. We believe it was not an accident, however, and you have already read our scenario. It is built on the inquest evidence plus a little bit of experience accumulated over the years. (Professor Usher used a similar phrase, remember, when he refuted Sir David Napley's suggestion that he would have to strain the imagination to believe a bruise found on Helen's nostrils was caused by an assailant's hand.) That experience is of how people behave in relation to alcohol, sex, claustrophobic expatriate atmospheres and each other. It had to be our experience because we were not told at the inquest. We never knew the real Richard Arnot, the real Martin Fleischer, the real Helen Smith, so we have to make educated guesses.

Helen, ah yes. How we wish this book was not about you, that you were still alive and well. How we wish we were writing about someone else, but it does not work because if we were writing about someone else we would still wish we were not. We cannot help feeling twinges of unease about making words from someone else's life – someone we never knew.

The inquest did not do justice to Helen Smith. It did not do justice to her father. To have done so it would have needed to examine in detail the fun-starved, work-saturated party guests rather than 'fun-loving' Helen. It would have had to try to understand Jeddah and its expatriate community rather than dismissing it as one of the problems facing the jury. It would have had to examine fully the much wider issues of British-Saudi relations. It barely tried and it certainly never linked these facets together to produce a whole picture. The end result was a mirage where justice only appeared to be seen to be done.

The question remaining at the end of this inquest (apart from how she died) was not, has the British State covered up the death of Helen Smith because of its wider interests, but whether it had the right to do so. Put like that, the question becomes philosophical and we can dismiss it with a shrug of the shoulders. View it through the blood, sweat and tears of Ron Smith's three-and-a-half-year campaign that brought this inquest and we realise its full impact. It is not a pretty sight, even though it may conjure up visions of David and Goliath.

But in opening our eyes just a little more as to what goes on in the world, Ron Smith has done us all a great service. What a shame we cannot thank Helen too.

STOP PRESS: Thursday 10 March 1983

A photograph appeared in today's *Daily Mirror* showing Helen lying in the courtyard of the block of flats. It is an official Saudi police photograph which Coroner Gill told the *Mirror* he recieved in mid-February, over two months after the inquest ended.

The photograph shows that Helen is up against the wall of the flats – in other words, in the recess caused by the setting back of the first-floor balcony. It is most improbable that she could have landed in this position in a fall from the sixth-floor balcony. She is also on her face, not on her side. She is fully clothed and her pants appear to be on both legs.

The photograph adds great weight to the theory presented in this book that Helen Smith died in the Arnot flat and her body was then dumped outside.

Index